POLITICAL PHILOSOPHY IN
THE TWENTIETH CENTURY

This book demonstrates the rich diversity and depth of political philosophy in the twentieth century. Catherine H. Zuckert has compiled a collection of works recounting the lives of political theorists, connecting each biography with the theorist's life work and explaining the significance of his or her contribution to modern political thought. The works are organized to highlight the major political alternatives and approaches. Beginning with essays on John Dewey, Carl Schmitt, and Antonio Gramsci, representing the three main political alternatives – liberal, Fascist, and communist – at midcentury, the book proceeds to consider the lives and works of émigrés such as Hannah Arendt, Eric Voegelin, and Leo Strauss, who brought a continental perspective to the United States after World War II. The second half of the collection contains works on recent defenders of liberalism, such as Friedrich Hayek, Isaiah Berlin, and John Rawls, and on liberalism's many critics, including Michel Foucault, Jürgen Habermas, and Alasdair MacIntyre.

CATHERINE H. ZUCKERT is currently Professor of Political Science, as well as Editor-in-Chief of *The Review of Politics*, at the University of Notre Dame. She has written several books, the most recent of which is *Plato's Philosophers: The Coherence of the Dialogues*. Her books have won several awards, including the R. R. Hawkins Award for the Best Scholarly and Professional Book in 2009; the PROSE Awards for Best Book in Philosophy and Excellence in the Humanities; and the PSP Award for the Best Book in Philosophy and Religion in 1990. Zuckert has had articles published in *Political Theory*, *The Journal of Politics*, *History of Political Thought*, *The Review of Politics*, *Philosophy & Rhetoric*, *Epoché*, *Review of Metaphysics*, *Polity*, *Interpretation*, and *The Claremont Review of Books*.

T0364310

POLITICAL PHILOSOPHY IN THE TWENTIETH CENTURY

Authors and Arguments

Edited by

CATHERINE H. ZUCKERT
University of Notre Dame

CAMBRIDGE
UNIVERSITY PRESS

CAMBRIDGE UNIVERSITY PRESS
Cambridge, New York, Melbourne, Madrid, Cape Town,
Singapore, São Paulo, Delhi, Mexico City

Cambridge University Press
32 Avenue of the Americas, New York, NY 10013-2473, USA

www.cambridge.org
Information on this title: www.cambridge.org/9780521185066

First published 2011
Reprinted 2012

A catalog record for this publication is available from the British Library.

Library of Congress Cataloging in Publication Data

Political philosophy in the twentieth century : authors and arguments / edited by
Catherine Zuckert.
    p. cm.
Includes bibliographical references and index.
ISBN 978-1-107-00622-5 (hardback) – ISBN 978-0-521-18506-6 (paperback)
1. Political science – Philosophy – History – 20th century.   2. Political scientists –
History – 20th century.   I. Zuckert, Catherine H., 1942–   II. Title.
JA83.P5628   2011
320.01–dc22   2011011457

ISBN 978-1-107-00622-5 Hardback
ISBN 978-0-521-18506-6 Paperback

Contents

Contents

Contributors

RUTH ABBEY is Associate Professor of Political Science at the University of Notre Dame. She is the author of *Nietzsche's Middle Period* and *Philosophy Now: Charles Taylor*, as well as editor of *Contemporary Philosophy in Focus: Charles Taylor*.

MICHAEL BACON is Lecturer in Political Theory at Royal Holloway, University of London. He is the author of *Richard Rorty: Pragmatism and Political Liberalism*, as well as articles on Rorty, pragmatism, and deliberative democracy.

JOSEPH BUTTIGIEG is William R. Kenan Jr. Professor of English and Co-Director of Italian Studies at the University of Notre Dame. He is president of the International Gramsci Society, as well as editor and translator of the multivolume, complete critical edition of Antonio Gramsci's *Prison Notebooks*.

JOHN M. FINNIS is Professor Emeritus of Law and Legal Philosophy at Oxford University and Biolchini Family Professor of Law at the University of Notre Dame. One of H. L. A. Hart's most famous students, Finnis is also a member of the British Academy. He is the author of *Natural Law and Natural Rights*, among numerous other works.

DAVID FOTT is Associate Professor of Political Science at the University of Nevada, Las Vegas, where he is also Director of the Great Works Academic Certificate program. He is the author of *John Dewey: America's Philosopher of Democracy*, as well as articles and book chapters on Dewey, Cicero, Machiavelli, Montesquieu, U.S. presidential power, and Jane Austen.

TIMOTHY FULLER is Lloyd E. Worner Distinguished Service Professor of Political Science at Colorado College. He has published many essays and has edited numerous books, including *Reassessing the Liberal State*; *Leading and Leadership*; *The Voice of Liberal Learning: Michael Oakeshott on Education*; *Michael Oakeshott on Religion, Politics, and the Moral Life*; and *Something of Great Constancy: Essays in Honor of the Memory of J. Glenn Gray*.

WILLIAM GALSTON is Ezra K. Zilkha Chair in Governance Studies at the Brookings Institution. His books include *Justice and the Human Good*, *Liberal Purposes*, and *Liberal Pluralism: The Implications of Value Pluralism for Political Theory and Practice*, of which chapter 5 deals explicitly with the liberalism of Isaiah Berlin.

ERIC MACK is Professor of Philosophy at Tulane University. He is the author of *Locke* in Continuum Press's Major Conservative and Libertarian Thinkers series, as well as articles on the foundation of moral rights, property rights and distributive justice, and the legitimate scope of coercive institutions.

ARTHUR MADIGAN, S. J., is Professor and Chair of the Department of Philosophy at Boston College. He has published "Plato, Aristotle, and Professor MacIntyre" in *Ancient Philosophy*, as well as books on Alexander of Aphrodisias and Aristotle's *Metaphysics*.

WILLIAM LEON MCBRIDE is Arthur G. Hansen Distinguished Professor of Philosophy at Purdue University and president of the International Federation of Philosophical Societies. His publications include *Social and Political Philosophy*, *Sartre's Political Theory*, *Philosophical Reflections on the Changes in Eastern Europe*, and *From Yugoslav Praxis to Global Pathos: Anti-Hegemonic Post-Post-Marxist Essays*.

ALAN MILCHMAN co-edited (with Alan Rosenberg) *Foucault and Heidegger: Critical Encounters, Postmodernism and the Holocaust*, and *Martin Heidegger and the Holocaust*. He is Lecturer in the Department of Political Science at Queens College of the City University of New York.

WALTER NICGORSKI is Professor in the Program of Liberal Studies and Concurrent Professor of Political Science at the University of Notre Dame. His essays on Cicero, liberal and character education, the American founding, Leo Strauss, and Allan Bloom have appeared in collections and such journals as *Political Theory*, *Interpretation*, and the *Political Science Reviewer*. He is a former editor of *The Review of Politics*.

ALAN ROSENBERG co-edited (with Alan Milchman) *Foucault and Heidegger: Critical Encounters, Postmodernism and the Holocaust*, and *Martin Heidegger and the Holocaust*. He is Professor of Philosophy at Queens College of the City University of New York.

ELLIS SANDOZ is Hermann Moyse Jr. Distinguished Professor of Political Science and the Director of the Eric Voegelin Institute for American Renaissance Studies at Louisiana State University, as well as founder of the Eric Voegelin Society. He edited *The Collected Works of Eric Voegelin* (34 vols.) and is the author or editor of twenty other books, including *Political Apocalypse: A Study of Dostoevsky's Grand Inquisitor* and *Republicanism, Religion, and the Soul of America*.

Contributors

WILLIAM E. SCHEUERMAN is Professor of Political Science at Indiana University, Bloomington. He is the author of *Between the Norm and the Exception: The Frankfurt School and the Rule of Law*; *Carl Schmitt: The End of Law*; *Frankfurt School Perspectives on Globalization*; and *Hans J. Morgenthau: Realism and Beyond*.

STEVEN B. SMITH is Alfred Cowles Professor of Political Science and Master of Branford College at Yale University. His recent publications include *Spinoza, Liberalism, and the Question of Jewish Identity*; *Spinoza's Book of Life*; *Reading Leo Strauss*; and *The Cambridge Companion to Leo Strauss*.

TRACY B. STRONG is Distinguished Professor of Political Science at the University of California at San Diego. He is the author of *Friedrich Nietzsche and the Politics of Transfiguration*, as well as "Dimensions of the New Debate around Carl Schmitt," the introduction to Carl Schmitt's *The Concept of the Political*, and the foreword to Carl Schmitt's *Political Theology: Four Chapters on the Concept of Sovereignty*.

DANA R. VILLA is Packey J. Dee Professor of Political Science at the University of Notre Dame. He is the author of *Arendt and Heidegger: The Fate of the Political*, *Socratic Citizenship*, *Public Freedom*, and *Politics, Philosophy, Terror: Essays on the Thought of Hannah Arendt*, as well as editor of the *Cambridge Companion to Arendt*.

PAUL WEITHMAN is Professor of Philosophy at the University of Notre Dame. He is the author of *Religion and the Obligations of Citizenship*. He studied with Rawls at Harvard and co-edited (with Henry S. Richardson) *The Philosophy of Rawls: A Collection of Essays* (5 vols.).

CATHERINE H. ZUCKERT is Nancy Reeves Dreux Professor of Political Science and Editor-in-Chief of *The Review of Politics* at the University of Notre Dame. Her publications include *Plato's Philosophers*, *Postmodern Platos*, and (with Michael Zuckert) *The Truth about Leo Strauss*.

Introduction: political philosophy in the twentieth century

CATHERINE H. ZUCKERT

Political Philosophy in the Twentieth Century began as a special issue of *The Review of Politics* intended to illustrate the variety and depth of philosophical analyses of politics in the face of the purported demise of political philosophy.[1] With the addition of ten new essays this book expands the range of positions and arguments represented.

We thought it desirable to demonstrate the richness and vitality of philosophical reflection on political issues in the twentieth century in response to the many observations of its weakness, if not death. As Dana Villa observes as the beginning of his chapter on Arendt, "in the 1970s and 1980s, students of political theory invariably encountered the cliché that political theory and philosophy died sometime in the 1950s, only to be revived in 1971 by the publication of John Rawls's *A Theory of Justice*." Much as he admires Rawls's work, Villa is nevertheless "taken somewhat aback by the radical foreshortening of the history of political thought implied by this cliché. After all, the 1950s and early 1960s saw the publication of some of the most interesting – and enduring – works of political theory of the past sixty years or so." A few "landmarks" of "what was, in retrospect, a remarkably fertile period for political thought" include Leo Strauss's *Natural Right and History* (1953), Eric Voegelin's *Order and History* (1956–7), Isaiah Berlin's *Four Essays on Liberty* (1969), Jürgen Habermas's *Structural Transformation of the Public Sphere* (1963), Michael Oakeshott's *Rationalism and Politics* (1962), and Arendt's *Origins of Totalitarianism* (1951), *The Human Condition* (1958), and *On Revolution* (1963).

In his chapter on H. L. A. Hart, John Finnis observes, moreover, that the revival of political philosophy attributed to Hart and Rawls was weak and partial. They broke the bounds of political philosophy as conceived by

[1] *The Review of Politics* 71, no. 1 (2009).

I

many in their analytic philosophical circle by going beyond generalizations about historically given institutions to offer sober accounts of what human persons and groups need and rationally desire. Hart and Rawls also proposed arrangements that are *universally* valuable (good) for beings with the nature we have. But they were not willing to admit the implication – namely, that the asserted autonomy of political from moral philosophy was not sustainable. Nor were they willing to take up the full range of issues raised by the tradition stemming from Plato and Aristotle.

In a speech he was asked to deliver at the Library of Congress on June 9, 1999, Pierre Manent thus lamented,

The twentieth century has witnessed the disappearance, or withering away, of political philosophy.... However highly we might think of the philosophical capacities and results of Heidegger, Bergson, Whitehead, or Wittgenstein, we would not single out any of them for his contribution to *political* philosophy.... It is true that... authors like Sir Karl Popper and Raymond Aron have been worthy contributors to both general epistemology and political inquiry.... And some modern representatives of that venerable tradition of thought, Thomism, have offered serious reflection on moral, social, and political problems within a comprehensive account of the world. But despite such countervailing considerations, the general diagnosis seems to me to be inescapable: no modern original philosopher has been willing or able to include a thorough analysis of political life within his account of the human world, or, conversely, to elaborate his account of the whole from an analysis of our political circumstances.[2]

As indicated by the title of his speech, "The Return of Political Philosophy," however, Manent also saw some movement toward a revival. He mentioned several of the authors featured in this volume – Hannah Arendt, Michael Oakeshott, and Leo Strauss – as having taken important steps in this direction.

The wide array of authors and approaches featured in this collection is intended to demonstrate that the three authors Manent named are by no means the only twentieth-century thinkers who perceived the need to bring the rigor of philosophical analysis to bear on questions of politics. Like Socrates, they have continued to ask the question that is first for us, if not first in itself: How can we best live, not merely as individuals, but also in communities that have to coexist, if not actively cooperate, in an ever more closely interrelated world? That is the enterprise of political philosophy in which all the authors featured in this volume have engaged.

---

[2] Pierre Manent, "The Return of Political Philosophy," *First Things* 103 (May 2000): 15.

Sources of the crises – philosophical and political

Why, then, has political philosophy seemed to be such a highly questionable, if not moribund, endeavor to many observers? The answer to that question can be given briefly in two words: science and history.

In the early nineteenth century G. W. F. Hegel famously announced that philosophy as literally the search for wisdom had come to an end, because it had culminated in his work in the possession of science or knowledge. Even more famously Karl Marx stood Hegel on his head by agreeing that there was a necessary course of historical development that was coming to its end, but arguing that this development was determined by the material conditions of production, not by ideas. The neo-Kantian philosophers who succeeded both Hegel and Marx contested the latter's contention that ideas were merely reflections of, or ideological justifications for, underlying economic conditions by arguing that human beings do not have any knowledge of the "world" independent of mental categories or constructions; and Vladimir Lenin transformed "Marxism" from an argument for historical inevitability into a "Marxist-Leninist" political program that provoked vehement responses from right, center, and left. Yet neither the philosophical critique of the historical inevitability thesis offered, for example, by Friedrich Nietzsche, nor the gradual revelation of the repressive policies undertaken by proponents of socialism in one country, prevented academic commentators such as George Sabine and Anthony Quinton from arguing that the great works in political philosophy were simply descriptive accounts of political institutions and activities along with recommendations about the ideal ends that reflected their authors' time and place.[3] Having concluded that all thought was historically conditioned and therefore limited, these scholars did not deem it possible for thinkers to rise above or beyond their particular circumstances in a way that would enable them to consider, much less determine, the best way for human beings to live – as individuals or in communities.

Although the terrible events associated with World War II made members of the generation who experienced the horrors question the validity of all arguments concerning historical inevitability, much less progress, Hegel's thesis about the "end of history" was revived after the fall of the Berlin Wall

---

[3] George Sabine, *A History of Political Theory* (New York: Holt, 1937); Anthony Quinton, ed., *Political Philosophy* (London: Oxford University Press, 1967), 1.

and the conclusion of the so-called Cold War in 1989.[4] This time the claim about the "end" rested less on a claim about the possession of complete knowledge, however, and more on the purportedly universally satisfying social and political arrangements that had been found and established in liberal social-welfare democracies. As the chapters in this volume make clear, that explicitly normative claim has been vigorously contested.

It is impossible to inquire about the best life for a human being, the way traditional political philosophers did, if one is convinced that human thoughts and deeds are historically determined. Why ask about something that cannot be changed? Why strive for a suprahistorical perspective that is impossible for a human being to achieve? Although all the authors featured in this collection agree on the necessity of taking historical circumstances into account, both in reading the works of past authors and in proposing improvements in contemporary conditions, none agrees that human thought and action are historically, materially, or biologically determined. These authors contest deterministic theses, however, on different grounds. Whereas some affirm that there is such a thing as human nature that persists from one historical period to another, others maintain that human life is historically contingent. The predictions or analyses of the authors who argue that human life is essentially contingent are necessarily conditional, and their recommendations tentative. Yet the authors who rest their analyses of political possibilities on assertions about human nature confront the challenge posed by modern natural science, the second major source of doubts about the possibility or validity of what is called political philosophy.

The challenge posed by modern natural-scientific analyses of the world to human freedom and agency was recognized long before the twentieth century. Because the nexus of cause and effect described by modern natural science left no room for human freedom or morality, at the end of the eighteenth century Immanuel Kant was led to posit a transcendental source, or ground. Unhappy with the gap Kant left between the intelligible and the sensible worlds, Hegel famously tried to bring the two back together by means of a historical synthesis. Later critics were not satisfied with Hegel's account of modern natural science or with his description of the final, best state of human affairs. Neo-Kantian philosophers such as Hermann Cohen again took modern natural science to be the paradigm of human knowledge,

---

[4] The most famous exponent of the revived thesis was, of course, Francis Fukuyama in his *The End of History*. See Tim Burns, ed., *After History? Francis Fukuyama and His Critics* (Lanham, MD: Rowman & Littlefield, 1994) and Jacques Derrida, *Specters of Marx*, trans. Peggy Kamuf (New York: Routledge, 2006) for some of the better-known direct critical responses.

but they argued that the progress of science would be accompanied by the development of a freer and more moral political order. Hegel-influenced but distinctly American "pragmatic" philosophers such as Charles Peirce and William James developed a less systematic and logical, more empirical, hypothetical, and incrementally cumulative understanding of natural science. As David Fott reminds us in the first chapter in this volume, John Dewey argued that this more "pragmatic," experiment-based understanding of modern natural science was not merely completely compatible with but could actively promote the spread of democratic political institutions and practices. Unfortunately, as the chapters on the émigrés in the second section of this volume show, both popular and philosophical faith in the essential compatibility of the progress of modern natural science and democratic politics were shattered by two world wars and the development of nuclear weapons.

Continuing to take modern natural science as the paradigm of knowledge, "logical positivists" like A. J. Ayer contended that the only things we can know are "facts" based on empirical observations that can be replicated and so verified.[5] They held that it is possible to analyze what we mean when we use "concepts" such as "the state," "obligation," or "law." Indeed, this became the business of an "analytical," linguistic political philosopher. Such analyses cannot tell us what to do or provide us with political "ideals," however, because all judgments of good and bad or "values" are merely expressions of emotional responses having no cognitive status. These admirers of modern natural science did not appear to see, as Nietzsche had, that science (knowledge or truth) is itself a value; human beings would not pursue it if they did not believe that it was good. Although the arguments of the positivists have been thoroughly criticized, if not refuted, by "moral realists," such positivist views still dominate American social science, and American modes of social science are rapidly spreading throughout the rest of the world.[6]

Responses to the crises – political and philosophical

The authors featured in this volume all respond to the challenge posed by the apparent success of modern natural science by arguing that the frameworks, methods, and models employed by modern natural scientists

---

[5] A. J. Ayer, *Language, Truth and Logic* (London: V. Gollancz, 1938).
[6] See the centennial issue of *The American Political Science Review* (*APSR* 100, no. 4 [Nov. 2006]: 463-665).

do not capture what is distinctive about human action and thought. To understand what kind of knowledge modern natural science represents as well as its value, they urge that it is necessary to investigate its source, that is, the human beings who seek knowledge, why they seek it, and with what results. Human beings do not merely react to external stimuli, these authors observe; human beings act, which is to say that they choose to act or not to act in certain ways under specified circumstances, and their actions have effects – intended as well as unintended. None of these authors would endeavor to discover how human beings can best live, which is to say, none of these authors would engage in the enterprise generally called political philosophy, if they did not think that human beings have or at least can have some degree of agency. And they would not think that human beings have agency if they thought that human life was historically, materially, or biologically determined.

Beyond an agreement on the possibility, if not fact, of human agency or freedom, the authors featured in this volume disagree markedly about both politics and philosophy. The sheer variety of political positions taken and the philosophical arguments used to support those positions demonstrate the existence of a rich and vibrant tradition of reflection and debate about the most fundamental issues of human existence. And the disagreements among these authors about the answers to such questions as "what is distinctively human?" and "what is the best political order?" speak very much against those commentators who would convince us that we are at "the end of history." The persistence of disagreement about such fundamental questions nevertheless tempts many observers to believe that these questions cannot be answered and that political philosophy is therefore a fruitless endeavor.

The authors featured in this collection also advance arguments to show how human beings can and should face the dual challenges posed by the successes of modern natural science, on the one hand, and history, on the other. Some, such as John Dewey and Friedrich Hayek, urge us to rely on gradually evolving social orders and experiments that incorporate modern natural science. Others, such as Leo Strauss, Eric Voegelin, and Yves R. Simon, look to philosophy to preserve not merely the memory but also the substance of a distinctively human way of life. Some liberal political philosophers, such as Isaiah Berlin and H. L. A. Hart, emphasize the limitations of human reason and knowledge in arguing that a space or spaces should be created and preserved in which human beings can and should remain free to direct their own lives – individually as well as politically. Others, such as John Rawls and Richard Rorty, argue that more extensive state action is required not merely to protect but also to provide individuals with the resources they need to develop and follow a life plan of their own. All these liberal political philosophers explicitly jettison the claims about human "nature" made by older "social contract" theorists, however, to avoid the difficulties that modern natural science and history have raised about the grounds of such claims in appeals to "nature" or nature's God.

Recognizing that there is no necessity that change will constitute progress if human life is not biologically or historically determined, other twentieth-century political philosophers find an opportunity for active self-definition, if not self-creation, in that very nondeterminism. These more explicitly activist stances vary, from Carl Schmitt's contention that a people forms itself in a life-or-death decision beyond the law, to Hannah Arendt's argument that individuals can show themselves to be distinctive only in public deliberations, to Michel Foucault's late advocacy of a critical philosophy that would reveal the conditions under which "subjects" can transform themselves. Impressed by the power of modern industrial organization and technology to oppress individuals and communities as well as to free them from economic necessity, Jean-Paul Sartre and Jürgen Habermas have articulated different understandings of freedom – individual and communal – as well as means of securing it. Equally impressed by the homogenizing tendencies of modern technologies and state use of them, Michael Oakeshott and Alasdair MacIntyre have both urged their readers to adopt more tradition- and practice-based understandings of politics and community. Yet where Oakeshott is at bottom a radical individualist, MacIntyre condemns both the modern state and its capitalist economy for its fundamental selfishness. Charles Taylor has tried to combine a liberal concern for preserving individual freedom and diversity with a recognition of the fundamentally social character of the dialogical understandings we develop of ourselves and our communities. In some way his work represents a return to the Hegel-based attempt by Antonio Gramsci to adapt Benedetto Croce's liberal recognition of the infinite diversity of concrete human historical experience to socialist politics.

The accounts presented in this volume of these diverse responses to the challenges posed by modern natural science and history to both politics and philosophy in the twentieth century are organized in the following manner, partly chronological and partly thematic.

Part I features three chapters on three thinkers who represent the three major political alternatives in the first half of the twentieth century: John Dewey (1859–1952), Carl Schmitt (1888–1985), and Antonio Gramsci (1891–1937). On his ninetieth birthday the *New York Times* announced that John Dewey was "America's Philosopher." As David Fott explains, Dewey thought that science and democracy would and should progress at the same time, in the same ways. Carl Schmitt's famous rediscovery of "sovereignty" in the "state of exception" beyond the law and the "concept of the political" in the conflict of friends and enemies was intended to attack and undermine exactly the kind of progressive liberal politics Dewey espoused as well as to respond to the communist threat from the left. As Tracy Strong reminds us, Schmitt was a leading jurist under the Weimar Republic in Germany who joined the Nazi Party in 1933 and never recanted. Although Schmitt did not have a particularly high opinion of Hitler as an individual, he apparently thought that Hitler had demonstrated his ability to realize Schmitt's understanding of "political theology" by making extralegal sovereign decisions. Antonio Gramsci was one of the founders of the Italian Communist Party in 1921. According to Joseph Buttigieg, Gramsci opposed the positivist doctrines and scientism dear to many more-orthodox Marxist-Leninists. He argued that the socialist goal of liberating the majority of humanity from the rule of the minority would not be brought about by the laws of nature or the inexorable march of history, but rather by "intelligent reflection, at first by just a few people and later by a whole class."

Part II contains essays on the reflective responses to World War II, the Holocaust, and the development of weapons of mass destruction articulated by a group of philosophically trained émigrés from the continent of Europe: Leo Strauss (1899–1973), Eric Voegelin (1901–85), Yves R. Simon (1903–61), and Hannah Arendt (1906–75). All four became U.S. citizens and publicly argued for the superiority of American political institutions and practices to those of the European nations (Germany and France) from which they had come. Yet all four also suggested that American political life rested on an inadequate understanding of politics that needed to be more historically and philosophically informed. All four gave penetrating critiques of American social science, but their responses to the novel and in many ways frightening political developments of the twentieth century were very different. Strauss, Voegelin, and Simon all suggested that the weakness that the modern liberal democracies had displayed in the face of the threat posed by the totalitarian regimes was ultimately a moral failure; all three looked to the history of philosophy, more or less broadly construed, for resources to shore up the faltering moral resolve of their fellow citizens. However, they put forward very different understandings of that history. Whereas Strauss argued that the vitality of the Western tradition arose from the fundamental conflict between reason and revelation, both Voegelin and Simon maintained that there was a fundamental continuity. As Steven Smith reminds us, Strauss suggested that a philosopher might need to write esoterically to avoid persecution by the authorities; yet, as Ellis Sandoz and Walter Nicgorski show, both Voegelin and Simon insisted that the philosopher's supreme duty was to proclaim the truth in the face of a hostile community.

As Dana Villa tells us, Arendt's investigation of the "origins of totalitarianism" led her to a very different analysis of the problem. By depriving human beings of any public or social space for free movement and discourses and by stripping them of the capacity for spontaneity by means of ideological conditioning and constant terror, totalitarian regimes had shown they could transform human nature. Asking how this dehumanization could have been carried out in the heart of civilized Europe, Arendt thought she had found the source of the problem in the history of philosophy itself: "From the Platonic analogy between the structure of the soul and that of the 'just' polity, to Aristotle's insistence on 'natural' relations of hierarchy, to Hobbes's and Rousseau's doctrines of a unitary sovereign will (whether monarchical or popular), to, finally, the Marxian idea of a society without class divisions that has 'overcome' politics . . . the tradition [had effaced] the *sine qua non* of authentic politics: the discursive relations of *plural* equals." Arendt attempted, therefore, to resuscitate a prephilosophical, ancient Greek understanding of politics as "the activity of debate, deliberation, and decision exercised by . . . diverse civic equals in a legally and institutionally articulated public space" that is diametrically opposed to Schmitt's more violent and moral "concept of the political."

Part III includes chapters on six different attempts on the part of two generations of Anglo-American political philosophers to articulate new and better defenses of liberal democratic political institutions in the face of challenges they faced from both left and right. Friedrich Hayek (1899–1992), Michael Oakeshott (1901–90), and Isaiah Berlin (1909–97) presented three very different arguments for limiting government to preserve what has come (to a considerable extent as a result of Berlin's work) to be known as "negative" rather than "positive" freedom. These chapters are followed by accounts of the arguments given by H. L. A. Hart (1907–92), John Rawls (1921–2002), and Richard Rorty (1931–2007) to support liberal political principles and practices. Whereas Hart and Rawls attempted to revive modified forms of social contract theory, Rorty argued that such theory should be jettisoned entirely.

Hayek, Oakeshott, and Berlin all raised questions about both the rationality and the beneficial results of attempts by the central government to plan and direct economic or other forms of development. In contrast to earlier "social contract" thinkers, however, their arguments in favor of preserving liberty by limiting government did not rely on claims about human nature or an original compact. All three were too aware of historical contingency and change. As a result, all three emphasized the essential diversity, plurality, and incommensurability of the varied goods or goals human beings seek.

As Eric Mack shows, Hayek extended the economic analysis of "spontaneous," unintended, and evolving order derived from Adam Smith to biology, language, morality, and law. Government was or ought to be one of the specialized associations that are intentionally created to serve a particular function – in this case, the enforcement of the "just rules of conduct" that secure the liberties of individuals. Hayek generally presented himself as an empirical social scientist whose findings were "value-free," but Mack wonders whether Hayek could or should have so understood his prescriptions with regard to the rules of just conduct.

Reflecting his Hegelian education, Oakeshott, like Dewey, denied the validity of the empiricist suggestion that there is a difference between "the world" and the world of our experience. Yet, as Timothy Fuller reports, Oakeshott emphasized the differences among the modes of interpreting that experience that human beings invent for themselves. In particular, he argued that science, which understands the world in terms of stable, quantitative relationships; history, which makes sense of the world by treating all experience as past; and practice, which, including both politics and religion, understands the world as a tension between "what is" and "what ought to be," are essentially different. In seeking knowledge of the whole, philosophy must thus investigate and expose the limitations of each of these modes. Rather than constituting a form of "politics by other means," political philosophy for Oakeshott thus became a critique of attempts to make politics scientific or to begin everything anew, abstracting from history and tradition.

Whereas Oakeshott insisted on differentiating philosophy from history and history from practice, Berlin, as William Galston informs us, tended to fuse them:

He argued against what he called moral monism – the view that "all ethical questions have a single correct answer, and that all these answers can be derived from a single coherent moral system." His opposition was in part practical: He was convinced that monistic claims had helped bolster modern tyrannies. It was in part historical, derived from his study of different cultures and thinkers. . . . It was also empirical. He insisted that ordinary experience reveals the reality of deep moral conflicts rooted not in confusion but rather in the clash of worthy goods, and he refused to sacrifice the phenomena of moral life to the demands of theoretical coherence.

Rather than trying to protect individual liberty from ideological, political, and economic domination, H. L. A. Hart, John Rawls, and Richard Rorty all suggested that more extensive governmental powers and intervention in the lives of individuals were needed to enable them to formulate and carry out life plans of their own. Hart and Rawls have both been heralded as the revivers of political philosophy within the linguistic, or analytic, tradition; in doing so, both recurred to modified forms of the social contract tradition originated by Hobbes.

In *The Concept of Law*, John Finnis explains, Hart not only argued that there are two different kinds of rules of law serving two different functions, "obligation-imposing rules" and "power-conferring rules." He also specified a "minimum content of natural law," beginning with the universal human "aim" of survival and recognizing such "truisms" as that human beings are approximately equal to each other in strength and vulnerability; limited in their "altruism," understanding, and strength of will; and subject to scarcity of resources; he concluded that it is therefore rational for human beings to cooperate voluntarily in a coercive system.

According to Paul Weithman, reflections on the extreme violence of two world wars and the Holocaust led John Rawls to conclude that the task of political philosophy in the twentieth century was to defend a reasonable faith in the possibility of a just constitutional regime. In *A Theory of Justice* Rawls sought to show that such a regime was possible by arguing, on the basis of what he thought were plausible assumptions about human psychology drawn from social contract theory, that members of a just society would acquire a sense of justice as a normal part of their moral development and that they would affirm that their disposition to cooperate is good for them. However, in *Political Liberalism* Rawls later explicitly jettisoned any such assumptions about human nature. In contrast to previous political philosophies, like those of Kant and Mill, Rawls insisted that his own view was founded not on ambitious philosophical claims about human beings anywhere and everywhere, but on ideas about the nature of citizenship that are common in the liberal democracies to which his work was addressed.

As Michael Bacon shows, Richard Rorty went even further than Rawls in arguing that liberal political institutions were historically contingent developments that could not be philosophically defended on the basis of untenable, theologically derived conceptions of human nature and natural rights. Such institutions could and should nevertheless be embraced on the "pragmatic" grounds that they have worked well for us in the past. By limiting the public sphere, liberal political institutions allow every individual to develop his or her own life story. "Liberal ironists" nevertheless have a duty to become aware of the many ways in which human beings continue to be cruel to others and to work for social reforms to ameliorate human suffering.

Part IV contains accounts of the critiques of, and alternatives to, liberal political philosophy articulated by Jean-Paul Sartre (1905–80), Michel Foucault (1926–84), Jürgen Habermas (1929–), Alasdair MacIntyre (1929–), and Charles Taylor (1931–). All five of these twentieth-century political thinkers begin with insights taken from Hegel or Marx, but all depart from Hegel and Marx in two fundamental respects: None argues that history has a necessary course or direction, and none thinks that human life is completely determined by material conditions. These thinkers all see selves or subjects and societies not as naturally given, but rather as historical entities that develop by interacting with others. It is not surprising, then, that most of these thinkers take an activist political stance. Like the liberal political philosophers featured in Part III, these critics of liberalism worry about concentrations of power, but they worry as much if not more about the economic power concentrated in a few hands in "late-capitalist" societies as they do about the government.

Like Arendt, Sartre began as a student of philosophy, William McBride shows, but became involved in politics as a result of his experience during World War II. Like Arendt, Sartre was deeply influenced by Heidegger, but also like Arendt, Sartre did not follow Heidegger politically. At the end of World War II Sartre became world famous as a proponent of "existential" freedom, which he then tried to meld with Marxism in analyzing the stages of development of human society. He consistently resisted the determinism associated with orthodox Marxism, however, and dissociated himself from it at the end of his life.

Foucault criticized both liberals and Marxists for their "juridical" understanding of political power as exercised by a central government that could be seized. Power is not only diffused in and through everything, he argued; it is also productive. Knowledge is power, and power produces knowledge. Human beings have become "subjects," in both the passive and the active sense of the word, as a result of a complex set of historical contingencies. Yet, as Alan Milchman and Alan Rosenberg point out, Foucault thought that we can now develop a kind of critical philosophy that does not seek to determine the conditions and limits of our possible knowledge, but instead seeks the conditions and indefinite possibilities of transforming ourselves.

Habermas also initially defined himself as a "critical theorist." As William Scheuerman explains, Habermas's portrayal of the decay of the classical liberal or "bourgeois" public sphere and its replacement by a late-capitalist "manufactured" public sphere in *The Structural Transformation of the Public Sphere* laid the foundation for his lifelong attempt to sketch out a defensible deliberative model of politics and law, grounded in a rigorous theory of communicative action; this model has put him in dialogue with Anglophone liberal political theorists. Although Habermas has criticized Hegelian-Marxist holistic models of planned democratic socialism for neglecting the rightful autonomy of market mechanisms and has largely jettisoned the Marxist framework of his early work, he has also persistently faulted Schmitt's political existentialism and antirationalism, most recently in defending a pacific, nonstatist form of cosmopolitan global governance.

Alasdair MacIntyre also began as a Marxist, Arthur Madigan reminds us, and the rejection of contemporary liberalism remains one of the constants in MacIntyre's thought. In *After Virtue* (1981) MacIntyre moved away from his early Marxism by arguing that the Enlightenment project of providing a rational justification for morality was bound to fail, because it attempted to justify an inherited morality separated from its basis in a teleological understanding of human nature. The classical exponent of such a teleological understanding of human nature is Aristotle, and MacIntyre has attempted to revive an Aristotelian understanding of a political community as a necessarily small group in which people know each other and develop their capacity to deliberate rationally about what is good both for each individual and for the community. Because neither the modern state nor the capitalist economy it defends constitutes such a community, MacIntyre argues, we should concentrate our attention on smaller, subpolitical communities and practices.

Like Foucault, Charles Taylor identified himself as a young man with the "New" as opposed to the old Marxist left, and he took his philosophical inspiration more from Hegel than from Marx. Like Habermas and MacIntyre, however, Taylor understands politics to be a kind of practice and that practice to consist, fundamentally, in a kind of rational deliberation. As Ruth Abbey explains, Taylor advances a conception of the self as dialogical and thinks about politics in the same terms: "Practices are intersubjectively formed and perpetuated: The meanings they contain are . . . 'not . . . the property of one or some individuals' . . . so . . . the individual cannot be the basic unit of analysis." Like Gramsci, Taylor thus concludes that, to change the world, critics must challenge the regnant interpretations held by their fellows. That, as he sees it, is the primary task of political theory.

The collection

This collection celebrates the lives and works of extraordinary individual thinkers who have tried not merely to understand but also to improve the political communities in which they found themselves. One of the many issues about which they are divided is the extent to which understanding, or "theory," and practice can or should be linked. Does political involvement and activity follow logically from a theorist's analysis of the world and his or her place in it, or does passionate engagement with the issues of the day cloud the clarity, if not objectivity, of that thought? The presentation of the varied responses offered by these thinkers, as individuals, to the political and philosophical crises of the twentieth century is based on the observation that philosophy is an activity undertaken by embodied human beings living at specific times and places. Although their thought is not bound or determined by their particular circumstances, they are provoked to think and write by problems they perceive in the world around them; they tend, moreover, to address their countrymen and contemporaries first, although by no means exclusively.

As a reader will see by consulting the description of the contributors at the front of the volume, each chapter is written by a scholar not only knowledgeable about but also sympathetic to the approach taken by the author in question. Some of the chapters nevertheless conclude by raising questions about the adequacy of that author's approach; in other words, they are not merely uncritical celebrations or praise. Much of the debate and criticism of the various approaches emerges, however, from the juxtaposition of the different authors and their various arguments in a single volume. Although we have attempted to indicate the breadth as well as the depth of the varied philosophical responses to political developments in the twentieth century, we make no claim to present an encyclopedic or comprehensive account. There are other authors who could and perhaps should have been included; for example, Jacques Maritain, Simone de Beauvoir, Raymond Aron, Georg Lukacs, Herbert Marcuse, Robert Nozick, and Michael Walzer. The authors and arguments featured in this volume represent the major political and philosophical alternatives, both before and after World War II. Contrary to the premature announcements of its demise, their work shows that, in the twentieth century, political philosophy was very much alive.

Part I

The three basic alternatives in the early twentieth century

I

John Dewey: philosophy as theory of education

DAVID FOTT

A graduate of the University of Vermont, John Dewey (1859–1952) taught high school in Pennsylvania and Vermont before beginning graduate school in philosophy and psychology at Johns Hopkins University. There he became attracted to neo-Hegelian philosophy because of its organic conception of the universe, including human society. Ten years as a professor at the University of Michigan and the University of Minnesota were followed by ten years at the University of Chicago, where he taught philosophy and psychology and established the Laboratory School. His growing recognition of the success of science in solving problems by beginning with ordinary human experience led to his rejection of any sort of Hegelian reliance on an Absolute to guarantee the validity of ideas. Dewey's pragmatism envisioned the role of thought as experimentally determining the consequences of proposed actions for the purpose of evaluation, instead of discerning fixed principles of action.

In 1904 Dewey became professor of philosophy at Columbia University and remained there until retirement in 1930. His major works of this period were *How We Think* (1910, revised 1933), *Democracy and Education* (1916), *Reconstruction in Philosophy* (1920, revised 1948), *Human Nature and Conduct* (1922, revised 1930), *Experience and Nature* (1925, revised 1929), *The Public and Its Problems* (1927), and *The Quest for Certainty* (1929).

In the 1930s Dewey's most important books were *Art as Experience* (1934) and *Logic: The Theory of Inquiry* (1938). His publications included many

I thank Katherine Philippakis and Catherine Zuckert for comments on earlier drafts of this chapter. I acknowledge permission from Rowman & Littlefield to use material from my book, *John Dewey: America's Philosopher of Democracy*. I give more attention to some points raised in *Democracy and Education* in my chapter "John Dewey's Alternative Liberalism," in *History of American Political Thought*, ed. Bryan-Paul Frost and Jeffrey Sikkenga (Lanham, MD: Lexington Books, 2003), 585–97.

articles for a wider audience, especially in *The New Republic*. A supporter of American involvement in World War I, he was a leading figure afterward in the outlawry of war movement, and he opposed American participation in World War II until the Japanese attack on Pearl Harbor, on the grounds that violence would promote militarism and capitalism, not democracy. Dewey was a socialist, but he gave scant attention to institutional means for implementing socialism. In 1937 he served as chair of the Commission of Inquiry in Mexico City that found Leon Trotsky not guilty of Joseph Stalin's charges of treason and murder, although he voiced his opposition to the communists' use of violence to achieve allegedly egalitarian goals.

In this chapter, a deeper analysis of Dewey's philosophy is achieved through an examination of one of his books (with reference to other writings). I choose *Democracy and Education* not only because it is his most influential book but also because Dewey thought that it came the closest to summarizing his "entire philosophical position."[1] The purpose of *Democracy and Education* is to "state the ideas implied in a democratic society and to apply these ideas to the problems of the enterprise of education" (3).[2]

Dewey divides the book into four parts (331–3). The first part (chapters 1–5) considers education in general as a social need and then in particular as a democratic need, along with the general features of education. The second part (chapters 6–14) treats democratic aims in education and articulates principles of method and subject matter. Part three (chapters 15–23) begins by considering aspects of the curriculum, but is mainly devoted to practical and philosophical impediments to the democratic ideal. In what may initially seem an odd theme for the conclusion, the final part (chapters 24–6) concerns the nature of philosophy.

Part 1: growth

It is significant that Dewey begins by treating education in terms of the preservation of social groups (5). Rarely in his writings does he recognize

---

[1] John Dewey to Horace M. Kallen, July 1, 1916. Horace M. Kallen Papers, American Jewish Archives, Hebrew Union College, Cincinnati, Ohio. Cited in Robert B. Westbrook, *John Dewey and American Democracy* (Ithaca, NY: Cornell University Press, 1991), 168.

[2] References to Dewey's work are to the critical (print) edition, *The Collected Works of John Dewey, 1882–1953*, ed. Jo Ann Boydston, 37 vols. (Carbondale: Southern Illinois University Press, 1969–91), published in three series as *The Early Works* (EW), *The Middle Works* (MW), and *The Later Works* (LW). These designations are followed by volume and page number. "LW 1.14," for example, refers to *The Later Works*, vol. 1, p. 14. All sources cited are Dewey's works unless otherwise noted. Parenthetical references in the text are to the page numbers of MW 9, which contains *Democracy and Education*.

a purpose of education that is not social. Communities strive to maintain their shared beliefs and practices, and toward that end education occurs almost constantly – wherever there is communication. Informal education, he suggests, is more important than formal schooling (7). However, it does not follow that formal education should mimic what happens in the larger community. The school has three functions: to simplify the social environment, to purify it, and to enable each individual "to escape from the limitations of the social group in which he was born" (24–5). The last function exists because of the heterogeneity of modern societies. All three functions necessitate direction, conscious or unconscious, of the young by adults.[3] Conscious control may be necessary when children cannot foresee the consequences of their actions (32). More desirable is the subtle guidance that appeals to children's interests as a means of developing their understanding of their environment. This conclusion appears to be dictated by Dewey's belief that the mind develops as individuals increasingly understand the use of things around them through association with other people, and understanding is enhanced when they take an interest in the use of those things – that is, when they are on a more equal footing with one another (38).

Lest we draw the conclusion that Dewey considers a purified adulthood the standard by which education should be conducted, he argues that immaturity should not be regarded as a negative condition. Immaturity implies the potential for development or growth, and viewing childhood as the absence of the ideal adulthood leads to a neglect of the child's native powers, as ideals are imposed on the child from above (55). Moreover, adults need to develop as much as children do (47). In other words, education should not be viewed entirely as preparation for the future; it is only partly so (61). Another mistake is to see education as a passive adjustment to a fixed environment. Indeed, one difference between civilized and savage people is that, to a greater extent, the former adapt to their environment by introducing means of control (52). Neglect of this point in education means that children fail to develop the ability to cope with new situations (55). Dewey never makes habits the enemy, but he does insist that they be seen as flexible: "A habit means an ability to use natural conditions as means to ends. It is an active control of the environment through control of the organs of action" (51). The view of habits as rigid yields "an undue

---

[3] See *Experience and Education* (1938), in LW 13.8, 21, 46–7 for Dewey's repudiation of the position that educators should leave children to act on their desires with little or no guidance.

emphasis upon drill and other devices which secure automatic skill at the expense of personal perception" (55).

The previous paragraph may be summarized by Dewey's claim that "the educational process has no end beyond itself' (54): "Not perfection as a final goal, but the ever-enduring process of perfecting, maturing, refining is the aim in living. . . . Growth itself is the only moral 'end.'"[4]

James H. Nichols Jr. has suggested that Dewey's philosophy does not clearly distinguish growth from its opposite: When Dewey says that growth is what enables more growth to occur, he appears to rely ultimately on the Hobbesian test of survival.[5] This issue is clearly important to Dewey because, in a passage from *Experience and Education*, his last major book on education, he asks whether a person can truly "grow" as a criminal:

Does this form of growth create conditions for further growth, or does it set up conditions that shut off the person who has grown in this particular direction from the occasions, stimuli, and opportunities for continuing growth in new directions? What is the effect of growth in a special direction upon the attitudes and habits which alone open up avenues for development in other lines? I shall leave you to answer these questions, saying simply that when and *only* when development in a particular line conduces to continuing growth does it answer to the criterion of education as growing.[6]

That Dewey leaves those questions to the reader might be interpreted as an admission of weakness in his argument. Alternatively, that passage may suggest fairly clear answers to the questions. Dewey seems to imply that a burglar or a corrupt politician (those are his examples) is shut off from further stimuli, which include other people, that are required for continuing growth. Perhaps he leaves us to supply the seemingly incontrovertible premises that we cannot all survive together as burglars or corrupt politicians and that no one can survive alone.

Part 2: the democratic conception

As we begin to look at the second part of *Democracy and Education*, we note that Dewey might make two other replies to Nichols's charge that growth is no more than the means to survival. First, in chapter 7, titled "The Democratic Conception in Education," he advances the following

---

[4] *Reconstruction in Philosophy* (1920), in MW 12.181.
[5] James H. Nichols Jr., "Pragmatism and the U.S. Constitution," in *Confronting the Constitution*, ed. Allan Bloom (Washington, DC: AEI Press, 1990), 382. I have greatly benefited from Nichols's essay.
[6] *Experience and Education*, in LW 13.19–20 (emphasis in original).

standards for gauging the worth of a form of association: "How numerous and varied are the interests which are consciously shared? How full and free is the interplay with other forms of association?" (89). Growth, then, as measured by the number and variety of shared interests, is the increasing harmonization of individuals within society. Because this harmonization is more than is needed for mere survival, growth is not reducible to survival.

Second, Dewey devotes a good deal of thought to moral growth. What constitutes moral growth in an individual, he and James H. Tufts argue elsewhere, is a movement from the stage of (1) acting according to habit to (2) paying attention to the meaning of that habit to (3) acting according to a higher, or more thoughtful, habit. This movement uses reason as "an element in determining what shall be sought."[7] Paying attention means using one's reason; thus reason is not exclusively, or even necessarily primarily, for the sake of survival. Instead, reason leads to a higher goal, growth, where the higher goal can be distinguished from a lower one according to the degree of harmonization.

Thus Dewey's ability to avoid the problem raised by Nichols depends on his thesis that more social harmonization is better than less. Dewey sees nothing in human nature – not reason, or passion, or anything else – the development of which would render social harmonization either impossible or undesirable.[8]

Dewey rejects both natural development and social efficiency as educational goals. As for the former, which sees growth as "natural" development in the sense of spontaneous or unhindered, he objects to Jean-Jacques Rousseau's *Emile*. Dewey says that children lack the already determined futures of seeds and that all growth requires external help (119–21): "A stunted oak, or a stalk of maize with few ears of scattered grains, exhibits natural development as truly as the noblest tree or the prize-winning ear of maize."[9] To appeal to nature as the goal is to fail to see that the "natural, or native, powers furnish the initiating and limiting forces in all education; they do not furnish its ends or aims" (121). The conception of social efficiency as the aim of education can take the form of industrial competency, in which case it tends to favor the status quo, or it can take the form of good citizenship, which has the advantage of greater concreteness but may

---

[7] John Dewey and James H. Tufts, *Ethics* (1908), in MW 5.17.
[8] See "Human Nature" (1932), in LW 6.31; "Does Human Nature Change?" (1938), in LW 13.286–7.
[9] "The Need for a Philosophy of Education" (1934), in LW 9.196.

be interpreted too narrowly. True social efficiency, he says, requires the possession and use of leisure, art, and recreation (127).

The second part of the book also stresses the commonality that Dewey sees between a model democratic society and an ideal community of scientific inquirers – a point worth examining in some detail. First, he attempts to show the inadequacy of epistemological rationalism (the view that knowledge begins with an act of pure mind or reason) as opposed to pragmatic empiricism (to be explained in the next paragraph). Thus he objects to our "making an entity out of the abstract noun 'consciousness'" (110). Mental states do not constitute a purely private realm but are instead bound up with physical objects (132, 147). Mind–body dualism is "the root of the dualism of method and subject matter" in education (173).

To that rationalism, Dewey opposes a notion of reason as a "reflective" process consisting of several steps, which constitute the scientific method: (a) "perplexity," (b) "a conjectural anticipation," (c) "a careful survey" of all considerations, (d) "elaboration of the tentative hypothesis to make it more precise and more consistent," and (e) acting on the hypothesis to test it (157). These steps are guidelines, not rigid rules to be followed in every scientific inquiry. He characterizes a liberal intelligence as "playing freely upon the subjugation of the world for human ends" but not manipulating others for selfish aims (143). Thus for Dewey science means thinking and acting with purpose – not taking a chance on one's fortune, but instead taking responsibility for the consequences of one's actions (110, 153).

Dewey sees the scientific method as logically connected to democratic method:

It is of the nature of science not so much to tolerate as to welcome diversity of opinion, while it insists that inquiry brings the evidence of observed facts to bear to effect a consensus of conclusions. . . . Freedom of inquiry, toleration of diverse views, freedom of communication, the distribution of what is found out to every individual as the ultimate intellectual consumer, are involved in the democratic as in the scientific method.[10]

Yet how solid is this kinship? On the one hand, comparison to science may lift up democratic practice by giving it a goal to strive for – the truth or reasonable desire – instead of the desire of the moment. On the other hand, science does not always operate through democratic means; in fact,

---

[10] *Freedom and Culture* (1939), in LW 13.135.

some of the greatest scientific achievements have come when at least one of the five steps mentioned by Dewey has been violated, or when diverse views have not been fully tolerated, or when one person has worked alone (e.g., Isaac Newton was reluctant to communicate his work). Moreover, as Dewey is well aware, science does not always operate for democratic ends.[11]

Part 3: the curriculum

The third part of *Democracy and Education* begins by considering aspects of the curriculum. Dewey takes up at greater length the theme of play and work, inside and outside school, briefly mentioned in the analysis of science. He rejects the typical, economic distinction between play and work in favor of a more nuanced distinction: Like play, work "signifies purposeful activity and differs *not* in that activity is subordinated to an external result, but in the fact that a longer course of activity is occasioned by the idea of a result. The demand for continuous attention is greater, and more intelligence must be shown in selecting and shaping means" (212; emphasis in original). In neither play nor work should activity be a *mere* means to a desired end, but in both play and work activity is undertaken for the sake of an end. The difference is that with work more attention is paid to the results attained than with play. Work done with a playful spirit should be considered "art" (214).

When we come to the specifics of the curriculum, Dewey's emphases are more controversial. History and geography are "the information studies *par excellence* of the schools" because they "enrich and liberate the more direct and personal contacts of life by furnishing their context, their background and outlook" (218). He sees a deeper relation between those two subjects – at least between geography and one aspect of history – than is commonly recognized. Geography has a primary focus on the study of nature, and "economic history is more human, more democratic, and hence more liberalizing than political history" because it deals with the human conquest of nature and not mainly with princes or military commanders (223–4). Thus he emphasizes history and geography rather than mathematics, literature, or art, as those three subjects are usually construed, because history and geography uniquely prepare the way for education in the scientific method

[11] Ibid., in LW 13.156.

for social purposes. Dewey has frequently been criticized for advocating the teaching of basic literacy and mathematics in the context of practical activities and neglecting the necessary role of memorization.[12] That criticism has also been made of progressive education, the child-centered excesses of which he has often been unfairly associated with.

Dewey maintains that literature and the fine arts can provide training in methods or skills of various sorts, and they can be socially useful. However, their primary function is to promote "an intensified, enhanced appreciation" of the things in human life (246). Humanistic studies should include a study of nature; otherwise they will become as remote from most people's lives as is knowledge of ancient Greek and Roman civilizations, which is valuable but less accessible than science (238). The particular problem of education in science is to convey the "belief in the possibility of the direction of human affairs by itself" (233).

For the remainder of the third part of the book, Dewey is concerned with combating impediments, theoretical and practical, to his conception of democratic education. He begins with the isolation of social classes, which separates those who labor from those who enjoy the fruits of labor, thereby preventing work from being art. He traces the isolation of classes to ancient Greece, alleging that Plato's and Aristotle's works reflect and endorse this unfortunate social development (259–70). Consequent to that social development was the separation of intellectual studies from practical studies (271–85), of social studies from physical studies (286–99), and of the individual from the world (300–15). Dewey appears to find the root cause – at least the intellectual cause – of all of these false dichotomies in the advent of the field of epistemology: "The identification of mind with the self, and the setting up of the self as something independent and self-sufficient, created such a gulf between the knowing mind and the world that it became a question how knowledge was possible at all" (302). If reformers such as Galileo Galilei and René Descartes had seen more clearly, they "would have perceived that such disconnection, such rupture of continuity, denied in advance the possibility of success in their endeavors" (304).

As I have noted, the central goal of Dewey's metaphysics is to advance recognition of the existential "continuity" between mind and world – "organism" and "environment," as he says.[13] He attempts to use scientific

---

[12] See *Schools of To-Morrow* (1915), in MW 8.248–93.
[13] *Experience and Nature*, 2nd ed. (1929), in LW 1.9, 211–25, 259–62.

method to disprove metaphysical dualisms, such as that between mind and body. The key to this effort is the continuity, or continuum, that he claims may be found within "experience" itself: Experience "recognizes in its primary integrity no division between act and material, subject and object, but contains them both in an unanalyzed totality."[14] If the situation consists of a mind internal to a person and an external world (including the body connected to that mind) separate from it, how can the mind connect to the world? However, if "mind" and "world" are conceived as analytical distinctions from an original whole, rather than as separate existences, then the problem dissolves. Knowledge is something that occurs, and we may usefully describe it as an activity in terms such as "mind" and "world," as long as we do not distort their significance.

Part 4: philosophy

The goal of chapter 24, which begins the final part of *Democracy and Education*, is to clarify the notion of philosophy implied in the previous chapters. Our puzzlement that this should be the end of a book on democratic education is somewhat lessened when we are told that philosophy is "*the general theory of education*" (338; emphasis in original). As we have seen, according to Dewey, philosophy is born of societal divisions or conflicts; for example, the philosophical separation between theory and practice derives from the social separation between the leisure and working classes. In other words, philosophical issues reflect certain dispositions, and the only way to resolve social separations is through a change in dispositions; hence the need for education and the connection between philosophy and education.

One prerequisite of progress is recognition of the distinction between knowledge and thinking. Dewey equates "grounded knowledge" with science: "[I]t represents objects which have been settled, ordered, disposed of rationally." Philosophy is identified with thinking, which "is occasioned by an *un*settlement and . . . aims at overcoming a disturbance. Philosophy is thinking what the known demands of us – what responsive attitude it exacts" (336; emphasis in original). It appears, then, that for Dewey philosophy is merely reactive, a response to science, just as thinking is a response to knowledge.

---

[14] Ibid., in LW 1.18.

That appearance is partially deceptive, however. Dewey does maintain that philosophy must respect science in the sense that it must recognize the valid claim of science to be the sole avenue to truth. Philosophy takes its bearings from the conclusions of scientific method.[15] Yet it does not follow that philosophy is left with no initiative of its own. Indeed, in an earlier age philosophy paved the way for scientific advancement by criticizing premodern institutions.[16] To a great extent, he believes, divisions in society are caused by the incomplete progress made by science and its practical applications; philosophy itself remains a mixture of old and new thinking.[17] Now philosophy must make a "systematic" effort "to subject the 'morals' underlying old institutional customs to scientific inquiry and criticism."[18] "Its business is criticism of experience as it exists at a given time and constructive projection of values, which, when acted upon, will render experience more unified, stable, and progressive."[19]

According to Dewey, one aspect of that work is development of a theory of knowledge. Other theories tend to dichotomize empirical and rational knowing, learning as a storehouse of material and learning as doing, passivity and activity, emotions and intellect, theory and practice. By contrast, his theory assumes the notion of continuity (343). He then presents two main arguments for continuity – in this context, continuity of mind and body. First, progress in physiology and psychology has demonstrated the connections among the mind, the nervous system, and the body: "[T]he nervous system is only a specialized mechanism for keeping all bodily activities working together.... While each motor response [to a stimulus] is adjusted to the state of affairs indicated through the sense-organs, that motor response

---

[15] See, e.g., "Philosophy and Democracy" (1918), in MW 11.41–8; "Philosophy" (1928), in LW 3.115, 118–21; "A Résumé of Four Lectures on Common Sense, Science and Philosophy" (1932), in LW 6.428–9; "Lessons from the War – in Philosophy" (1941), in LW 14.316–19, 329–31; *John Dewey and Arthur F. Bentley: A Philosophical Correspondence, 1932–1951*, ed. Sidney Ratner and Jules Altman (New Brunswick, NJ: Rutgers University Press, 1964), 629.

[16] See the introduction to the 1948 reprint of *Reconstruction in Philosophy*, in MW 12.264; "Modern Philosophy" (1952), in LW 16.414–15.

[17] See, e.g., "Has Philosophy a Future?" (1949), in LW 16.367.

[18] Introduction to the 1948 reprint of *Reconstruction in Philosophy*, in MW 12.266. Dewey does not mean that philosophers should do the work of scientists, but that their methods in grappling with moral problems should resemble the method of natural science. See ibid., in MW 12.270, 273; compare "Philosophy's Future in Our Scientific Age: Never Was Its Role More Crucial" (1949), in LW 16.375, 379n.

[19] "The Determination of Ultimate Values or Aims through Antecedent or A Priori Speculation or through Pragmatic or Empirical Inquiry" (1938), in LW 13.255–6.

shapes the next sensory stimulus" (346).[20] Second, the discovery of biological evolution teaches

> continuity of simpler and more complex organic forms.... As activity becomes
> more complex, coordinating a greater number of factors in space and time, intel-
> ligence plays a more and more marked role, for it has a larger span of the future
> to forecast and plan for. The effect upon the theory of knowing is to displace the
> notion that it is the activity of a mere onlooker or spectator of the world, the notion
> which goes with the idea of knowing as something complete in itself. (347)

Here Dewey's principle of continuity implies a notion of growth, not merely
a continuum. Thus a theory of knowledge has social and political relevance:
"[S]ince democracy stands in principle for free interchange, for social continuity, it must develop a theory of knowledge which sees in knowledge the
method by which one experience is made available in giving direction and
meaning to another" (354–5). Similarly, a superior theory of morals will
build on the observation that learning follows from activities having a social
purpose and proceeding from normal social situations: "[T]he measure of
the worth of the administration, curriculum, and methods of instruction of
the school is the extent to which they are animated by a social spirit" (368).

Because he concludes his book as he does, Dewey invites evaluation
of his view of democratic education on the basis of his understanding of
philosophy. As we have seen, he defines philosophy as "the general theory
of education." By "theory" here he means not a giving of answers but an
asking of questions. The phrase "philosophy of education" refers to "an
explicit formulation of the problems of the formation of right mental and
moral habitudes in respect to the difficulties of contemporary social life"
(341).

However, the goal of philosophy is limited not only because of the
unique access of science to knowledge but also because of the narrow
validity that ideas or principles can attain – a point Dewey makes most
clearly regarding political philosophy: "The fundamental defect" of early
political liberalism "was its lack of perception of historic relativity."[21] The
idea of the individual in the state of nature in full possession of liberty
prevented early liberals from recognizing that governmental intervention

---

[20] Dewey here implicitly draws on his own seminal article "The Reflex Arc Concept in Psychology"
(1896), in EW 5.96–109.
[21] "The Future of Liberalism" (1935), in LW 11.290. See also *Liberalism and Social Action* (1935), in LW
11.26; "Introduction to *Problems of Men*: The Problems of Men and the Present State of Philosophy"
(1946), in LW 15.162–3.

might be necessary to ensure political liberty against opposing forces in society, especially concerning economic matters. "Ideas that at one time are means of producing social change have not the same meaning when they are used as means of preventing social change. This fact is itself an illustration of historic relativity."[22] Yet, we may ask, is not the statement of that fact itself a refutation of historic relativity? To the best of my knowledge, Dewey offers no solution to that conundrum.

It might appear that the orientation toward science that Dewey gives philosophy would also provide boundaries that transcend time and place. Does not science disclose things as they are? Yet Dewey sees a close connection between the scientific method and historical relativism: Science teaches us that principles that succeed in solving one problem may fail in solving another problem. Thus he claims, "The connection between historic relativity and experimental method is intrinsic."[23] Because, as we have seen, philosophy must respect science, it will not challenge the teaching of historical relativism.

According to Dewey, the experimental approach to life "is itself a theory to be tested by experience."[24] The reader of this chapter may have noticed the frequency of the word "experience." Recall Dewey's thesis that "experience" includes both the organism and its environment; his standard is not merely a subjective one. To validate science, he relies on immediate experience, which consists of material from the world presented to a person's senses. We may *feel* qualities of things in our experience without *thinking* about them.[25] What is true, what we are warranted to assert, does not exhaust the domain of what is real. The stuff out of which reflective experience, or science, is made, then, is not prescientific knowledge, but feelings. In turn those feelings may change as the result of reflective experience. Evaluations of things should occur in that way. The interrelation between immediate and reflective experience enables Dewey to judge – not merely to feel – that science may have deleterious consequences as well as beneficial ones.[26] Yet we may want to ask him, how much scientific reflection is necessary *to know* that nuclear war would be bad?

In his later years, Dewey had the misfortune of seeing his profession become even more impressed with science than he was: Under analytic

---

[22] "Future of Liberalism," in LW 11.291.
[23] Ibid., in LW 11.292.
[24] *German Philosophy and Politics* (1915), in MW 8.201.
[25] See, e.g., "The Postulate of Immediate Empiricism" (1903), in MW 3.158–67.
[26] See, e.g., "Has Philosophy a Future?" in LW 16.364–5.

philosophy and logical positivism, ethics was banished to an inferior realm of "normativity." Dewey managed to avoid that trap. Yet his failure to think more rigorously about the relation between philosophy and science allowed Richard Rorty, his most famous recent spokesman, to claim Dewey's thought for his own, postmodern ends more plausibly than would otherwise have been possible.

Suggested secondary reading

Alexander, Thomas M. *John Dewey's Theory of Art, Experience, and Nature: The Horizons of Feeling*. Albany: SUNY Press, 1987.

Diggins, John Patrick. *The Promise of Pragmatism: Modernism and the Crisis of Knowledge and Authority*. Chicago: University of Chicago Press, 1994.

Fott, David. *John Dewey: America's Philosopher of Democracy*. Lanham, MD: Rowman & Littlefield, 1998.

Hook, Sidney. *John Dewey: An Intellectual Portrait*. New York: John Day, 1939.

Pappas, Gregory Fernando. *John Dewey's Ethics: Democracy as Experience*. Bloomington: Indiana University Press, 2008.

Ryan, Alan. *John Dewey and the High Tide of American Liberalism*. New York: Norton, 1995.

Smith, John E. *Purpose and Thought: The Meaning of Pragmatism*. New Haven: Yale University Press, 1978.

Thayer, H. S. *Meaning and Action: A Critical History of Pragmatism*. 2nd ed. Indianapolis: Hackett, 1981.

Westbrook, Robert B. *John Dewey and American Democracy*. Ithaca, NY: Cornell University Press, 1991.

2

Carl Schmitt: political theology and the concept of the political

TRACY B. STRONG

One calls to me from Seir: "Watchman, is the night almost gone? Watchman, is the night almost gone?"

The Watchman said: "Even if the morning cometh, it still remains night. If you wish to inquire, then come again and inquire." (Isaiah 21:11–12)

Carl Schmitt (1888–1985) was perhaps the leading jurist during the Weimar Republic (1919–33). Born the son of a Catholic Westphalian businessman, he was educated as a lawyer and legal theorist at several universities, taking his *habilitation* eventually in Strasbourg (then part of Germany) in 1915. He taught at several German universities, becoming a professor of law at the University of Köln in 1932 and in Berlin in 1933. It is worth noting here that being professor in the German academic system (the title precedes that of doctor) also meant being a (very) high-ranking civil servant and, as such, subject to the regulations governing the behavior of civil servants. Although Schmitt's work was in legal theory and the theory of sovereignty, it was shaped by the concerns raised by the conflicts and difficulties of the Weimar Republic.

In May 1933, he joined the National Socialist Workers Party, or NSDAP (the Nazi Party), the same month as did Martin Heidegger, the leading philosopher in Germany. In November of that year he became the president of the National Socialist Jurists Association. He published works that were supportive of the Nazi Party, including some that were anti-Semitic.[1] However, all did not go smoothly: One tends to forget that there were diverse factions in Nazism, as there are in all political movements, and Schmitt found himself on the losing side of several controversies. Severely

---

[1] Schmitt's anti-Semitism is well documented in Heinrich Meier, *The Lesson of Carl Schmitt* (Chicago: University of Chicago Press, 1998).

criticized in several official organs, he was protected by Hermann Goering, commander-in-chief of the Luftwaffe, the German Air Force. He remained a member of the Nazi Party as well as professor of law at the University of Berlin from 1933 to 1945; he was detained after the war by the victorious Allies. Never charged with crimes, he never recanted nor apologized for his membership in the NSDAP. He continued to write and was in personal and epistolary contact with many prominent postwar intellectuals, including the Hegelian-Marxist Alexandre Kojève, the philosopher-theologian Jacob Taubes, and the politically unplaceable Ernst Jünger. He died in the town in which he was born, Plettenburg, in April 1985.

Before World War II, indeed before 1934 or 1935, Schmitt had been of importance to thinkers across the entire political spectrum. Although always a man of the right, he influenced prominent members of what was to become the "Frankfurt School," a group of left-wing critical thinkers strongly influenced by Marx that included Max Horkheimer, Theodor Adorno, and Walter Benjamin. Recent work has found important traces of his influence in the work of people such as Hannah Arendt and even in so-called postmodernists such as Lyotard. (Derrida devotes several chapters of *The Politics of Friendship* to Schmitt.) At the center of the political spectrum, important liberals such as Carl Friedrich and Hans Morgenthau found significant insights in Schmitt.[2] Yet Schmitt was a willing member of the Nazi Party, and he expressed anti-Semitic statements both before and after World War II (albeit with greater restraint in the postwar period). Why should one pay attention to him?

Anyone writing on Schmitt has an obligation to give an account of what in his work is worth the effort. This is neither a matter of "freedom of thought" (which would reduce interest in Schmitt to subjective preference) nor of "knowing your enemy" (the question is rather to know *who* your enemy is and for what reasons).[3] Necessarily any such account must be substantive. In my view, Schmitt gives us purchase on questions such as these:

[2] See my "Dimensions of the New Debate around Carl Schmitt," foreword to *The Concept of the Political*, by Carl Schmitt, ed. George Schwab (Chicago: University of Chicago Press, 1996), x–xii and the references given there for further discussion of these events. For this chapter, I draw on this foreword, as well as on my foreword to *Political Theology*, by Carl Schmitt, ed. George Schwab (Chicago: University of Chicago Press, 2005).

[3] See Etienne Balibar, "Le Hobbes de Schmitt, le Schmitt de Hobbes," introduction to *Le Léviathan dans la doctrine de l'état de Thomas Hobbes*, by Carl Schmitt (Paris: Seuil, 2002), for similar thoughts.

What are the reasons for the gradual and apparently continuing domination of executive over legislative power in Western democracies during the last century? What is the relation between the various faces of Western industrial democracies – on the one hand their adherence to rights, liberty, and social welfare, and on the other their repressive, disciplinary qualities, not just domestically but, given power, internationally (for example, imperialism, colonialism, support for authoritarian regimes)? In historical terms, are we to think of Fascism as a development of tendencies in modernity or as an aberration? Schmitt's work also raises important questions about what serious attention to these questions entails.

Political Theology, first published in 1922, represents Schmitt's most important initial engagement with the theme that was to preoccupy him for most of his life: that of sovereignty, that is, of the locus and nature of the agency that constitutes a political system. The core of a political decision, Schmitt tells us, is a "demanding and moral decision."[4] The first sentence of *Political Theology* is famous: It locates the realm in which Schmitt asserts the centrality of sovereignty, and it also constitutes the full first paragraph of the work. Schmitt writes, "Sovereign is he who decides on the exceptional case" (*Soverän ist, wer über den Ausnahmezustand entscheidet*) (PT 5). The decisive matter comes from the fact that *über* here is ambiguous: It can mean "he who decides *what* the exceptional case is" or "he who decides *what to do* about the exceptional case." This ambiguity is centrally important to grasping what Schmitt wants to say: It is the essence of sovereignty *both* to decide what is an exception *and* to make the decisions appropriate to that exception; indeed, the one without the other makes no sense at all.

Thus it is not only the case that "exceptions" are obvious, as they would be if we think of them as being produced by severe economic or political disturbance. It would be natural to read what Schmitt says in Germany through the prism of the years of hyperinflation or the economic depression of 1929. However, *Political Theology* was published in March 1922 and cannot be understood as simply the response to these or any other developments. (Hyperinflation hit only in 1923.)

A second issue with the opening sentence comes from the understanding of *Ausnahmezustand*. What the meaning attributed to *über* might seem to reinforce (the absolute, dictatorial, and unlimited quality of the decision), this second concern might seem to mitigate. Schmitt sometimes uses more

---

[4] Schmitt, *Political Theology*, 65. Henceforth cited in the text as PT, followed by the page number. Here and throughout, I have modified Schwab's translation as I thought necessary.

general words when speaking of this question, including "state of exception" (*Ausnahmefall*), "crisis" or "state of urgency" (*Notstand*), and, even more generally, "emergency, state of need" (*Notfall*). However, the idea of an *Ausnahmefall* has more of a legal connotation: It is narrower than an "exception." Thus the same issue is raised as with the word *über*: Can the understanding of what counts as an "exception" be defined in legal terms, or is it more of what one might think of as an open field?

Note here that he is not talking simply about dictatorship. In *Die Diktatur*, published one year before *Political Theology*, Schmitt differentiates between "commissarial dictatorship" – he cites Lincoln in the Civil War as an example – and "sovereign dictatorship." The former defends the existing constitution, whereas the latter seeks to create the conditions for a new one, given the collapse of the old – one might think of de Gaulle in 1958. *Die Diktatur* is a theory of dictatorship; *Political Theology*, however, is a theory of sovereignty and an attempt to locate the state of emergency in a theory of sovereignty. More importantly, *Political Theology* discusses that which for Schmitt underlies the commissarial and sovereign dictatorship and makes both of them possible.

I again do not think this linguistic glide on Schmitt's part is accidental. Rather than seeking to determine what precisely is an *Ausnahmezustand* (or *Notfall*, *Notstand*, etc.), the problem should be looked at from the other direction. For Schmitt, no preexisting set of rules can be laid down that will tell anyone if a given situation is, in actual reality, an exception. It is of the essence of Schmitt's conception of the state that there can be no preset, rule-fixed definition of sovereignty. Why not? What is clear here is that the notion of sovereignty contains, as Schmitt tells us, his general theory of the state (PT 5). As he remarks in the preface to the second edition (1933), the nature of the sovereign is the making of "a genuine decision" (PT 3). Thus it is not simply the making of a decision, but of a "genuine" decision that is central. The obvious question is what makes a decision "genuine" and not simply an emanation of a "degenerate decisionism." Schmitt is never "simply" a decisionist, if by that one means simply that choice is necessary and any choice is better than none.

What constitutes a "genuine decision" is a complex matter. To understand Schmitt's position one must realize why politics (or, here, "the political") is not the same for him as "the state,"[5] even if the most usual framework for

---

[5] This is a theme from Schmitt's earliest work, including his *Habilitationsschrift*, *Der Wert des Staates und die Bedeutung des Einzelnen* (The value of the state and the meaning of the individual) (Hellerau, 1917). See Reinhard Mehring, *Carl Schmitt: Zur Einführung* (Hamburg: Junius, 2001), 19–21.

the concretization of politics in modern times has been the state. In *Political Theology II* (1969), taking up the themes of *Political Theology*, Schmitt writes, "Today one can no longer define politics in terms of the State; on the contrary what we can still call the State today must inversely be defined and understood from the political."[6] Underlying the state is a community of people – necessarily not universal – a "we" that, as it defines itself necessarily in opposition to that which it is not, the state presupposes and that is defined by conflict. It derives its definition from the friend/enemy distinction. That distinction is an us/them distinction, in which the "us" is of primary and necessary importance.

This claim is the basis of Schmitt's rejection of what he calls "liberal normativism": the assumption that a state can in the end rest on a set of mutually agreed-on procedures and rules that trump particular claims and necessities. Thus pluralism is not a condition on which politics nor, therefore, eventually the state can be founded. Politics rests rather on the equality of its citizens (in this sense Schmitt is a democrat, although not a liberal!) and thus their collective identification distinguishing them from other such groups: This is the "friend/enemy" distinction or, more accurately, the distinction that makes politics possible. It is, one might say, its transcendental presupposition.[7] The hostility to pluralism also explains (some of) Schmitt's anti-Semitism. Much like what Hobbes thought about Catholics and their allegiance to the Holy See, Schmitt holds that Jews are always divided in their loyalty and are thus dangerous elements in the state.[8]

Politics is thus different from economics, in which one has "competitors" rather than friends and enemies, and from debate, where one has "discussion opponents."[9] Nor is it a private dislike of another individual. Rather it is the actual possibility of a "battling totality" that finds itself necessarily in opposition to another such entity. "The enemy," Schmitt notes, "is *hostis* [enemy] not *inimicus* [disliked] in the broader sense; *polemios* [belonging to war], not *echthros* [hateful]."[10]

These considerations are made in the context of several other arguments. The first comes in Schmitt's discussion of Hans Kelsen. At the time that

---

[6] Carl Schmitt, *Politisches Theologie II* (Berlin: Duncker & Humblot, 1996), 21.

[7] This is confirmed explicitly in a letter from Leo Strauss to Schmitt, September 4, 1932, printed in Heinrich Meier, *Carl Schmitt and Leo Strauss: The Hidden Dialogue* (Chicago: University of Chicago Press, 1995), 124.

[8] It explains *part* of his anti-Semitism. See footnote 1 for a more extensive discussion.

[9] Schmitt, *Concept of the Political*, 28.

[10] Ibid.

Schmitt wrote *Political Theology*, Kelsen was a leader in European jurisprudence, a prominent Austrian jurist and legal scholar as well as a highly influential member of the Austrian Constitutional Court. A student of Rudolf Stammler, Kelsen was a neo-Kantian by training and temperament, and shortly before the publication of *Political Theology* he published *Das Problem der Souveränität und die Theorie des Völkerrechts* (*The problem of sovereignty and the theory of international law*), in which he set out the foundations for what he would later call a "pure theory of law," a theory of law from which all subjective elements would be eliminated. In other words, Kelsen sought a theory of law that would be universally valid for all times and all situations. It is worth noting here that Schmitt's quarrel with him is analogous to the quarrel between Heidegger and Carnap, between thought with its feet in the earth and what one might call *freischwebende Gedanken* – free-floating thought.

Against Kelsen's "pure theory of law," Schmitt insists that "all law is situational law" (PT 13). What he means is that in actual, lived human fact it will always be the case that, precisely at unpredictable times, "the power of real life breaks through the crust of a mechanism that has become stiff by repetition" (PT 15). In other words, Schmitt requires that his understanding of law and politics respond to the fact of the ultimately unruly and unruled quality of human life. If life can never be reduced or adequately understood by a set of rules, no matter how complex, then this means that in the end, rule is of humans and not of law, or rather that the rule of humans must always existentially underlie the rule of law. For Schmitt, to pretend that one can have an ultimate "rule of law" is to set oneself up to be overtaken by events at some unpredictable but necessarily occurring time and to lose the human element in and of our world.

This is a powerful and important theme in Schmitt. It is not a claim that law is not centrally important to human affairs, but that in the end human affairs rest on humans and cannot ever be independent of them. For instance, in his discussion of Locke, he criticizes Locke on the grounds that although he said the "law gives authority," he "did not recognize that the law does not designate to whom it gives authority. It cannot be just anybody" (PT 32). Schmitt contrasts this to Hobbes's discussion (and in doing so brings out qualities often overlooked in discussions of Hobbes). He cites *Leviathan*, chapter 26, to the effect that sovereign power, and not truth, makes laws. He then drives the point home by citing Hobbes to the effect that "Subjection, Command, Right and Power are accidents not of

37

Powers but of Persons." For Hobbes, "Persons" are beings constituted or authorized to play a certain role or part in the political realm.[11]

Schmitt's insistence on the necessarily and irreducibly *human* quality of political and legal actions is key. Those who would elaborate a set of rules by which decisions can be made take the politics out of human life; Schmitt is concerned to keep them in human life. (It is for reasons such as this that some object to John Rawls's *A Theory of Justice* and even more to his *Political Liberalism* for what appears to them to be an overly legalistic reliance on courts.) Human society can thus never be made to rest on the determination and application of rules to individual situations. Decisions and judgments will always be necessary. In this, Schmitt may be deemed an initiator (albeit an unacknowledged one) of contemporary developments such as critical legal studies on the left and the law and economics movement on the right.

Thus, for Schmitt, the state is not cofounded with the legal order, and in exceptional situations the juristic order that prevails is "not of the ordinary kind" (*keine Rechtsordnung* [PT 12])[12] and "normatively speaking is born from a nothingness" (*normativ betrachtet* [*ist*] *aus einem Nichts geboren* [PT 31–2]). Therefore the point of this notion of sovereignty ultimately unconstrained by formal rules is "to create a juridical order" (*Recht zu schaffen*) under conditions that threaten anarchy (PT 13). Only when freed from normative ties is the authority absolute. This is why this is a political *theology* – God is neither good nor evil in himself, and his authority is not ethical. To be able to create or recover a judicial order when the existing one is threatened by chaos, the sovereign must decide both that a situation is exceptional and what to do about that exception. Ethics and the juridical order are grounded in *das Nichts*, and it was from *das Nichts* that God created the world.

The necessarily extraordinary quality of sovereignty is made clear in the analogy Schmitt uses to explain his point: "The exception in jurisprudence is analogous to the miracle in theology" (PT 36). What does it mean to refer to the exception as a miracle? Clearly, this reference has to do with "political theology." To move toward an answer one should look first at the author who remained Schmitt's touchstone. In *Leviathan*, chapter 37, Hobbes first identifies a miracle as an occurrence in which "the thing is strange, and the natural cause difficult to imagine," and he goes on to define

---

[11] PT 33–4. See my "Seeing the Sovereign: Theatricality and Representation in Hobbes," in *Letting Be: Fred Dallmayr's Cosmopolitan Vision*, ed. Stephen Schneck (Notre Dame, IN: University of Notre Dame Press, 2006).

[12] See the discussion in R. Howse, "From Legitimacy to Dictatorship – and Back Again," in *Law as Politics*, ed. David Dyzenhaus (Durham, NC: Duke University Press, 1998), 60–5.

it as "a work of God (besides his operation by the way of nature, ordained in the creation), done for the making manifest to his elect the mission of an extraordinary minister for their salvation." Hobbes's definition is apposite to Schmitt, because for him the exception is the *occasion for and the revelation of the true nature of sovereignty*. Thus for Schmitt the sovereign not only defines the "exception" but *he is also revealed by and in it*, which is why Schmitt must refer to a "genuine" decision.

What would be wrong with at least trying to rest human affairs on the rule of law? Schmitt finds two major problems. The first comes from the epistemological relationship between the exception and the norm. Sovereignty is what Schmitt calls a *Grenzbegriff*, a limiting or border concept. It thus looks in two directions, marking the line between that which is subject to law, where sovereignty reigns, and that which is not subject to law – potentially the space of the exception (PT 5). To look only to the rule of law will be to misunderstand the nature and place of sovereignty. According to Schmitt, we only understand the nature of the juridical order by understanding sovereignty, that is, by understanding that which opens onto the province of the exception.[13] This, he asserts, is because "the exception is more interesting than the rule" (PT 15). As the citation from Kierkegaard that Schmitt uses to support this claim argues, it is not because one cannot think about the rule or the "general," but because one does not notice anything in the general worth thinking about, and thus our thought in this realm would be "without passion" (ibid.). The point here is that the exception engages the human being in a way that the normal routine does not.

Second, it is important to realize that one can only have an exception if one has a rule. Therefore the designation of something as an exception is in fact an assertion of the nature and quality of rule. For example, if, as director of an exchange program, I say, "I am going to make an exception in your case and let you go on the exchange program to Germany despite the fact that you did not have the required grades," I am affirming both the rule and the fact that the rule is a human creation and hence does not control us automatically. I am also making a judgment that in this case, at this time, the good of all concerned indicates the need for this exception (and thus that I am not taking a bribe). Thus there can be no exceptions without there also being a rule.

---

[13] See the striking and informative discussion in William Scheuerman, *Between the Norm and the Exception: The Frankfurt School and the Rule of Law* (Cambridge, MA: MIT Press, 1994), 330 and passim.

Yet in affirming the human quality of the rule, what am I affirming? The claim about the exception and thus the grounding of rules on human actions are part of what Schmitt sees as the need to defend the political. When Max Weber described the workings of bureaucracy he asserted that bureaucratic (rationalized, rational-legal) relations are in no case relations between persons or human beings. Bureaucracy is the form of social organization that rests on norms and rules and not on persons. It is thus a form of rule in which there is "'objective' discharge of business . . . accordingly to calculable rules and 'without regard for persons.'"[14] What Weber meant is that it is in the nature of modern civilization to remove the nonrational from societal processes, replacing it with the formalism of abstract procedures. (He did not think that all parts of society were already like this, merely that this was the tendency.) For Weber the disenchantment of the world is the disappearance of politics – hence the disappearance of the human, hence the lessening of the role that the nonrational and the non-rule-governed play in the affairs of society. "Bureaucracy," he proclaims, "has nothing to do with politics."

Importantly the modern age is one in which an analog for transcendent authority must be sought, because "all conceptions of transcendence will no longer be credible to most educated people" (PT 50). Any theory of decisionism must therefore rest on *immanent* criteria. This is the essence of what Schmitt considers the political matter: to find the secular analog to the sacred. Such was the achievement of Hobbes, who, by creating an artificial yet transcendent sovereign, provided the model for the solution to the problem of modernity as Schmitt posed it.

These thoughts help explain the last chapter of *Political Theology*. There Schmitt argues that Joseph de Maistre, Louis Gabriel Ambroise de Bonald, and Juan Donoso Cortes exaggerate evil. They do so because they fail to see that the human striving for power not only renders people capable of great evil but also makes possible the domination of a certain class of leaders. Schmitt is certainly not opposed to the domination of a certain class of leaders; however, although the decision will emanate from nothingness (*das Nichts*), it must always be sanctioned by the will of the people (PT 66). One might say that Schmitt is not a counterrevolutionary in a reactionary sort of way. He accepts that legitimacy in this age must be in some sense democratic; it certainly cannot be monarchical. Thus, although it is clear that he thinks that Maistre, Bonald, and Cortes got the problem right, he

---

[14] Max Weber, *Economy and Society* (Berkeley: University of California Press, 1967), 975.

finds their solutions – monarchy for the Frenchmen and dictatorship for the Spaniard – unacceptable. As he notes on the last page of *Political Theology*, "Those counterrevolutionary philosophers of the state . . . heightened the moment of the decision to such an extent that the notion of legitimacy, their starting point, was dissolved. . . . This [decisionism] is however essentially dictatorship, not legitimacy" (PT 65–6).

Although Schmitt has sympathies for these theorists over and against the bourgeois liberal thinkers whom he and Cortes had stigmatized as a *clasa discutidora* (chattering class) (PT 62), the point of the analysis of the centrality of the exception for sovereignty is precisely to restore, in a democratic age, the element of transcendence that had been there in the sixteenth and even the seventeenth centuries. Hobbes, Schmitt believes, understood the problem exactly: He dealt with the problem of transcendence in an age when theological conflicts had apparently made any claim to transcendence inherently questionable. Recall that for Hobbes the sovereign was each of us, and the sovereign's authority was established by a creative covenant that placed what was written in hearts (the same in each heart) beyond question; it was an absolute authority, like that of scripture for Protestants.

Taken together, these elements in Schmitt's thought cast light on what we can surmise was the attraction for him of National Socialism. Schmitt came, as did Heidegger, from a rural, Catholic, petit-bourgeois upbringing. He describes his childhood, adolescence, and youth – the latter lasting until the end of World War I, during which he served as an officer and at the end of which he was thirty years old – as periods of getting rid of various influences: His Catholicism is *entortet* (dis-placed) and *enttotalisiert* (de-totalized); greater Prussianness is *enthegelianisiert* (de-Hegelized). Likewise, during his adulthood, Weimar Germany is *entpreusst* (de-Prussified).[15] Although Catholicism was always to remain important to Schmitt, this self-description is the portrait of a person whose ties to his various traditions are negative and are not replaced by a liberal faith in the future or in progress. One has to read his attacks on liberalism in conjunction with the accumulation of *ent-* verbs:[16] What remains when one has lost most of what one was?

---

[15] This is Schmitt's account in his contribution to *Complexio Oppositorum: Über Carl Schmitt*, ed. H. Quaritsch (Berlin: Duncker & Humblot, 1988), 105. See the discussion in Mehring, *Carl Schmitt*, 12–15, to which I owe this reference.

[16] And thus while left-wing antiliberals can "learn from" Carl Schmitt, it is not completely clear that it is Carl Schmitt that they are learning. See Paul Piccone and G. L. Ulmen, "Introduction to Carl Schmitt," *Telos*, no. 72 (Summer 1987): 14.

What, then, was the source of his attraction to Hitler? Clearly it did not stem from admiration of Hitler's particular qualities: Even if one discounts the occasion, the disdain he expresses during his interrogation at Nuremberg is palpable.[17] One might rather say that Hitler appeared to him something like the entity that God had sent to perform a miracle – as in the earlier citation from Hobbes – and the miracle was the recovery of a this-world transcendence to sovereignty and thus the human realm of the political. From this understanding, the person Hitler was nothing important, and Schmitt's relation to him could only be the relation one has to a miracle: acceptance or rejection.

This is all the more likely as Hitler very quickly seemed to many to behave as a true statesman in times of exception, legally elected but capable of making the hard, extralegal decisions that were necessary. When Hitler and Goering ordered the execution of all of the leadership of the SA on June 30–July 2, 1934, within two days almost all the press was congratulating them on having saved the country from civil war. Hindenburg sent (or was led to send) a telegram of thanks to the new chancellor. On August 1, 1934, Schmitt published a newspaper article entitled *Der Führer schützt das Recht* (The führer protects the legal order) defending Hitler's actions.[18] Thus it was the *reality of taking power* and manifesting sovereignty in the use of power that attracted Schmitt: *His understanding of law required that he support Hitler.* It was not a question of succumbing to the charisma of a prophet, true or false.

Thus, in his 1938 book on Hobbes, Schmitt attacks Hobbes for allowing privacy of belief. Such belief destroys, he says, the Leviathan from inside. Hobbes's sovereign, although of the same structure as Schmitt's, is much more restrained: There is no potential *Volksgeist* waiting to be awakened.[19] Perhaps this is the reason that Schmitt thinks Tocqueville to be the most

---

[17] "He [Hitler] was so uninteresting to me that I don't even want to talk about it" (Carl Schmitt, *Ex Captivate Salus: Experiences des années 1945–1947; Textes et commentaires*, ed. A. Doremus [Paris: Vrin, 2003], 41). This material is not in the German edition.

[18] The matter is a bit more complex. Ellen Kennedy, mainly on Schmitt's testimony, argues that he was forced to do so. Schmitt was identified with some elements of the SA, and there is some evidence that he was specifically exempted from the purge by Goering. In a somewhat self-pitying and self-aggrandizing poem he wrote for his sixtieth birthday, *Gesang des Sechzigjährigen* (Song of a sixty-year-old), Schmitt notes that he has been "three times in the belly of the fish." The first is 1934; the second, the attacks on him in 1936 in the Gestapo organ *Das schwarze Korps* (a moment he identifies to his interrogator in Nuremberg as when he "foreswore the devil"); and the last, his interrogation after the war when he appears to believe that he might be hanged.

[19] See George Kateb, "Hobbes and the Irrationality of Politics," *Political Theory* 17, no. 3 (August 1989): 355–91.

important contemporary historian. Tocqueville understood the irresistibility of the democratic spirit of equality. For Schmitt, as for Max Weber, there are only the resigned words of Isaiah that stand as an epigraph to this chapter.

Suggestions for further reading

Schmitt, Carl. *The Concept of the Political*. Edited by George Schwab, with a foreword by Tracy B. Strong. Chicago: University of Chicago Press, 1996.
———. *Political Theology*. Edited by George Schwab, with a foreword by Tracy B. Strong. Chicago: University of Chicago Press, 2005.

3
Antonio Gramsci: liberation begins with critical thinking

JOSEPH BUTTIGIEG

Antonio Gramsci (1891–1937) had been dead for a decade and absent from the political scene for twice that long when his letters from prison were published in Italy for the first time in 1947. Widely reviewed and highly acclaimed, the volume was declared a major literary work and awarded the prestigious Viareggio Prize. Largely unknown or forgotten outside communist circles, Gramsci burst onto the national scene posthumously in the immediate aftermath of the Fascist catastrophe, just when the country was most in need of narratives of heroic resistance to the dictatorship to assuage or attenuate its collective guilt and shame. The *Letters from Prison*, however, did more than document the sufferings borne with dignity by a political dissident who described himself as "an average man who has his own convictions and will not trade them away for anything in the world."[1] In his correspondence, Gramsci often discussed at considerable length the studies he was conducting in his prison cell, as well as the ideas and critiques he was elaborating in his notebooks. One could see from his letters that the prisoner had managed to defy the Fascist prosecutor's determination to "prevent this brain from functioning for twenty years."[2] What the Fascists feared most in Gramsci was his intellect, perversely mirroring his view that, in politics, ideas matter at least as much as the direct exercise of power and frontal opposition to it. Although unable to put a stop to Gramsci's intellectual labor, the regime nevertheless succeeded in keeping it hidden for the twenty years that followed his arrest. Once the letters were published, it was Gramsci's intellectual legacy that attracted the greatest attention. Benedetto Croce, who had long been regarded as Italy's preeminent philosopher and

---

[1] Antonio Gramsci, *Letters from Prison*, ed. Frank Rosengarten (New York: Columbia University Press, 1994), 1:140.
[2] Giuseppe Fiori, *Antonio Gramsci: Life of a Revolutionary*, trans. T. Nairn (London: Verso, 1970), 230.

intellectual arbiter – and aptly labeled "a kind of lay pope"[3] in one of the letters – declared in an enthusiastic review of the volume that "as a thinker [Gramsci] was one of us, of those who in the early decades of the century applied themselves to the task of developing in Italy a philosophical and historical mode of thinking adequate to the problems of the present; I, too, was among them in the role of an elder vis-à-vis the younger ones."[4]

Gramsci's prison notebooks were first published between 1948 and 1951 in six thematically organized volumes, the first of which collected the writings on historical materialism and the philosophy of Benedetto Croce. Their cultural and political impact was powerful and almost immediate, spurring numerous discussions and polemics. Within communist and socialist circles, Gramsci's systematic attack on positivism and economism caused deep consternation among the strict adherents and staunch defenders of Marxist-Leninist orthodoxy; at the same time, it encouraged and inspired those who were eager to break away from a dogmatic legacy that had become unbearable during the Stalinist ascendancy. Most conservative and Catholic intellectuals warned that, despite the singularity and apparent openness of his thought, Gramsci remained in the end a Marxist. Others found much to admire in the notebooks and, before long, were producing different readings of the complex texts that rendered their main concepts and arguments more or less compatible with their respective ideological leanings. The overall effect of these debates and of the rapid growth of publications they generated was the elevation of Gramsci's stature as an intellectual to a level that put him on a par with Croce. The *Prison Notebooks* inspired new directions in scholarship and criticism in many fields, including political theory, philosophy, historiography, literature, and sociology.

Croce's response was to dismiss the very possibility that Gramsci could have made any valid contribution to philosophy or to most other fields of knowledge, given that his political interests and goals prevented him from thinking with the kind of detachment required for an authentic search for truth. Recalling Marx's best-known axiom in the "Theses on Feuerbach" – "The philosophers have *interpreted* the world in various ways; the point, however, is to *change* it" – Croce argued that Gramsci's endorsement of it necessarily obliged him to subordinate thought to a practical need.[5]

---

[3] Gramsci, *Letters from Prison* 2:67.

[4] Benedetto Croce, "Lettere di Antonio Gramsci," in *Due anni di vita politica italiana, 1946–1947* (Bari: Laterza, 1948), 146. The review was first published in *Quaderni della Critica* in July 1947.

[5] Benedetto Croce, review of Gramsci's *Il materialismo storico e la filosofia di Benedetto Croce*, *Quaderni della Critica* 4, no. 10 (1948): 78.

In his criticism, Croce ignored the many different ways in which Gramsci put forward the notion that how humans interpret the world has much to do with whether a given sociopolitical order is preserved or transformed. Indeed, Croce's brief writings on Gramsci ignore all but a few minor details of the numerous pages devoted to philosophy in the prison notebooks; instead, he reiterates in a variety of ways the principle that a deep commitment to a political cause is incompatible with the dispassionate search for truth that alone merits the appellation of philosophy. In other words, from Croce's standpoint, what Gramsci calls the "philosophy of praxis" is not a philosophy at all and is a contradiction in itself.

There are other ways of constructing arguments that would arrive at Croce's conclusion that Gramsci cannot be legitimately considered a political philosopher. The entire thrust of Gramsci's life and work, one might say, propelled him in exactly the opposite direction from that of the philosopher whose quest for knowledge compels him or her to withdraw from the city. To be sure, incarceration isolated Gramsci from society, but it did not diminish his interest in or intellectual engagement with what he often called "this vast and tremendous world." Whether Gramsci could or should be included in the company of political philosophers obviously depends on how one defines philosophy and conceives of the political. Ultimately, however, his inclusion is not a question of great import, especially because it would shed little, if any, light on the most significant aspects of his work. It is much more fruitful to consider the place and role of philosophy in his political writings and activities.

Antonio Gramsci was born in 1891, the thirtieth anniversary of Italy's unification and a year marked by significant social unrest triggered by political instability, a weak economy, and high unemployment. Class conflict had become very pronounced, leading Pope Leo XIII to issue the encyclical *Rerum Novarum* on the relations between capital and labor. The first complete Italian edition of the *Communist Manifesto* was also published in 1891. That same year, a workers' congress in Milan ended with a resolution to form a national labor party. The Italian Workers Party was founded in 1892; three years later it changed its name to the Italian Socialist Party.

Gramsci's birthplace, Ales, and his mother's hometown, Ghilarza, where the family settled permanently in 1898, were both small towns in central Sardinia with an illiteracy rate of 60 percent or higher. Gramsci's father had come to Sardinia from the mainland as a civil servant in charge of the local registry. His mother, daughter of a small landowner and tax collector, was quite refined and cultured by the local standards of the time. Nevertheless, Gramsci had a very difficult childhood. Potts disease, which was misdiagnosed, left him frail, small of stature, and with a deformed spine. To make matters worse, his father was sentenced to nearly six years in prison for embezzlement. The family's straitened circumstances compelled Gramsci to suspend his schooling and work for two years after completing the elementary grades. At the age of fourteen, he was able to attend middle school at a nearby town and somehow did well enough to gain admission to the Dettori lyceum in the island's capital, Cagliari.

In Cagliari, Gramsci shared a room with his elder brother Gennaro, who had been drawn to socialism while completing compulsory military service in Turin. After his return to Sardinia, Gennaro had found employment in Cagliari where he also became secretary of the city's Socialist Party section. He helped introduce his sibling to politics. Although extreme poverty severely restricted Gramsci's socializing with his peers, he was able to attend talks and debates on current political and economic issues. He also had access to major newspapers and periodicals, which he devoured. In particular, he scoured the weekly *La Voce* for the writings of its editor Giuseppe Prezzolini (who launched it in 1908) and of other leading intellectuals of the time, such as Croce and Gaetano Salvemini. *La Voce* was not socialist, but many of the issues it addressed would become salient features in Gramsci's writings: the backwardness of the South, the urgent need for an intellectual and moral revitalization of Italian culture, the corrupting effects of transformism (i.e., the policy of avoiding necessary but disruptive change by accommodating the interests of every powerful social group), the role of intellectuals in society, the limitations of positivist thought, and Italian colonialism.

One essay Gramsci wrote during his last year at the Dettori has survived. "Oppressed and Oppressors" is a passionate indictment of the barbarism of colonial conquest and domination; it was probably inspired by the debates on the Italian colonial venture in Ethiopia and by the Sardinian autonomist movement that regarded Italian rule over the island as a form of colonialism. Toward the end of the essay, Gramsci makes an observation that would remain a major leitmotif throughout his writings: The great lesson of the French Revolution is that "social privileges and differences, being products of society and not of nature, can be overcome."[6] The greatest obstacle to the elimination of inequality, Gramsci would argue repeatedly, is not the repressive force that the powerful have at their disposal to quell rebellion, silence dissent, and preserve existing hierarchies. Rather, the powerless and the marginalized are all too often debilitated by their resigned acceptance of the existing order, in the belief that it is in the nature of things to be as they are. Throughout his life, Gramsci criticized every mode of thinking that compared or drew analogies between nature and society or between the natural and the human spheres. Nature is not created by humans and is governed by its own laws, whereas society and its institutions are created by humans who make their own history – this is a basic principle that Gramsci derived from Vico and the Italian school of philosophical idealism.

By the time he finished grammar school, Gramsci had read little by Marx and was only superficially acquainted with Marxist theory. His subsequent study of Marx's major works did not dilute his historicism. Quite the contrary – in refuting the orthodox Marxist theories of his contemporaries, Gramsci asserted in one of his notes, "As for this expression 'historical materialism,' greater stress is placed on the second word, whereas it should be placed on the first; Marx is fundamentally a historicist."[7] He argued vigorously and repeatedly against the notion that history is governed by its own iron-clad laws, and he never tired of demonstrating the pitfalls of adopting the methods of the natural sciences for the analysis of history, society, and politics. A quarter-century after "Oppressed and Oppressors," just before his deteriorating health forced him to abandon his studies, he wrote in one of his last notebooks: "But not everyone is Cuvier, and sociology, in particular, cannot be compared to the natural sciences. In sociology, arbitrary and bizarre generalizations are much more possible (and more harmful to practical life)."[8]

In 1911, Gramsci traveled to the Italian mainland for the first time to sit for the exams that would earn him a scholarship at the University of Turin. Penury and physical ailments made his first few years in the cold northern city extremely difficult; at times he was unable to attend classes or was forced to delay taking exams. He gradually drifted away from the university and never completed his degree. Still, he studied assiduously, and the courses he completed, the numerous lectures he attended, as well

---

[6] Antonio Gramsci, *Selections from Political Writings, 1910–1920*, ed. Quintin Hoare (London: Lawrence and Wishart, 1977), 5.
[7] Antonio Gramsci, *Quaderni del carcere*, ed. Valentino Gerratana (Turin: Einaudi, 1975), 1:433.
[8] Ibid., 3:2327.

as the relationships he established with professors and fellow students – among them, the economist Piero Sraffa and the future leader of the Italian Communist Party, Palmiro Togliatti – had an enormous impact on Gramsci's intellectual and political formation. An even more important factor in Gramsci's development was the city of Turin itself, where he observed and experienced firsthand modernity and the processes of modernization. Turin's rapid industrial growth was well under way by the time of Gramsci's arrival, with a high proportion of its half-million inhabitants working in factories. (The FIAT automobile company, founded in 1899, produced 3,000 cars in 1911, and it was still growing at a remarkable pace.) Through their membership in various organizations, including trade unions and the Socialist Party, workers were becoming an increasingly powerful political force. Deeply concerned with the growing power of organized labor, a number of business associations joined together in 1910 and founded the Italian Confederation of Industry with its headquarters in Turin. A year later, the growing strength of the best organized sector of the labor force led to the establishment of the Turin Consortium of Automobile Factories (comprising seven companies with 6,500 employees), aimed at diminishing trade union bargaining power and enforcing stricter control over the workplace.

The tensions between capital and labor in Turin reflected much broader phenomena: on the one hand, the fear inspired among political, economic, and social elite groups by the eruption of the masses (particularly, politicized workers in large urban centers) onto the social and political scene and, on the other hand, the heightened awareness among the swelling ranks of industrial workers of the advantages they stood to gain from solidarity, organization, and political engagement. Fear turned to alarm in 1912, when parliament approved an electoral reform law granting universal male suffrage, thus increasing the number of eligible voters by more than four million. Anticipating a large socialist advance in the 1913 general election, Catholic politicians and their conservative allies persuaded the Vatican to soften its prohibition of direct Catholic involvement in national state politics. This resulted in the clergy prompting Catholics to vote for candidates who publicly declared their adherence to church doctrine – which, in turn, triggered heated polemics about the religious threat to the secular character of the state. The election year was also marked by a three-month-long strike by car factory workers in Turin. Between or after lectures at the university, Gramsci and some of his friends would go to one of the city parks to meet and talk with the strikers. Later in the year, Gramsci spent some time in

Sardinia and wrote to his friend Angelo Tasca about how impressed he was "by the utter change caused by the participation of the peasant masses in the election."[9] On his return to Turin, Gramsci joined the Socialist Party.

The Italian Socialist Party that Gramsci joined while still a university student was a fractious political formation rife with internal disputes. "The main disputes within the party," Donald Sassoon points out, "arose not from theoretical questions, but from practical issues and particularly whether socialists should cooperate with non-socialist forces in order to extract reforms and concessions."[10] The struggles to preserve some semblance of party unity while simultaneously strengthening its presence within the existing parliamentary system were not conducive to the theoretical elaboration of a coherent ideology. A valuable source of theoretical inspiration was available in Antonio Labriola's classic works of Marxist philosophy, *Essays on the Materialistic Conception of History* (1896) and *Socialism and Philosophy* (1898); however, the neo-idealist and historicist foundations of his thought were antithetical to the positivist doctrines and scientism espoused by the socialist movement and its intellectual sympathizers. "As for those who . . . talk now of scientific philosophy," wrote Labriola, "it will suffice to say that they are simply fools."[11] In early twentieth-century Italy, Labriola's thought was kept alive primarily by Croce, his erstwhile student who turned into a conservative liberal. The spread of positivism, in Croce's view, impoverished Italian philosophy and culture in general, and he made it a primary target of his campaign for the intellectual and moral reform of the nation. Gramsci, in whose early writings the influence of Croce appears more pronounced than Labriola's, participated in that reform movement from within the ranks of the Socialist Party. He found a platform in the socialist newspapers of Turin.

The impoverished state of the national culture, the detachment of the intellectuals from the people, and the propagation by the socialists of a quasi-religious belief in historical determinism were among the major factors to which Gramsci attributed the lack of political preparedness among the masses, including the workers' movement; as a result, the masses were hindered from playing a decisive role in the transformation of the existing social order, which, everyone agreed, was extremely unstable. Gramsci's association of culture with politics set him apart from the mainstream of his

[9] Giuseppe Fiori, *Antonio Gramsci: Life of a Revolutionary*, 88.
[10] Donald Sassoon, *One Hundred Years of Socialism* (New York: The New Press, 1997), 14.
[11] Antonio Labriola, *Essays on the Materialistic Conception of History*, trans. C. H. Kerr (Chicago: Kerr & Co., 1908), 216.

party, and before long he found himself at odds with its most stalwart members. In 1916, Enrico Leone, a professor of economics at the University of Bologna who had written on revolutionary syndicalism, published an article in which he declared, "The modern worker learns much more from his class institutions than from any book of official knowledge.... There is no salvation except within workerism, within the classes of calloused hands and a brain uncontaminated by culture and by scholastic infection."[12] Gramsci used the provocation as a point of departure for his article "Socialism and Culture,"[13] which epitomizes views that he would develop extensively in his later writings on the inseparability of critical consciousness from effective politics and of philosophy from sociopolitical transformation.

Politics, Gramsci explains in "Socialism and Culture," starts with an intelligent reflection that enables the individual to acquire self-awareness and an understanding of his or her relation to others. He opens his exposition with a brief quotation from Novalis, who singled out "lacking a perfect comprehension of ourselves" as the "supreme problem of culture." Gramsci then turns to Vico's *New Science* to illustrate the political significance of Solon's maxim, "Know yourself." According to Vico, in the earliest Athenian aristocratic commonwealth, the nobles believed the plebeians to be of bestial origins, whereas they themselves were of divine origins. However, Solon "admonished the plebeians to reflect upon themselves to realize that they were of like human nature with the rulers and should therefore be made equal with them in civil rights." That was what gave rise to "all the institutions and laws that shape a democratic commonwealth," and not just in Athens; "the plebeians universally, beginning with Solon's reflection, changed the commonwealths from aristocratic to popular."[14]

Vico's narrative allowed Gramsci to formulate the argument that the socialist goal of liberating the majority of humanity from the rule of the minority will not be brought about by the laws of nature or the inexorable march of history but, rather, by "intelligent process, at first by just a few people and later by a whole class." This process requires "an intense labor of criticism, the diffusion of culture, and the spread of ideas among masses of men." By way of illustration, Gramsci offers the Enlightenment as a

---

[12] Antonio Gramsci, *Cronache Torinesi*, ed. S. Caprioglio (Turin: Einaudi, 1980), 103.
[13] Antonio Gramsci, "Socialism and Culture," in *Selections from Political Writings, 1910–1920*, 10–13. All the quotations from "Socialism and Culture" that follow are taken from this edition. For the Italian original, see *Cronache Torinesi*, 99–103.
[14] Giambattista Vico, *The New Science of Giambattista Vico*, trans. T. G. Bergin and M. H. Fisch (Ithaca: Cornell University Press, 1984), 133–4.

period of vigorous philosophical and cultural activity that "gave all Europe a bourgeois spiritual International in the form of a unified consciousness." It prepared the ground for the French Revolution and the spread of republican ideals elsewhere, including Italy. The immediate task of socialism, then, is simultaneously political and cultural: to foster the formation of a proletarian consciousness through a critique of capitalist civilization – and "critique implies culture," which starts with the self-awareness of which Novalis and Vico wrote.

The revolutionary developments in Russia presented Gramsci with an opportunity to reiterate even more forcefully the view that revolutions are not the inevitable outcome of mechanical or deterministic processes but the product of the human spirit. Enthused by the news arriving from Russia, he imagined a quasi-utopian transformation that would go far beyond the toppling of an autocratic regime and would create an entirely new culture: "What the revolution has created in Russia is a new way of life. It has not replaced one power by another. It has created a new moral order, it has replaced one way of life with another."[15] More than anything else, however, Gramsci was keen to demonstrate that the events in Russia disproved deterministic theories of history. The title of one of his articles describes the Bolshevik achievement as "the revolution against *Capital*." In it he declared,

This is the revolution against Karl Marx's *Capital*. . . . Events have exploded the critical schema determining how the history of Russia would unfold according to the canons of historical materialism. [Yet] if the Bolsheviks reject some of the statements of *Capital*, they do not reject its invigorating, immanent thought. These people are not "Marxists," that is all; they have not used the works of the master to compile a rigid doctrine of dogmatic utterances never to be questioned. They live Marxist thought – that thought which is eternal, which represents the continuation of German and Italian idealism, and which in the case of Marx was contaminated by positivist and naturalist encrustations. This thought sees as the dominant factor in history, not raw economic facts, but man, men in societies, men in relation to one another, developing through these contacts (civilization) a collective social will.[16]

This and other articles Gramsci wrote about the revolutionary developments in Russia are interesting only to the extent that they reflect his political thinking at the time, because they are based on very sketchy and often unreliable information gathered from newspapers that were subject to censorship while Italy was at war.

[15] Gramsci, *Selections from Political Writings, 1910–1920*, 30.
[16] Ibid., 34–5.

Years later, in his prison notebooks, Gramsci would produce a more complex analysis of the Russian Revolution and arrive at the conclusion that it could not be repeated in the liberal democracies of Western Europe. He would also decry Stalin's perverse transformation of the revolutionary impulse into an idolization of the absolutist state. In the aftermath of the Bolshevik success, however, he envisaged the adoption or adaptation of the Soviet model of direct democracy at the grassroots level in Italy. Immediately after the end of the war, Gramsci's political engagement became much more intense and militant. In 1919 he became an editor of the new Turin edition of the Socialist Party paper, *Avanti!*, with an initial circulation of 16,000 that tripled in a matter of months. In collaboration with other Socialist Party dissidents he also launched *Ordine Nuovo*, self-described in its masthead as "a weekly review of socialist culture." In addition to writing a prodigious number of articles and regular theater reviews, Gramsci was deeply involved in organizational activities. The wave of political unrest that swept through Europe gave rise to several new political formations in Italy, including the country's first Catholic mass party, Don Luigi Sturzo's Partito Popolare. In Milan, Mussolini organized the first Fascist cells. In Turin, Gramsci devoted much of his energy to the theorization of "workers' democracy" and the organization of factory councils. He envisaged a system of workers' and peasants' clubs, ward councils, and so forth, which would function as "a magnificent school of political and administrative experience and would involve the masses down to the last man"; in short, a remedy to the Socialist Party leadership's detachment from the grassroots. In all these endeavors, the words that recur with the greatest frequency in Gramsci's writings are "education" and "organization," both of which he identified with culture.

In the two "red years" of 1919–20, revolutionary fervor in Italy reached its peak: The socialists obtained one-third of the popular vote in the general elections; well over a thousand workers joined a strike in Turin promoted by the *Ordine Nuovo* group; in parliament, the governing coalition fell apart repeatedly; and another strike by a half-million industrial workers resulted in multiple factory occupations in Lombardy, Piedmont, and Liguria. Gramsci worked tirelessly during this period, organizing and supporting the workers' initiatives, but he was also extremely wary. When the factory occupations failed to gain the support of the major trade union organization and had to be abandoned, Gramsci predicted a fierce reaction. In fact, the reaction was already gathering momentum with violent attacks on socialist offices and personnel in multiple cities. The Italian Communist Party, of which he was a founding member, was launched in January 1921, a result of a split within the Socialist Party – a split that Gramsci characterized as another victory of the forces of reaction. With the left struggling to recover from a devastating defeat and Fascism on the rise, Gramsci did not just attempt to analyze what had gone wrong; he also set out to examine the deeper factors – historical, social, cultural, economic, demographic – that contributed to the failure of both liberal democracy and the Marxist movement in Italy. These were the issues he was addressing in his well-known essay "Some Aspects of the Southern Question," which his arrest and imprisonment prevented him from completing.

In September 1927, Gramsci wrote to his brother Carlo from prison: "I have become convinced that even when everything is or seems lost, one must quietly go back to work, starting again from the beginning."[17] He was able to get back to work about fifteen months later when he obtained permission to write in his cell. The notebooks that Gramsci composed in prison contain reflections on a vast range of topics as well as theoretical elaborations of several major concepts, of which none has been as widely discussed as hegemony. The term emerges early in the first notebook, in the course of a discussion of how the Moderate party had achieved "political hegemony" before assuming governmental power in the newly unified Italian state. According to Gramsci, one of the main reasons for the Moderates' success was that they "exercised a powerful attraction . . . over the whole mass of intellectuals in the country."[18] As becomes obvious in another note on the Moderates and the intellectuals, Gramsci was also thinking in broader terms: Any party with realistic aspirations to government power would first have to achieve hegemony among the intellectuals. To do so it would need to generate (a) "a general conception of life, a philosophy . . . that gives its adherents an intellectual 'dignity' to set against the dominant ideologies as a principle of struggle" and (b) "a scholastic program which interests the segment of intellectuals that is the most homogeneous and most numerous (teachers, from elementary school teachers to university professors)."[19] Of course, Gramsci examines many other aspects of hegemony in his notebooks, but none receive more extensive treatment than the role of intellectuals, philosophy, and education.

Gramsci composed three large blocks of notes in three separate notebooks under the general rubric "Notes on Philosophy. Materialism and Idealism." In these notes (and in later notebooks in which the materials are

---

[17] Gramsci, *Letters from Prison* 1:140.
[18] Gramsci, *Quaderni del carcere* 1:42.
[19] Ibid., 1:56.

better organized), Gramsci's aim is twofold: to disentangle what he calls the philosophy of praxis from the positivist and sociologistic version of Marxism expounded by Nikolai Bukharin in *Historical Materialism*, which had acquired the status of a catechism among orthodox Marxists, and to refute Croce's dismissal of the philosophical claims of Marxism while revealing the limitations of Italian neo-idealism. One of the objections that Gramsci raises vis-à-vis the two diametrically opposed philosophical traditions – that is, positivism and neo-idealism – is that they purport to explain all reality from a vantage point above or detached from history as lived experience. Of the positivists, Gramsci writes (and here he is echoing Labriola), in a note titled "The Reduction of the Philosophy of Praxis to a Sociology," that their work consists in "reducing a conception of the world to a mechanical set of formulas that gives one the impression of holding the entirety of history in one's pocket."[20] In his refutation of Croce, he uses a comparison derived from La Fontaine's fable "The Coach and the Fly": In Croce "history becomes a formal history, a history of concepts, and in the final analysis a history of intellectuals, or rather an autobiographical history of Croce's thought, a history of flies who believe they drive the coach."[21] In Gramsci's formulation, the distinctive character of the philosophy of praxis resides in its attentiveness to specificity, particularity, multiplicity, and difference. To emphasize this point he associates it with philology – defined as "the methodological expression of the importance of particular facts understood as definite and specific individualities" – and historicism. In one note, he asserts that "the experience upon which the philosophy of praxis is based cannot be schematized; it is history itself in its infinite variety and multiplicity."[22] In a later note he goes even further:

The basic innovation introduced by the philosophy of praxis into the science of politics and history is the demonstration that there is no "abstract" human nature, fixed and immobile (a concept derived from religious thought and from transcendentalism) but that human nature is the ensemble of historically determined social relations, that is, it is a historical fact which can be ascertained, within certain limits, by the methods of philology and criticism.[23]

Gramsci's deep interest in philosophy stemmed from his conviction that a political movement cannot succeed unless the worldview that animates

---

[20] Ibid., 2:1428.
[21] Ibid., 2:1241.
[22] Ibid., 2:1428.
[23] Ibid., 3:1598–9.

it is not only disseminated among the people but is also understood and consciously embraced by them. A sense of injustice, a state of desperation, anger, incitement, and so on, can and do sometimes give rise to rebellions that may even topple a government, but they will not change the basic equation of power. In hegemonic – as opposed to dictatorial – states, radical transformation can only come about through a substantial shift in the way people think of themselves, their relation to others, and their place in the world. Gramsci discusses this issue in several notes on the relation between philosophy and common sense. He characterizes common sense as the philosophy of nonphilosophers; it consists of a conception of the world that has been absorbed acritically from various social and cultural environments and is therefore disjointed, incoherent, and full of contradictions. One of the greatest failures of the socialist and workers' movements, Gramsci maintains, was that they did not seek to understand the common sense of the people they purported to lead, much less attempt to replace it with a coherent philosophy. Subaltern social groups will forever remain on the margins of history if they do not acquire the ability to think and speak for themselves. In modern societies, challenges to hegemonic power take place on the terrain of civil society. Subalterns cannot participate in civil society in any meaningful way as long as they have nothing to offer other than jumbled fragments of concepts acquired unconsciously from their surroundings.

Gramsci's approach to this problem starts with an assertion that, wittingly or not, everyone is a philosopher, followed by rhetorical questions that outline the fundamental reason why liberation starts with critical thought:

Having shown that everyone, in his own way, is a philosopher, that no normal human being of sound mind exists who does not participate, even if unconsciously, in some particular conception of the world, since every "language" is a philosophy – having shown this, one moves on to the second stage, which is that of criticism and consciousness. Is it preferable to "think" without being conscious of doing so, in a disjointed and inconsistent manner? Is it preferable to "participate" in a conception of the world "imposed" from the outside by some social group (which can range from one's village to one's province or can come from one's parish priest, or the old patriarch whose "wisdom" is law, or the little old woman who practices witchcraft, or the minor intellectual embittered by his own stupidity and ineffectiveness)? Or is it preferable to elaborate consciously and critically one's own conception of the world and, through the labors of one's own intellect, choose one's sphere of activity, participate actively in the creation of universal history, etc.?[24]

---

[24] Ibid., 2:1063.

A health crisis brought an end to Gramsci's writing in the spring of 1935. He died in a clinic in Rome two years later, just as his prison sentence ended. His wife and two sons were in the Soviet Union, where Stalin's great purges were well under way. Mussolini was intensifying his ties with Germany, and Italian socialists and communists were forging a union to combat Fascism.

In the immediate postwar period, the Italian Communist Party played a crucial role in restoring democracy in Italy and, in the process, drew heavily on its Gramscian inheritance to become a powerful presence in the cultural politics and political culture of the newly established Republic of Italy. The publication and dissemination of Gramsci's writings also inspired other socialist and communist activists outside the Soviet bloc – first in Latin America and, soon after, in other parts of Europe – to challenge the Marxist-Leninist orthodoxies to which their parties were wedded. The Eurocommunist movement regarded Gramsci as its intellectual precursor – an undogmatic Marxist untainted by Stalinism and a founding member of a party with strong democratic credentials. By the early 1980s, substantial segments of his large body of work had been translated into several languages, including English, Spanish, and French. Much of the interest he generated and continues to generate arises out of his elaboration of the concept of hegemony, that is, his analysis and theorization of the ineluctable relationship between culture and politics as well as the rapport between civil society and political society in modern democratic states. Another aspect of Gramsci's thought that has come into sharper relief over the past decade is his treatment of the historical and political status of subaltern social groups. Gramsci devoted one of his very late notebooks to the topic, thus returning to the issues that led to his political involvement in the first place.

Suggestions for further reading

Gramsci, Antonio. *Letters from Prison.* Edited by Frank Rosengarten. 2 vols. New York: Columbia University Press, 1994.
_____. *The Prison Notebooks.* Edited by Joseph A. Buttigieg. 3 vols. New York: Columbia University Press, 1992–2007. (The three sets of notes that Gramsci originally composed under the heading "Notes on Philosophy. Materialism and Idealism" are reproduced in their entirety in vol. 2, 137–99, and vol. 3, 136–76, 300–50.)
_____. *Selections from Political Writings, 1910–1920.* Edited by Quintin Hoare. London: Lawrence and Wishart, 1977.

Part II
Émigré responses to World War II

4

Philosophy as a way of life:
the case of Leo Strauss

STEVEN B. SMITH

The highest subject of political philosophy is the philosophic life: philosophy – not as a teaching or as body of knowledge, but as a way of life – offers, as it were, the solution to the problem that keeps political life in motion.[1]

Leo Strauss was born in the Hessian town of Kirchhain in Germany on September 20, 1899.[2] He was raised in an Orthodox Jewish family and received a pre–World War I *gymnasium* education. He took degrees at the University of Marburg and the University of Hamburg, where he studied with the neo-Kantian philosopher Ernst Cassirer. In a postdoctoral year at Freiburg, he worked with the phenomenologist Edmund Husserl, but was more impressed with Husserl's young assistant, a man named Martin Heidegger. Strauss's professional career began as an assistant at the Academy for Jewish Research in Berlin where he coedited some of the early volumes of the jubilee edition of the writings of Moses Mendelssohn. It was here also that he wrote his first book, *Die Religionskritik Spinozas*, which was dedicated to the memory of Franz Rosenzweig.[3]

---

[1] Leo Strauss, "On Classical Political Philosophy," in *What Is Political Philosophy? and Other Studies* (Glencoe, IL: Free Press, 1959), 91.
[2] There has yet to be written a full-length biography of Strauss. A partial step in this direction has been taken by Eugene R. Sheppard, *Leo Strauss and the Politics of Exile: The Making of a Political Philosopher* (Waltham, MA: Brandeis University Press, 2006). For other biographical overviews of Strauss's life, see Allan Bloom, "Leo Strauss (September 20, 1899–October 18, 1973)," *Political Theory* 2, no. 4 (1974): 372–92; Edward Banfield, "Leo Strauss," in *Remembering the University of Chicago: Teachers, Scientists, and Scholars*, ed. Edward Shils (Chicago: University of Chicago Press, 1991), 490–501; Steven B. Smith, "Leo Strauss: The Outlines of a Life," in *The Cambridge Companion to Leo Strauss*, ed. Steven B. Smith (Cambridge: Cambridge University Press, 2009), 13–40.
[3] Leo Strauss, *Die Religionskritik Spinozas als Grundlage seiner Bibelwissenschaft* (Berlin: Akademie Verlag, 1930). This appeared in English translation as *Spinoza's Critique of Religion*, trans. E. M. Sinclair (New York: Schocken Books, 1965).

Strauss left Germany in 1932 to spend a year in Paris before moving to England to carry out research on Thomas Hobbes. In 1938 he emigrated with his wife Miriam to the United States; at the age of almost forty he took up his first teaching position at the New School for Social Research in New York, where he spent the next decade. In 1949 he accepted a position in the Department of Political Science at the University of Chicago where he was to have his greatest influence. Several important works, including *Persecution and the Art of Writing* (1952), *Natural Right and History* (1953), *Thoughts on Machiavelli* (1958), and *What Is Political Philosophy?* (1959), followed in rapid succession. Strauss retired from the university in 1968, and after spending a year at Claremont Men's College in California, he joined his old friend Jacob Klein at Saint John's College in Annapolis, Maryland. He continued to write and publish to the very end of his life, his last competed book being a study of Plato's *Laws*.[4] Strauss died on October 18, 1973.

Strauss has done as much as any contemporary to revive the serious study of political philosophy, a field that was considered all but moribund during his lifetime. His emphasis on the "quarrel between the ancients and the moderns," his recovery (or rediscovery) of the tradition of esoteric writing, and his pointed attacks on the dominant academic schools of historicism and social-scientific positivism made him inevitably controversial. Strauss gathered generations of devoted students but equally devoted critics. Among the most persistent criticisms have been that Strauss's writings convey a secret teaching that contains dangerous, antidemocratic sentiments and that he favored the rule of a philosophical elite, believing the masses should be held in check through the judicious use of religion and other "noble lies."[5] This chapter is less concerned with answering such charges – often presented in a scurrilous and ideological manner – than in presenting the case for Strauss as a philosopher who ceaselessly homed in on and devoted his work to exploring the most fundamental yet rarely asked question, namely, "Why philosophy?"

---

[4] Leo Strauss, *The Argument and the Action of Plato's "Laws"* (Chicago: University of Chicago Press, 1975).

[5] Strauss's most devoted critic over the years has been Shadia Drury: see Drury, *The Political Ideas of Leo Strauss* (New York: St. Martin's Press, 1988). For more recent criticism, see Nicholas Xenos, *Cloaked in Virtue: Unveiling Leo Strauss and the Rhetoric of American Foreign Policy* (New York: Routledge, 2008). For a response to many of the political attacks, see Catherine Zuckert and Michael Zuckert, *The Truth about Leo Strauss: Political Philosophy and American Democracy* (Chicago: University of Chicago Press, 2006).

Why philosophy?

A generation ago, an English critic, Myles Burnyeat, wrote an excoriating attack on Strauss in the pages of the *New York Review of Books*.[6] Among other things, Burnyeat declared that, although Strauss's writings contained much discussion of "the philosopher," there was "no sign of any knowledge, from the inside, of what it is to be actively involved in philosophy."[7] If true, this would be a damning indictment. However, the question is whether it is true and whether Burnyeat's confidence in identifying what it means to be "actively involved in philosophy" is justified.

Burnyeat does not bother to define what he understands by being "actively involved in philosophy," but he may have in mind one of two possibilities. First, the idea of philosophy, at least in the Anglo-American world, was shaped to a large degree in the post–World War II years by the "ordinary-language" approach adopted by J. L. Austin and the later Wittgenstein. Philosophy meant here the analysis of concepts found in everyday language. The analytical movement, as it became known, assumed that all philosophical problems were linguistic in nature and that these problems could be solved with ever more careful scrutiny of ordinary usages. More recently, and to some degree in opposition to the ordinary-language approach, some philosophers have opted to engage in more ambitious, reconstructive attempts to address substantive moral and political issues. Philosophers such as John Rawls and Jürgen Habermas have attempted to engage in this kind of public discourse.

Strauss is clearly not a philosopher in either of these two senses mentioned above. His understanding of philosophy is marked by a return to an older – a much older – meaning of the word. In its oldest sense philosophy is *philo-sophia* or, literally, the love of wisdom. Yet what does it mean to love wisdom? Long before philosophy became a name for an academic discipline nested within divisions of the humanities, it was associated with a way of life. To practice philosophy did not necessarily mean to adhere to a specific set of doctrines or a method, much less to anything like a system of ideas, but rather to practice a certain manner of living. Philosophy was not just a theoretical exercise, but a practical one designed to answer the questions, "How ought I to live?" or "What is the best way of life?" or simply "Why philosophy?"

---

[6] Myles Burnyeat, "Sphinx without a Secret," *New York Review of Books*, May 30, 1985, pp. 30–6.

[7] Ibid., 32.

There is some evidence of recent interest in this older conception of philosophy as a way of life.[8] In *Philosophy as a Way of Life* the French classicist Pierre Hadot argues that the ancient philosophical sects – Platonists, Stoics, Epicureans – all understood philosophy first and foremost as a "spiritual exercise" designed to liberate the mind and free their members from the grip of the passions.[9] Their aim was to create spiritual communities in which individual members could seek to live freely and in friendship with others who had chosen a similar way of life. In a similar vein Alexander Nehamas has sought to revive the idea of philosophy as "the art of living." Although denying that he is urging readers to return to a philosophical way of life, he wants to remind analytical philosophers in particular that the type of philosophy one espouses affects the type of person one is: Philosophical discourse, like the great works of literature, shapes character. According to Nehamas, the greatest proponents of philosophy as the art of living have been Socrates, Montaigne, Nietzsche, and Foucault.[10]

It is only when we think of philosophy in this older sense, as a way of life, that we can begin to appreciate Strauss's role in recent philosophical debate. However, for Strauss, philosophy is not the kind of "spiritual exercise" Hadot associates with certain ancient ascetic cults; nor is the philosophical way of life a form of individual self-construction, as Nehamas maintains. As Strauss understands it philosophy is less a constructive or architectonic activity than a skeptical one. Philosophy for Strauss is zetetic or, as he puts it, "skeptic in the original sense of the term," that is, knowing that one does not know, or knowing the limits of knowledge.[11] The task of the philosopher is not so much to propound answers, but to anticipate problems. At the moment when the certainty of our solutions outweighs the awareness of their problematic character, the philosopher ceases to be a philosopher. In many ways this is a rigorous and demanding conception of philosophy.

---

[8] For two recent examples, see James Miller, *Examined Lives from Socrates to Nietzsche* (New York: Farrar, Straus and Giroux, 2011); Sarah Bakewell, *How to Live: Or, a Life of Montaigne in One Question and Twenty Attempts at an Answer* (New York: Other Press, 2011).

[9] Pierre Hadot, *Philosophy as a Way of Life*, trans. Michael Chase, ed. Arnold I. Davidson (Oxford: Blackwell, 1995).

[10] Alexander Nehamas, *The Art of Living: Socratic Reflections from Plato to Foucault* (Berkeley: University of California Press, 1998).

[11] Leo Strauss, "Restatement on Xenophon's *Hiero*," in *On Tyranny*, rev. ed., Victor Gourevitch and Michael S. Roth (Chicago: University of Chicago Press, 2001), 196; see also Strauss, "Progress or Return?" in *The Rebirth of Classical Political Rationalism*, ed. Thomas Pangle (Chicago: University of Chicago Press, 1989), 259–60.

To use a modern category to express a Socratic insight, the philosopher must be a practitioner of "negative dialectics."[12]

This passage, in which Strauss defines philosophy as "skeptic in the original sense of the term," provides the key to how he understands philosophy as a way of life. He addresses the following questions: What kind of life is it? What promises and responsibilities does it hold out for its followers? And, most fundamentally, what can justify the choice of philosophy as a way of life?

The primacy of politics

Strauss is, of course, most famous as a student of political philosophy, but his understanding of political philosophy cannot dispense with some general account of philosophy. Philosophy, he explains, is quest for "universal knowledge," or knowledge of "the whole."[13] By "the whole" he does not mean some kind of encyclopedic inventory, a *catalogue raisonée*, of everything that exists, but a knowledge of "the natures of things," that is, the basic categories of being that allow us to ask questions of the form "What is...?" We know a thing by knowing its nature or the category to which it belongs. Philosophy strives for categorical knowledge, not knowledge of things in their particularity. Strauss gives as examples of these categories the knowledge of God, humans, and world.

Philosophy as a distinctive enterprise emerges because knowledge of these natures is not immediately accessible. We have a variety of more or less reliable opinions about things, but these opinions often exhibit internal inconsistencies, and even contradict one another. In Strauss's famous formulation, philosophy is "the attempt to replace opinions about the whole by knowledge of the whole."[14] Yet even as philosophy strives for knowledge of the whole, the whole is fundamentally elusive. We may have knowledge of the parts, but the whole remains mysterious, and even knowledge of the parts, without knowledge of the whole, remains incomplete knowledge. Strauss admits that the discrepancy between the loftiness of the ambition and

---

[12] For the emphasis on Strauss as a zetetic, or skeptical, thinker, see Daniel Tanguay, *Leo Strauss: An Intellectual Biography*, trans. Christopher Nadon (New Haven: Yale University Press, 2007). The language of "negative dialectics" belongs, of course, to Theodor Adorno.

[13] Leo Strauss, "What Is Political Philosophy?" in *What Is Political Philosophy?* 11; see also Strauss, *Natural Right and History* (Chicago: University of Chicago Press, 1953), 30–1.

[14] Strauss, "What Is Political Philosophy?" 11.

the puniness of the results "could appear as Sisyphean or ugly," but he then goes on to affirm that philosophy "is necessarily accompanied, sustained, and elevated by eros."[15] In other words, philosophy is first and foremost an erotic activity consisting more in the quest, the desire for knowledge, than in the completion or achievement of wisdom.

On occasion Strauss associates philosophy with a certain type of causal knowledge. "The philosopher's dominating passion is the desire for truth, i.e., for knowledge of the eternal order, or the eternal cause or causes of the whole."[16] Once again Strauss emphasizes the specific kind of desire or passion – eros – that characterizes philosophy. This passion is for knowledge of the causes of the whole, rather than knowledge of any particular kind of thing. In fact this desire for knowledge leads the philosopher to look askance at the human things that cannot but appear "paltry and ephemeral" in comparison to the eternal order.[17] Being chiefly concerned with causes – with the form or *eidos* of things – philosophy seems to care little about things, including human beings, in their individuality.

Strauss is aware – deeply aware – of an obvious objection to this conception of philosophy. The ancient or Socratic conception of philosophy as "knowledge of the whole" or of an "eternal order" seems to presuppose an "antiquated cosmology"; namely, one in which the universe appears as an ordered cosmos in which human beings and other species have their allotted roles. Such an idea is completely at odds with the modern notion of the infinitely expanding universe.[18] The teleological conception of nature seems as obsolete today as the claims of creationism and other pseudosciences. Does Strauss have an answer to this very pointed objection?

He does indeed. Strauss denies that the classical conception of human nature presupposes any specific cosmology or underlying metaphysics. The desire for knowledge of the whole remains precisely that, a desire; it does not dogmatically presuppose, much less claim to demonstrate, one or another specific cosmology. No doubt, modern natural science has vastly increased our power over nature in precisely the way imagined by Bacon and Descartes, but this is scarcely a guarantee that science has provided anything like a comprehensive understanding of nature, including human nature, unless one equates power with understanding. Strauss even toys with

---

[15] Ibid., 40.
[16] Strauss, "Restatement," 197–8.
[17] Ibid., 198.
[18] Strauss, *Natural Right and History*, 7–8; "What Is Political Philosophy?" 38–9.

the idea that the ancients considered this idea of science but rejected it as "destructive of humanity."[19]

Strauss claims that, unlike modern science, ancient philosophy understood the human situation in terms of "the quest for cosmology" rather than any specific answer to the problem of cosmology. It is this very openness to or skepticism about knowledge of the whole that distinguishes the ancients from modern natural science:

> Whatever the significance of modern natural science may be, it cannot affect our understanding of what is human in man. To understand man in the light of the whole means for modern natural science to understand man in the light of the sub-human. But in that light man as man is wholly unintelligible. Classical political philosophy viewed man in a different light. It was originated by Socrates. And Socrates was so far from being committed to a specific cosmology that his knowledge was knowledge of ignorance. Knowledge of ignorance is not ignorance. It is knowledge of the elusive character of the truth, of the whole.[20]

Strauss's understanding of philosophy begins with a desire for knowledge of the whole and concludes with an awareness of "the elusive character of the truth." How does he arrive at this conclusion?

Knowledge of the whole is necessarily preceded by knowledge of the parts. Because we cannot achieve knowledge of the whole immediately, as if "shot out of the barrel of a gun" (in Hegel's famous metaphor), our access to the whole must take the form of an "ascent," a movement from the things most immediate and known to us to those things that remain obscure and shrouded in mystery. Philosophy must proceed "dialectically" from premises that are generally agreed on.[21] This ascent begins with the opinions we share about those things that are "first for us," namely, about the foundations of the political community, the rights and duties of its members, the relation of law and liberty, and the imperatives of war and peace. It is the "political" that provides our clearest point of access to the whole. Why is this?

Political philosophy is not simply a branch of general philosophy, like ethics, logic, or aesthetics. For Strauss, political philosophy is a kind of first philosophy. The investigation of political things requires that we begin with the investigation of the opinions about the better and worse, the just and unjust, that give shape and direction to political life. All politics is governed

---

[19] Strauss, "Restatement," 178.
[20] Strauss, "What Is Political Philosophy?" 38.
[21] Ibid., 93.

by opinion, and political philosophy takes as its starting point the investigation of opinion – the often authoritative opinions as handed down in laws,
statutes, and other official documents – that governs a community. These
opinions, although not philosophy itself, nevertheless share something with
philosophy, namely, a concern for the political good, the good of the community. Yet what distinguishes the political philosopher from even the best
citizen or statesman is not knowledge or concern for the well-being of this
or that political community, but a certain breadth of perspective: a search
for the "true standards" that shape "the good political order."[22]

The political community is from one point of view a category of being,
merely one aspect or part of the whole, but from another it is the very
microcosm of the whole. The political is the most comprehensive human
grouping within the order of nature. As such, the political order provides
the basic structure or ranking of all other orders. Of all the perishable
things, the heterogeneity of the political order is the closest expression of
the heterogeneity of the eternal order. Knowledge of the whole must begin
with political philosophy. Whether political philosophy becomes an end in
itself or a means to an understanding of metaphysics is a problem not clearly
resolved by Strauss.

Throughout his various writings Strauss emphasizes that his approach
to philosophy was given its canonical expression in the writings of the
classical political philosophy of Plato and Aristotle. This was not simply
because theirs was chronologically first, but because the ancients stood
in a privileged position in relation to the political opinion that shaped
their communities. These opinions – Strauss refers to them as forming the
"natural consciousness" or the "prephilosophic consciousness" – form the
horizon out of which the fundamental concepts and categories of political philosophy arose and against which they can be checked.[23] Classical
political philosophy was related directly to political life, whereas all subsequent philosophies represent modifications of this tradition and hence could
only experience their world indirectly, viewing it, so to speak, through a
glass, darkly. Natural experience has become further distorted through a
tradition of philosophy that has become at various times intermingled with
theology, science, and, more recently, history. Consequently, we experience
the world today through a prism of concepts that prevents access to the

---

[22] Ibid., 12.
[23] Ibid., 75–6.

"original position" – apologies to John Rawls – of philosophy vis-à-vis the city.[24]

How, then, can we recover these opinions, this "prephilosophic consciousness" that has been blocked or encrusted with layers of theoretical abstraction? Strauss's project, to some degree like Rousseau's genealogical approach, consists of peeling away, onion-like, the layers of congealed tradition that have succeeded in obscuring the natural consciousness that it presupposes. There have always been and there always will be certain natural obstacles to the philosophical life: Strauss mentions natural ignorance, the power of the imagination, and superstition. What blocks our access today is a set of wholly artificial "pseudophilosophies" – historicism, scientism, economism – that have distorted our relation to experience. Strauss's paradoxical answer is that only through historical studies carried out not in the spirit of the reigning academic historicism but by reacquiring the art of careful reading can we think ourselves back into the original situation of philosophy.[25] Only through reading certain "old books" will we be able to begin the slow and painstaking ascent from the artificial cave we now inhabit back into the "natural cave" that is the foundation for all later philosophy.[26]

Philosophy and the city

All philosophy is political philosophy in another sense for Strauss. He puts this assertion in the form of a syllogism: Philosophy is the attempt to replace opinion, including opinions about political things, by knowledge; opinion is the medium of society; therefore philosophy is necessarily at odds with society. Strauss drew from this syllogism the following conclusion: Philosophy is necessarily a function of the "few" or an elite that must conceal its activity from the hostility of the "many."[27] It is this tension

---

[24] The idea that there remains some primordial, prephilosophical ground of experience derives from Husserl, but is left undertheorized in Strauss. See *Natural Right and History*, 31–2; for some interesting comments on the problem, see Robert B. Pippin, "The Unavailability of the Ordinary: Strauss on the Philosophical Fate of Modernity," *Political Theory* 31, no. 3 (2003): 335–58, esp. 341–4.

[25] For the philosophical importance of historical studies, see Strauss, "How to Study Spinoza's *Theologico-Political Treatise*," in *Persecution and the Art of Writing* (New York: Free Press, 1952), 142–201, esp. 142–62; "On Collingwood's Philosophy of History," *Review of Metaphysics* 5, no. 4 (1952): 559–86.

[26] For the "second cave" image, see Strauss, "How to Study Spinoza's *Theologico-Political Treatise*," 155–6.

[27] This is the central thesis of Strauss in "Persecution and the Art of Writing," in *Persecution and the Art of Writing*, 22–37; see also Strauss, "On a Forgotten Kind of Writing," in *What Is Political Philosophy?* 221–2.

between philosophy and society, given its most vivid expression in Plato's *Apology of Socrates*, which constitutes the political situation of philosophy. The philosopher's way of life is forced to pay homage to politics.

Strauss's most developed thoughts on the tension between philosophy and politics occur in his exchange over the nature of modern tyranny with the Hegelian-Marxist philosopher Alexandre Kojève. Strauss's *On Tyranny* was an attempt to resuscitate the ancient concept of tyranny as presented in Xenophon's dialogue *Hiero* to better understand the phenomenon of twentieth-century totalitarianism. Unlike many of his contemporaries who emphasized the novelty of totalitarianism, Strauss somewhat counterintuitively saw a continuity between ancient and modern tyranny. Strauss did not deny that modern tyrannies supported by the powers of technology and ideology have become vastly more dangerous than tyrannies in the past, but he wondered whether this changed the essential nature of the phenomenon ("Tyranny is a danger coeval with political life").[28] In the course of their exchange, Strauss and Kojève turned the debate over tyranny into a discussion of the philosopher's responsibility to the city.[29]

The Strauss-Kojève debate begins by considering the philosopher's motives, the peculiar desire or eros that drives the philosophic quest. For Kojève, it is recognition above all that intellectuals crave, the desire to have their ideas "realized" by being put into practice, whether it be by a court, a president, or a tyrant. The test of the truth of an idea is its success in the public sphere. For Strauss, however, it is not public recognition but the satisfaction that derives from philosophy itself that is its own reward. The justification of philosophy is entirely internal to philosophy. "We do not have to pry into the heart of any one in order to know that, insofar as the philosopher, owing to the weakness of the flesh, becomes concerned with being recognized by others, he ceases to be a philosopher," Strauss retorts. "According to the strict view of the classics he turns into a sophist."[30]

Kojève's complaint is that Strauss's understanding of philosophy remains isolated from the life of the city, from political praxis, and from the historical process. This retreat has historically taken the form of the Epicurean garden,

---

[28] Strauss's introduction to *On Tyranny*, 22.
[29] The best commentary on this debate remains Victor Gourevitch, "Philosophy and Politics, I" and "Philosophy and Politics, II," *Review of Metaphysics* 22, nos. 1 and 2 (1968): 58–84 and 281–328. See also Robert B. Pippin, "Being, Time, and Politics: The Strauss-Kojève Debate," *History and Theory* 32, no. 2 (1993): 138–61; Steven B. Smith, "Tyranny Ancient and Modern," in *Reading Leo Strauss: Politics, Philosophy, Judaism* (Chicago: University of Chicago Press, 2006), 131–55.
[30] Strauss, "Restatement," 203.

the Republic of Letters, or the academic ivory tower, which all represent efforts to escape the judgment of history by retreating into some kind of inner citadel. Strauss accepts that the philosopher's quest is a lonely one that requires liberation from "the most potent natural charm" of attachment to the city, but this does not render it absolutely self-regarding. Fully aware of the fallibility of the mind, philosophers must seek out others of their kind with whom to share, challenge, and test their ideas. The cultivation of friendship becomes one of the highest duties of philosophy.[31]

To be sure, Strauss agrees with Kojève regarding the danger of self-referentiality that comes from "the cultivation and perpetuation of common prejudices by a closely knit group of kindred spirits."[32] He seems to be fully cognizant of all the dangers later associated with "Straussianism." Yet if one danger to philosophy comes from "the snobbish silence and whispering of the sect," an even greater danger derives from the desire to turn philosophy into a mass doctrine ("propaganda"). The idea of a public philosophy is an oxymoron. "*If* we must choose between the sect and the party," Strauss writes, "we must choose the sect."[33] There will always be rival philosophical sects that check and balance one another in the search for truth. The true danger to philosophy is when it is turned into an ideology that would eliminate all competition.

It is in this context that Strauss confirms the skeptical or zetetic nature of philosophy referred to earlier. Philosophy is a matter of knowledge, but knowledge of one's ignorance, of knowing the limits of knowledge:

Philosophy as such is nothing but genuine awareness of the problems, i.e., of the fundamental and comprehensive problems. It is impossible to think about these problems without becoming inclined toward a solution, toward one or the other of the very few typical solutions. Yet as long as there is no wisdom, but only quest for wisdom, the evidence of all solutions is necessarily smaller than the evidence of the problems. Therefore the philosopher ceases to be a philosopher at the moment at which the "subjective certainty" of a solution becomes stronger than his awareness of the problematic character of that solution. At that moment the sectarian is born.[34]

This is Strauss's boldest statement on the nature of philosophy and surely refutes the charge that there is "no sign of any knowledge, from the inside, of what it is to be actively involved in philosophy." Yet Strauss leaves many

---

[31] Ibid., 194–5.
[32] Ibid., 195.
[33] Ibid.; emphasis added.
[34] Ibid., 196.

questions unanswered. His affection for Socratic moderation and nonsectarianism notwithstanding, where exactly does one draw the line between knowledge and ignorance? Even if we accept the claim that the evidence for the problems of philosophy is greater than the evidence for the solutions, does this render all solutions equally problematic? Are we not entitled to claim that some solutions are preferable to others, even if they lack certainty? Is the only choice that between absolute wisdom or zetetic skepticism? More seriously, Strauss's zetetic understanding of philosophy seems to undercut the ground of political judgment. If, as he remarked earlier, one cannot think about the problems without becoming "inclined" toward a solution, on the basis of what should one be so inclined? If knowledge of the right or good political order remains fundamentally problematic, what standard can be used for judgment in political life?

Strauss probably exaggerates philosophy's radical detachment from the concerns of the city. He recognizes that the philosopher "cannot help living as a human being who as such cannot be dead to human concerns."[35] Among these concerns are the philosopher's twin responsibilities to both philosophy and the city. The philosopher's first and primary concern must always be to philosophy itself, to ensure its survival even in the most dangerous times: "The philosopher must go to the market place in order to fish there for potential philosophers."[36] The city will necessarily see these fishing expeditions as an attempt to corrupt the young by weaning them away from politics and business to philosophy. In this way philosophers are forced to defend themselves and their way of life, not only before other philosophers but also before the tribunal of public opinion.

In what does the philosopher's responsibility to the city consist? Recognizing that philosophy can only take place within the context of the city, the philosopher must show a decent respect for the opinions on which the city is based. To be sure, the philosopher's public responsibilities are entirely exoteric. It is sufficient to satisfy the city "that the philosophers are not atheists, that they do not desecrate everything sacred to the city, that they reverence what the city reverences, that they are not subversives, in short, that they are not irresponsible adventurers but good citizens, and even the best of citizens."[37] Knowing that true happiness is found only in the activity of philosophy, philosophers will find it relatively easy to

---

[35] Ibid., 199.
[36] Ibid., 205.
[37] Ibid., 205–6.

accommodate themselves to the *nomoi* of the city. Plato's allegory of the cave always remained Strauss's Exhibit A for the intransigent hostility between philosophy and even the best social order.

Strauss's philosophical politics raises the troubling question of the limits of the philosopher's accommodation to the city. Does this accommodation include acquiescence to tyranny as something "coeval with political life"? How far must the philosopher maintain the fiction that philosophy is not atheistic but reveres the gods of the city? Must tyrannical regimes be tolerated as one of the evils "inseparable from the human condition"?[38]

Strauss's answer to these questions is best summed up in a phrase he uses in regard to Judah Halevi: "[T]he line of demarcation between timidity and responsibility is drawn differently in different ages."[39] He might also have added "and according to the temperament and judgment of each individual." Strauss's own philosophical politics clearly displayed a combination of inner radicalism and outer conformity. There will always remain the lingering question of how far Strauss was recommending such a strategy to his own readers. To what degree does esotericism remain a historical thesis about the interpretation of the thought of the past or a responsibility of philosophy even in the present?[40] This is a theme on which Strauss remained tantalizingly and, I believe, deliberately opaque. It is certainly far from evident that a strategy adopted by Halevi, Alfarabi, and Maimonides, writing in times of considerable hostility to philosophy, remains applicable in a modern democratic age where the demands for intellectual probity and "transparency" have become not just private but public virtues.[41]

Reason versus revelation

The philosopher may believe – Strauss may even believe – that the philosophical life is best. The question is what makes it so. Strauss refers to the sense of satisfaction bordering on "self-admiration" felt by the philosopher. Yet this is not so much a proof as an expression of the philosophical life. It is also less than clear how knowledge of one's ignorance contributes to

---

[38] Ibid., 200.

[39] Strauss, "The Law of Reason in the *Kuzari*," in *Persecution and the Art of Writing*, 110.

[40] Strauss regards society's hostility to philosophy as a danger "coeval with philosophy." See the introduction to *Persecution and the Art of Writing*, 21.

[41] For the importance of "probity," see Leo Strauss, "Preface to *Spinoza's Critique of Religion*," in *Liberalism Ancient and Modern* (New York: Basic Books, 1968), 255–6; for Strauss's references to the Nietzschean origins of this concept, see ibid., 258 nn. 24–8.

the sense of satisfaction or happiness experienced by the philosopher, but as Strauss would say, "be that as it may." Can philosophy justify itself and its way of life before the most serious alternatives? This is perhaps the central question of Strauss's philosophical writings.

The most serious alternative, in fact the only real alternative, to philosophy is the challenge posed by divine revelation.[42] Other choices and other life plans – even the classical conflict between the philosophical and the political life – pale in comparison. The alternatives of reason and revelation, or, in Strauss's idiom, Athens and Jerusalem, remain the sharpest and most comprehensive contrast that philosophy must confront in defending itself and its way of life. The difference between Athens and Jerusalem centers on their respective views of the role of morality in the overall economy of human life. For adherents of Jerusalem, it is the passionate quest for righteousness that represents the pinnacle of humanity, whereas for partisans of Athens, morality is at most instrumental to the attainment of a kind of contemplative autonomy. This contrast, even more than the famous "quarrel between the ancients and the moderns," remains *the* philosophical question because if philosophy cannot defend itself against the adherents of revelation then philosophy threatens to become just another faith based on an arbitrary decision or an act of will.[43]

Strauss states this contrast nowhere more starkly than in the pages of *Natural Right and History*:

Man cannot live without light, guidance, knowledge; only through knowledge of the good can he find the good that he needs. The fundamental question, therefore, is whether men can acquire that knowledge of the good without which they cannot guide their lives individually or collectively by the unaided efforts of their natural powers, or whether they are dependent for that knowledge on Divine Revelation. No alternative is more fundamental than this: human guidance or divine guidance.[44]

There seems, then, to be a standoff between philosophy and revelation. Can either side refute the other?

---

[42] For Strauss's treatment of this theme, see "Progress or Return?"; "Preface to *Spinoza's Critique of Religion*"; Strauss, "Jerusalem and Athens: Some Preliminary Reflections," in *Studies in Platonic Political Philosophy*, ed. T. Pangle (Chicago: University of Chicago Press, 1983), 147–73; Strauss, "Reason and Revelation," in *Leo Strauss and the Theologico-Political Problem*, by Heinrich Meier (Cambridge: Cambridge University Press, 2006), 141–80.

[43] The claim that the entire Straussian project rests on a Nietzschean "will to power" has been argued provocatively by Stanley Rosen, *Hermeneutics as Politics* (Oxford: Oxford University Press, 1987), 107–23; see also Laurence Lampert, *Leo Strauss and Nietzsche* (Chicago: University of Chicago Press, 1996), who treats Strauss as a weak Nietzschean.

[44] Strauss, *Natural Right and History*, 74.

In Socratic fashion Strauss considers a variety of opinions on both sides of the argument. Consider the matter first from the side of theology. Within the Jewish tradition what is called the "Call of God" is often said to be verified by a long line of tradition.[45] This Call was given to Moses on Mount Sinai, handed down to Joshua, and then to the elders and the prophets, all in an unbroken chain of tradition stretching to the rabbis. Is this tradition reliable?

Strauss questions the validity of this kind of historical proof. The Call of God cannot be distinguished from those who claim to have experienced the Call. In other words, the Call is only as reliable as the individuals who claim to have received it. Yet this makes the Call dependent on the interpretation of the believer, and such interpretations will inevitably vary from person to person and from sect to sect. A believing Jew will interpret the Call very differently from a believing Muslim. Furthermore, those who claimed to be witnesses to the revelation or the inheritors of this revelation are in all known cases already adherents of the faith. There are no impartial or neutral witnesses apart from the believers themselves.[46]

Strauss considers and rejects the various arguments used to defend the primacy of revelation, but how do things look from the standpoint of philosophy? No better. Philosophy demands that revelation defend itself before the bar of reason, our human reason. Yet revelation resolutely refuses to do so. The argument that revelation must justify itself rationally is circular. It presupposes what it needs to prove, namely, that revelation is a rational experience. At most, philosophy can claim to have refuted the various theological arguments in defense of revelation; it has not disproved the possibility of revelation itself.

Strauss considers several more specific arguments against revelation drawn from historical and archaeological criticism of the Bible and from modern scientific theories (Darwinism), but he pays the greatest respect to the claims of philosophical theology or what goes by the name of natural theology. According to the argument of natural theology, God's attributes are in principle knowable and accessible to human reason. The opening axioms and demonstrations of book 1 of Spinoza's *Ethics* constitute the clearest proof-text of this approach. According to Spinoza, we can know the attributes of God because God *is* nature and the operations of nature can be known through the application of unaided human intelligence.

---

[45] See the Coen brothers' movie *The Big Lebowski*: "Three thousand years of beautiful tradition from Moses to Sandy Koufax – you're damn right I'm living in the past." The chronology may be slightly off, but the point is well taken.

[46] Strauss, "Progress or Return?" 261–2.

Just as everything exists within the ordered sphere of nature, so can everything be known according to the principle of sufficient reason. According to this principle, there is a perfect unity between reason and nature, and this unity is God.

Strauss takes Spinoza's argument with the utmost seriousness, but in the end finds it just as arbitrary as the assertion of revelation. The attributes of God proposed by Spinoza have all been preselected to prove God's perfect rationality and intelligibility, to deny all mystery to the universe. Whether Spinoza's disenchantment of the universe represents a form of concealed atheism or a higher form of piety is not a question that concerns Strauss. His point is that the Spinozist conception of God as *Deus sive natura* may well follow the criteria for clarity and distinctness, but clarity and distinctness are not a guarantee of truth. A clear and distinct proof for the existence of God is only clear and distinct from our point of view, from the standpoint of philosophy; it cannot begin to penetrate the existence of an infinite being whose ways may not be our ways. The *Ethics* remains a castle built on sand.

The conflict between Athens and Jerusalem seems to have concluded with a draw. Strauss writes, "All alleged refutations of revelation presuppose unbelief in revelation, and all alleged refutations of philosophy presuppose faith in revelation."[47] No common ground or neutral standpoint seems possible. Yet a standoff between philosophy and faith would seem to tilt the balance in favor of faith. If philosophy cannot prove – rationally demonstrate – its superiority to revelation, if every proof against revelation turns out to be hypothetical or to rest on "unevident premises," then one must accept that the philosophical life is itself based on faith, that is, an act of will or decision that cannot in the last instance be rationally grounded. In such a competition the adherents of faith would win on a technicality.[48]

Strauss goes out of his way to make the strongest case for revelation or, what amounts to the same thing, to create the highest possible hurdle for philosophy. He often seems to demand a much higher burden of proof from philosophy than from theology. Theology merely needs to hold open the possibility of revelation, whereas philosophy is required to refute its very premises. Anything less must be taken as an admission of failure. Strauss was himself a product of the early twentieth-century "reawakening of theology" associated with Karl Barth and Franz Rosenzweig, who "appeared to make

---

[47] Ibid., 269.
[48] For the theistic interpretation of Strauss's thought, see Kenneth Hart Green, *Jew and Philosopher: The Return to Maimonides in the Jewish Thought of Leo Strauss* (Albany: SUNY Press, 1993); Susan Orr, *Jerusalem and Athens* (Lanham, MD: Rowman & Littlefield, 1995).

it necessary to investigate how far the critique of orthodox theology – Jewish and Christian – deserved to be victorious."[49] Strauss clearly took it for granted that the critique of theology had not yet proved deserving of victory.

Although the reawakening of theology alerted Strauss to the failure of the Enlightenment critique of religion, it would be a mistake to place him in the camp of Counter-Enlightenment political theology, to turn him into a defender of faith, as some have tried to do. Through his dissatisfaction with Spinoza, Strauss fought his way back not to a reaffirmation of orthodoxy but to a much older conception of philosophy as zetetic philosophy. This, I take it, is the meaning of his statement that a return to premodern philosophy is not an impossibility but only a very difficult task.[50]

Strauss's "return" to classical political philosophy – a return he always described as "tentative or experimental" – is not an endorsement of natural hierarchy or any other form of ancient biology or eugenics.[51] His understanding of ancient philosophy has to do with the political problem of philosophy or the issue of the philosophical life and not a philosophy of politics, as it is usually understood. This has certainly not inhibited all manner of interpreters from attributing all manner of doctrinal positions to him from neoconservatism to a nihilistic antimodernity.[52] His concern was with the original position of philosophy as a mode of questioning and not with the defense of any particular philosophical school or sect, much less a political movement or cause.

Strauss makes clear that the philosophical life is to be understood as a form of zetetic questioning. This is the meaning of "Platonic political philosophy" in its original sense.[53] Even here zeteticism is a return not to the questions of the Stoa but to a whole range of topics unknown to the ancients, mainly the problem of Athens and Jerusalem, or what he later called the "theologico-political problem" ("*the* theme of my investigations").[54] Zetetic

---

[49] Leo Strauss, "Preface to *Hobbes Politische Wissenschaft*," in *Jewish Philosophy and the Crisis of Modernity*, ed. Kenneth Hart Green (Albany: SUNY Press, 1997), 453.

[50] Strauss, "Preface to *Spinoza's Critique of Religion*," 257.

[51] For the provisional nature of Strauss's project, see Strauss, *The City and Man* (Chicago: University of Chicago Press, 1964), 11.

[52] For two of the best studies on the uses and misuses of Strauss, see Zuckert and Zuckert, *The Truth about Leo Strauss*; Peter Minowitz, *Straussophobia: Defending Leo Strauss and Straussians from Shadia Drury and Other Accusers* (Lanham, MD: Lexington, 2009).

[53] This may help explain why Strauss planned a book titled *Studies in Platonic Political Philosophy* that contained only two essays specifically dealing with Plato. The term "Platonic" meant for him a certain style of philosophizing rather than a doctrine or system attributable to Plato.

[54] Strauss, "Preface to *Hobbes Politische Wissenschaft*," 453.

or Platonic philosophy does not claim to have found an answer, much less the answer, to the reason–revelation problem, but rather to keep that problem alive for future investigation. Zetetic understanding is precisely what protects the philosopher from the twin dogmatisms of faith and unbelief. Yet neither can withstand the test of rational justification. Only the philosopher who lives in constant awareness of and engagement with the conflict between Athens and Jerusalem, who is able to engage each side with the claims of the other, is in a position to justify philosophy as a way of life.[55]

Conclusion

If Strauss is correct that we have lost sight of the question of the philosophical life, then it is hardly surprising that many today fail to see him as a philosopher, often mistaking him for a commentator, a historian of ideas, or even some kind of political guru. Strauss's interests were not with the techniques or methods of philosophy, much less with advancing knowledge of concepts and propositions; they were with the prior question, "Why philosophy?" This is obviously not a question one would ask of activities such as military strategy or business enterprise where the ends in question (victory, profit) are not fundamentally controversial. Yet the ends of philosophy are and will always remain an open question. More specifically, Strauss was concerned with what the philosophical life is and what value, if any, it confers on the life of the community. His single-minded examination of this question fulfills the offices of philosophy to the highest degree.

Suggestions for further reading

Smith, Steven B., ed. *The Cambridge Companion to Leo Strauss*. Cambridge: Cambridge University Press, 2009.

———. *Reading Leo Strauss: Politics, Philosophy, Judaism*. Chicago: University of Chicago Press, 2006.

Strauss, Leo. *Natural Right and History*. Chicago: University of Chicago Press, 1953. See esp. the introduction and chap. 1, "Natural Right and the Historical Approach."

———. "Progress or Return?" In *The Rebirth of Classical Political Rationalism*, edited by Thomas Pangle, 227–70. Chicago: University of Chicago Press, 1989.

---

[55] Strauss, "Progress or Return?" 270; see also the following remark from Goethe, cited by Strauss in "The Law of Reason in the *Kuzari*," 107 n. 35: "The actual, only and most profound theme of world and human history, the theme under which all others are subsumed, remains the conflict between unbelief and belief."

———. "What Is Political Philosophy?" In *What Is Political Philosophy? and Other Studies*, 9–55. Glencoe, IL: The Free Press, 1959.

Tanguay, Daniel. *Leo Strauss: An Intellectual Biography*. Translated by Christopher Nadon. New Haven: Yale University Press, 2007.

Zuckert, Catherine, and Michael Zuckert. *The Truth about Leo Strauss: Political Philosophy and American Democracy*. Chicago: University of Chicago Press, 2006.

5

The philosopher's vocation: the Voegelinian paradigm

ELLIS SANDOZ

In his personal and scholarly demeanor, Eric Voegelin's stance was overtly and explicitly that of a philosopher and teacher professing truth and resisting corruption. The mark of his life was intellectual integrity in the Weberian sense, and his only professional commitment was that of a partisan of truth. This was more than academic duty, however. It was quite distinctly a vocation – or *calling (klesis)*[1] – of the highest order and responsibility, one intrinsic to the paradigm of philosophizing that Voegelin accepted from Plato and Anselm and demonstrated in his own life and work. It is exemplified and directly evoked in the "Introduction to Political Science" he taught as a lecture course at the University of Munich in the spring semester, 1964, now published under the title *Hitler and the Germans*.[2] Yet it can be traced everywhere in his writings, beginning in the 1930s, as a constant and defining attitude.[3] The implications are important not only for Voegelin but also for philosophy itself when it is rightly done as embracing the science of human affairs, palpably akin to that first elaborated in antiquity by Aristotle. It is this decisive, unfashionable, and somewhat elusive contextual dimension of *Hitler and the Germans* that I explore here.

---

[1] 2 Thess. 1:11; 1 Pet. 2:9 (AV): "You are a . . . royal priesthood . . . that you should show forth the praises of him who has called you out of darkness into his marvelous light." Said of all believers under the dispensation of Grace who, living in immediacy to God, are sons of the heavenly *Rex et Sacerdos*. Cf. Rom 1:1–6, a passage Voegelin repeatedly read in his last days. It is a commonplace of Christian faith that "conversion and vocation were for [St. Paul] one and the same event (Gal. 1:15–16)" (Franz J. Leenhardt, *The Epistle to the Romans: A Commentary*, trans. Harold Knight [London: Lutterworth, 1961], 39).

[2] Published as *Collected Works of Eric Voegelin* (hereafter CW), vol. 31, ed. Detlev Clemens and Brendan Purcell (Columbia: University of Missouri Press, 1999). A German-language edition of the course of lectures basic to the text of this book appeared as Eric Voegelin, *Hitler und die Deutschen*, ed. Manfred Henningsen (Munich: Wilhelm Fink Verlag, 2006). References herein are to the English-language version unless otherwise indicated.

[3] As in the remarks on the "concept of the person" in the *Theory of Governance*, in CW, vol. 32, ed. William Petropulos and Gilbert Weiss (Columbia: University of Missouri Press, 2003), 226–55.

Calling and authority

The responsive center of the philosopher's calling lies in the divine–human partnership, understood as participation in the process-structure governing metaxic-reality-experienced – the only reality we have – with the philosopher cast in the role of representative man. Voegelin announces the calling and its authoritative consequences in his essay "The Oxford Political Philosophers," in which he writes, "This is a time [1953] for the philosopher to be aware of his authority, and to assert it, even if that brings him into conflict with an environment infested by dubious ideologies and political theologies – so that the word of Marcus Aurelius will apply to him: 'The philosopher – the priest and servant of the gods.'"[4]

Even more energetically, Voegelin traces the transfer of authority from corrupt public institutions to the philosopher to the climax of the *Gorgias*, with plain allusions to his own totalitarian experience:

The man who stands convicted as the accomplice of tyrannical murderers and as the corruptor of his country, does not represent spiritual order, and nobody is obliged to show respect to his word. The authority of public order lies with Socrates. . . . The situation is fascinating for those among us who find ourselves in the Platonic position and who recognize in the men with whom we associate today the intellectual pimps for power who will connive in our murder tomorrow. It would be too much of an honor, however, to burden Callicles personally with the guilt of murder. The whole society is corrupt, and the process of corruption did not start yesterday.[5]

The same applies to Hitler and the Germans, as Voegelin emphasizes:

And now we pass to the problematic of crime when the society is not intact, as a problematic that has come to light through the mass murder during the Third Reich. But, as I again and again emphasize, we are speaking, not about the problem of National Socialism, but about Hitler and the Germans. . . . I have continually spoken of moral degeneracy; it does not exist abstractly. . . . It is, rather, a matter of this whole process of intellectual and spiritual degeneration [infecting every level of personal and institutional life with rot]. . . . All of these people are accomplices. I have forgotten nobody [clergy, judges, generals, professors]. . . . I will not here, for heaven's sake, defend the professors. When in the early 1930s, after Hitler had come into power, a whole series of professors, not only Jews, were relieved of their posts, none of the others . . . ever refused to occupy with pleasure one of the posts vacated

---

[4] Voegelin, "The Oxford Political Philosophers," in CW, vol. 11, ed. Ellis Sandoz (Columbia: University of Missouri Press, 2000), 46.

[5] Voegelin, *Order and History*, vol. 3, *Plato and Aristotle* (Baton Rouge: Louisiana State University Press, 1957), 38, 37. For the structure of corruption see the summary at ibid., 79.

through this dismissal. Since I was myself dismissed in 1938, I have always [had] a particularly keen eye for people who became tenured professors in Germany after 1933. So there is this kind of aiding and abetting, one always goes along, there is no one who offers resistance.... That does not happen.[6]

Truth and ecumenicity

The language of truth is spoken in many dialects, and no absolute partition between revelation and *noesis* is empirically or theoretically supportable, whatever the institutional differentiations. As Voegelin informed his political science students in Munich from time to time, you cannot ignore revelation and pretend it never occurred. If apperceptive experience forms the empirical ground of philosophical inquiry and exegesis, then one must attend to insights from that and every other quarter, whenever they arise, as events of consciousness in concrete individual human beings to form the articulate experiences-symbolizations of noetic exploration. That *philosophy* by this accounting must be in some sense empirically grounded, and not merely imaginative word play or logorrhea however brilliant, if it is to be epistemologically cogent, immediately puts Voegelin at odds with both ideologues devising imaginary second realities (for whom experience is terribly "inconvenient") and much else that otherwise passes for contemporary "autonomous" philosophizing.[7] That it bridges the distance between pneumatic and noetic discourse to embrace both offends the self-appointed custodians of both revelation and academic philosophy. (So there goes the readership.) Nonetheless Voegelin makes this firm reiterated conclusion:

We can no longer ignore that the symbols of "Faith" express the responsive quest of man just as much as the revelatory appeal, and that the symbols of "Philosophy" express the revelatory appeal just as much as the responsive quest. We must further acknowledge that the medieval tension between Faith and Reason derives from the origins of these symbols in the two different ethnic cultures of Israel and Hellas, that in the consciousness of Israelite prophets and Hellenic philosophers the differentiating experience of the divine Beyond was respectively focused on the revelatory appeal and the human quest.... The reflective action of [Plato and Aristotle] is a quest by concrete human beings in response to a divine appeal from the Beyond of the soul.[8]

---

[6] Voegelin, *Hitler*, 230–5.
[7] Cf., however, David Walsh, "Voegelin's Place in Modern Philosophy," *Modern Age* 49, no. 1 (Winter 2007): 12–23.
[8] Voegelin, "The Beginning and the Beyond," in CW, vol. 28, ed. Thomas A. Hollweck and Paul Caringella (Columbia: University of Missouri Press, 1990), 211. See the late (1981) summarizing

Yet it is of utmost importance to grasp that the relationship and process of communion with the divine are not reserved for grandiose personalities. That communion is the common coin of open existence available to every human being as the precious mark of their humanity is confirmed in apperceptive experience. Thus, in noting that *reason* is "due to God's grace" even according to Aquinas, Voegelin remarks that this understanding applies today and to wherever we may be as well: "You are sitting here asking questions. Why? Because you have that divine *kinesis* in you that moves you to be interested.... It is the revelatory presence, of course, that pushes you or pulls you. It's there. We are talking."[9] "The consciousness of being caused by the Divine ground and being in search of the Divine ground – that is reason [*nous*]. Period."[10]

Personal action

At the concrete level of political action, an array of consequences follow that give texture to the critique of the Nazi period recounted in *Hitler and the Germans* and elaborate the cardinal principle energetically asserted in Voegelin's *Antrittsvorlesung* (inaugural lecture). This principle connects the philosopher as a representative figure with every individual, to wit: "The spiritual disorder of our time, the civilizational crisis of which everyone so readily speaks, does not by any means have to be borne as an inevitable fate; on the contrary, everyone possesses the means of overcoming it in his own life.... No one is obliged to take part in the spiritual crisis of a society; on the contrary, everyone is obliged to avoid this folly and live his life in order."[11]

---

statement on these subjects titled "The Meditative Origin of the Philosophical Knowledge of Order": "In my view there is neither natural reason nor revelation, neither the one nor the other. *Rather we have here a theological misconstruction of certain real matters that was carried out in the interest of theological systematization*" (CW, vol. 33, ed. William Petropulos and Gilbert Weiss [Columbia: University of Missouri Press, 2004], 385–6, italics added).

[9] *Conversations with Eric Voegelin*, in CW 33:328, 330–1. The attitude experientially validates the flux of ubiquitous divine presence in human consciousness implicit in Jesus's promise at the end of the Gospel of Matthew: "and, lo, I am with you always, even unto the end of the world" (Matt. 28:20 [AV]). On the pushes and pulls (*helkein*) in experiences of divine reality as recounted in Greek philosophy as well as in biblical revelation, see Voegelin's comparative analysis in "The Gospel and Culture," in CW, vol. 12, ed. Sandoz (Columbia: University of Missouri Press, 1990), 184–91; see also "Reason: The Classic Experience," in CW 12:281.

[10] CW 33:329.

[11] Voegelin, *Science, Politics and Gnosticism*, in CW, vol. 5, ed. Manfred Henningsen (Columbia: University of Missouri Press, 1999), 261.

Divine–human partnership

The first lecture of the course identifies the transcendent source of order in terms of the immanent present of time and political action as occurring in the "presence under God":[12] "It is for everyman: to place the immanent present within the immanent process under the judgment of the [divine] presence." As Plato showed in the *Republic* and in the *Gorgias*, "to place oneself under the presence, under the presence of God, and according to that to adjudicate what one does as man and how one forms the order of one's own existence and the existence of society, that for Plato is an act of judgment. That means that man is always under judgment." He is persuaded by the logic of his heart to live his life continuously *sub specie mortis*, under the aspect of death and eternity.[13] It is the calling of the philosopher to utter that judgment and to claim the authority of public order when necessary, for example, under conditions of social schism and disintegration when political and other institutional power and the truth of spirit separate.[14] Aleksandr Solzhenitsyn claims a similar role for the writer when he asks, "Why have literature at all?" and answers his own question by observing, "After all, the writer is a teacher of the people.... And a greater writer – forgive me, perhaps I shouldn't say this, I'll lower my voice – a greater writer is, so to speak, a second government. That's why no regime anywhere has ever loved its great writers, only its minor ones."[15]

Anthropology and the tension of existence

Every human being, Voegelin writes, is *imago Dei* and thereby *called* – a call the individual person in freedom can respond to, reject, or ignore – to fulfill the promise of his sacred destiny. Thus, man is *theomorphic*:

Through the seeking for the divine, the loving reaching beyond ourselves toward the divine in the philosophical experience and the loving encounter through the

---

[12] See Voegelin, *Anamnesis*: "There is no philosophy without philosophers, namely without men whose psychic sensorium responds to eternal being" (CW, vol. 6, ed. David Walsh [Columbia: University of Missouri Press, 2002], 313); "The concept most suitable to express the presence of eternal being in the temporal flow is *flowing presence*" (ibid., 329). See also the discussion in CW 33:182–3, 233, 264, 340–1.

[13] Voegelin, *Hitler*, 71; *Order and History* 3:92, 129.

[14] As Jürgen Gebhardt remarks, in the face of political and spiritual disaster "it is the philosopher-scholar who is called upon to accept the office of *magisterium* and defend it against intellectual usurpers" (Gebhardt, "The Vocation of the Scholar," in *International and Interdisciplinary Perspectives on Eric Voegelin*, ed. Stephen A. McKnight and Geoffrey L. Price [Columbia: University of Missouri Press, 1997], 18).

[15] A. Solzhenitsyn, *The First Circle*, trans. Thomas P. Whitney (New York: Bantam Books, 1981), 415.

Word in the pneumatic experience, man participates in the divine.... The specific dignity of man is based on this, on his nature as theomorphic, as in the form and in the image of God.... One cannot dedivinize oneself without dehumanizing oneself.[16]

By *spirit* we understand the openness of man to the divine ground of his existence: by *estrangement* from the spirit, the closure and the revolt against the ground. Through spirit man actualizes his potential to partake of the divine. He rises thereby to the *imago Dei* which it is his destiny to be. Spirit in this classical sense of *nous*, is that which all men have in common, the *xynon* as Heraclitus has called it. Through the life of the spirit, which is common to all, the existence of man becomes existence in community.[17]

Spokesmen for divine truth

At the conclusion of the lecture on the German university Voegelin again invoked the words of the prophet Ezekiel as fitting therapy for the pneumopathology of consciousness he had diagnosed and sketched in his meditation on the Nazi disorders. Ultimately, the faithful or responsive human being – whether citizen, soldier, philosopher, priest, or prophet – can do no more than make the public aware of such maladies, as Socrates in the name of truth had done in serving as a messenger of God to persuade the Athenians to tend their souls and serve justice. The message is not merely moralistic. It is soteriological and eschatological in content, pertaining to the salvation and destiny of individual human beings, society in history, and the structure-process of reality itself. Yet its seat is the participatory realm of the divine–human consciousness of concrete individual persons. Thus, the saving word reiterated by Voegelin came to Ezekiel from God:

So you, son of man, I have made a watchman for the house of Israel; whenever you hear a word from my mouth, you shall give them warning from me. If I say to the wicked, O wicked man, you shall surely die; and you do not speak to warn the wicked to turn from his way, that wicked man shall die in his iniquity; but his blood I will require at your hand. But if you warn the wicked to turn from his way, and he does not turn from his way, he shall die in his iniquity, but you will have saved your soul.[18]

Voegelin told his students to memorize this passage.

---

[16] Voegelin, *Hitler*, 87.
[17] Voegelin, "The German University and the Order of German Society," in CW 12:7.
[18] Ezek. 33:7–9 (RSV), quoted in ibid., 35; earlier quoted to the students, with instructions, in *Hitler*, 200.

As Manfred Henningsen, who was present at the lecture as one of Voegelin's graduate assistants, writes, the charged atmosphere was that of a "courtroom" with Voegelin the judge. The overall intent of Voegelin in these discourses was to elicit the conversion or "*metanoia*" of his auditors to truth analogous to that of the denizen in the cave recounted in Plato's *Republic*.[19]

Conclusion

At the beginning of his long study of order and history Voegelin defined philosophy: "Philosophy is the love of being through love of divine Being as the source of its order." This remained, enduringly, the pole star of his life and work.[20]

A consequence of the foregoing discussion is that anybody who is seriously interested in understanding Voegelin as he understood himself is obliged to come to grips with the issues briefly remembered here and clarified textually in numerous places over the decades as artifacts and way stations of the philosopher's own questing, meditative life.[21] A second consequence is plainly a substantial, even revolutionary, redefinition of the meaning of *philosophy* itself, especially on the decisive points of (a) underlining the loving tension toward divine Reality in open existence as central; (b) attenuating or abandoning the scholastic convention separating faith and reason as supernatural and natural, respectively; and (c) discarding as *egophany* the arrogant pretense of autonomous reason as its originator in self-sufficient human speculators.[22] The God of Abraham, Moses, Plato,

---

[19] Manfred Henningsen, editor's introduction to *Hitler und die Deutschen*, 29, 38. See Plato *Republic* 518de; Voegelin, *Order and History* 3:68, 112–17.

[20] Voegelin, *Order and History*, vol. 1, *Israel and Revelation* (Baton Rouge: Louisiana State University Press, 1956), xiv. See the discussion in Ellis Sandoz, *The Voegelinian Revolution: A Biographical Introduction*, 2nd ed. (New Brunswick, NJ: Transaction, 2000), 141–2.

[21] As one astute commentator writes, "It is as if he himself were a second Jeremiah, that Voegelin undertook his own effort to rebalance the consciousness of his own age.... His own purpose is clearly one that seeks to recover the prophetic impulse" (Geoffrey L. Price, "Recovery from Metastatic Consciousness: Voegelin and Jeremiah," in *Politics, Order and History: Essays on the Work of Eric Voegelin*, ed. Glenn Hughes et al. [Sheffield, UK: Sheffield Academic Press, 2001], 204). The able editors of *Hitler* remark that, as a political philosopher, Voegelin's authoritative appeal for conversion to truth in his auditors is founded "on his own life of bearing witness" (CW 31:34).

[22] For discussion of *egophany* see Sandoz, *Voegelinian Revolution*, 239–43 and the sources cited therein (among which see esp. Voegelin, *Order and History*, vol. 4, *The Ecumenic Age* [Baton Rouge: Louisiana State University Press, 1974], 260–71). For a preliminary elaboration of the revolutionary implications for philosophy per se, see *Voegelinian Revolution*, 189–216. This is a meditative and ontological revolution of mind and spirit, one involving a "change in being," not a political one in the streets, nor even in intractable prevailing climates of opinion, one is constrained to emphasize to help avoid misunderstanding.

and Paul *is one and the same God*, disclosed to spiritually sensitive people of all ages and communicated in equivalent language modalities and symbolisms. To make any other assumption about human communion with divine being would be extraordinary, if one acknowledges that there is one humankind and one reality of which the human being is ontologically the self-reflective, articulate part.[23] Openness and *responsiveness* to the luminous presence of ineffable It-reality within limits imposed by metaxic existence form the very essence of what it means to be a human being, on this accounting.[24] More discursively, Voegelin writes, "Things do not happen in the astrophysical universe; the universe, together with all things founded in it, happens in God."[25] Voegelin later adds that "the questioner's language reveals itself as the paradoxic event of the ineffable becoming effable. . . . In reflective distance, the questioner. . . experiences his speech as the divine silence breaking creatively forth in the imaginative word that will illuminate the quest as the questioner's movement of return to the ineffable silence."[26]

Philosophy, then, is the loving noetic search of the heights and depths of reality, conducted as faith seeking understanding and accepting as

[23] This is no mere inference; Voegelin is explicit in the matter: "Unless we want to indulge in extraordinary theological assumptions, the God who appeared to philosophers, and who elicited from Parmenides the exclamation 'Is!', was the same God who revealed himself to Moses as the 'I am who (or: what) I am,' as the God who is what he is in the concrete theophany to which man responds. When God lets himself be seen, whether in a burning thornbush or in a Promethean fire, he is what he reveals himself to be in the event" (*Order and History* 4:229). See also "Equivalences of Experience and Symbolization in History," in CW 12:115–33.

[24] Some of the implications are discussed in Paul Caringella, "Eric Voegelin: Philosopher of Divine Presence," in *Eric Voegelin's Significance for the Modern Mind*, ed. Ellis Sandoz (Baton Rouge: Louisiana State University Press, 1991), 174–205. Although Voegelin seems never to say so, the ultimate source of the symbol *It* as used in his work is clearly Pseudo-Dionysius, where the name "It" represents the ineffable "Super-Essential Godhead which we must not dare . . . to speak, or even to form any conception Thereof, except those things which are divinely revealed to us from the Holy Scriptures" (Ps.-Dionysius, *The Divine Names*, in *Dionysius the Areopagite: The Divine Names and the Mystical Theology*, ed. C. E. Rolt (Kila, MT: Kessinger, n.d.), 53; see 4–12. Note that the presentation here assumes the analysis given in Ellis Sandoz, *Republicanism, Religion and the Soul of America* (Columbia: University of Missouri Press, 2006), chap. 8, esp. 162–81. Behind Thomas's *Tetragrammaton* stands Dionysius's It, and behind that, the *epekeina* (Beyond) of Plato's *agathon* (Good), *kalon* (Beauty), *periechon* (Comprehending), and *to pan* (All), back to Anaximander's *apeiron* (Unbounded, Depth) and similar symbols – matters pertaining to nonexistent reality that must be left aside here. For an analysis of some of the issues, see Voegelin, *Order and History*, vol. 5, *In Search of Order*, ed. Sandoz [Baton Rouge: Louisiana State University Press, 1987], 100–03; see also Fran O'Rourke, *Pseudo-Dionysius and the Metaphysics of Aquinas* (Notre Dame: University of Notre Dame Press, 2005), esp. the section "Aquinas and the Good Beyond Being," exploring the difficulty "of expressing in concepts and terms appropriate to beings that which is supposedly nonexistent, i.e., prime matter, or which is beyond existence, namely, the divine Good" (201).

[25] Voegelin, *Order and History* 4:334.

[26] Voegelin, *Order and History* 5:103; see Sandoz, *Voegelinian Revolution*, 264.

authoritative truth the insights attained in the open quest of reality experienced – and the philosopher is the true type of human being.[27] The philosopher thus speaks as the oracle of God in manifesting receptivity to highest truth[28] – a role of urgent significance when the ordering institutions of a society founder and abdicate responsibility or collapse and pervert themselves into instruments of evil, injustice, and murderous destruction, as displayed in lurid detail in Hitler's Germany or Stalin's Russia, but not only there. As we have seen, Voegelin reminds all who will hear of the abiding obligation of *every* individual to live in accordance with truth and to resist evil and corruption to the limits of his or her capacities – thereby to serve justice and goodness so far as possible, the message of Ezekiel's watchman. The truth ascertained is neither dogmatic nor exhaustive but existential and self-augmenting, ecumenical and authoritative as in accordance with revelation and reason. To give Voegelin one last word:

I am indeed attempting to "identify" . . . the God who reveals himself, not only in the prophets, in Christ, and in the Apostles, but wherever his reality is experienced as present in the cosmos and in the soul of man. One can no longer use the medieval distinction between the theologian's supernatural revelation and the philosopher's natural reason, when any number of texts will attest the revelatory consciousness of the Greek poets and philosophers; nor can one let revelation begin with the Israelite and Christian experiences, when the mystery of divine presence in reality is attested as experienced by man, as far back as 20,000 B.C. . . . As far as my own vocabulary is concerned, I am very conscious of not relying on the language of doctrine, but I am equally conscious of not going beyond the orbit of Christianity when I prefer the experiential symbol "divine reality" to the God of the Creed, for "divine reality" translates the *theotes* of Colossians 2:9. . . . Moreover, I am very much aware that my inquiry into the history of experience and symbolization generalizes the Anselmian *fides quaerens intellectum* so as to include every *fides*, not only the Christian, in the quest for understanding by reason. . . . In practice this means that one has to recognize, and make intelligible, the presence of Christ in a Babylonian hymn, or a Taoist speculation, or a Platonic dialogue, just as much as in a Gospel.[29]

---

[27] See Voegelin, *The New Science of Politics* (Chicago: University of Chicago Press, 1952), 63–70. Cf. the fine analysis of Anselm in Robert McMahon, *Understanding the Medieval Meditative Ascent: Augustine, Anselm, Boethius, and Dante* (Washington, DC: Catholic University of America Press, 2006), esp. 202–10.

[28] Although it may at first sight appear to be novel, this is in fact the *ordinary* obligation and role of "every man" of faith (not only philosophers, prophets, and apostles) under the dispensation of grace as "good stewards of the manifold grace of God. If any man speak, let him speak as the oracles of God [*lógia theou*]; if any man minister, let him do it as of the ability which God gives him: that God may in all things be glorified" (1 Pet. 4:10–11 [AV, modified]).

[29] Voegelin, "Response to Professor Altizer," in CW 12:294.

Perhaps as clearly as any other text, this remarkable statement captures the revolutionary thrust of Voegelin's work. It is a set of claims to be pondered by anyone devoted to the study of order and disorders in human experience in its broadest amplitude, in service to truth and in resistance against deformation and evil. This is the philosopher's vocation.

Because we are interested in politics, it is well to be reminded of Voegelin's own actions to stem the tide in time and to rectify the effects of the Hitler calamity after the fact – the therapeutic intent of the *Hitler* lectures. He narrowly escaped the Gestapo and fled to Switzerland and the United States in 1938 after the *Anschluss* and after he was fired from his job as a professor at the University of Vienna; he thus avoided paying the almost certain ultimate price of an opponent of tyranny. Of his day-to-day activities while a member of the faculty of the University of Vienna in the years leading up to his dismissal by the Nazis, information is meager. His opposition was sufficiently well known through his publications, however, that he was regularly identified (in print) as a "Jew." His "mastering of the present," as he called it in the 1964 lectures,[30] consisted in publishing three books that methodically demonstrated the fallaciousness and reductionist virulence of National Socialist pneumopathology – two of them published in 1933 by German publishers – and condemning it as the apocalypse of evil and anti-Christianity. As Gregor Sebba later wrote, "When I read those two books, I knew that Voegelin would be on the Nazi list when Austria fell. I still wonder how he had the nerve to publish both books in Hitler's Germany, and how two German publishers could accept them."[31] The third of these took as its epigraph a line from Dante's *Inferno* (Canto 3, line 1): "Per me si va ne la città dolente" (Through me the way is to the city of woe).[32] The earthly Hell was at hand. As for Voegelin himself, there was no chariot of fire translating him to Heaven like Elijah, only the evening train to Zurich after a day spent eluding the Gestapo in Vienna, on the way to a new life in America, trembling as he went.[33]

---

[30] Voegelin, *Hitler*, 75.

[31] Gregor Sebba, "Prelude and Variations on the Theme of Eric Voegelin," in *Eric Voegelin's Thought: A Critical Appraisal*, ed. Ellis Sandoz (Durham, NC: Duke University Press, 1982), 11. Sebba was Voegelin's colleague and friend in Vienna, later professor at Emory University. The works in question, in English translation, are *Race and State* and *The History of the Race Idea*, in CW, vols. 2 and 3, ed. Klaus Vondung (Columbia: University of Missouri Press, 1997–98). Hannah Arendt regarded *Race and State* as "the best historical account of race-thinking" (Arendt, *Origins of Totalitarianism* [New York: Harcourt, Brace and Co., 1951], 158n).

[32] Voegelin, *The Political Religions*, in CW, vol. 5, ed. Henningsen (Columbia: University of Missouri Press, 1999), 20.

[33] See Voegelin, *Autobiographical Reflections*, rev. ed., in CW, vol. 34, ed. Sandoz (Columbia: University of Missouri Press, 2006), 71, 82–3.

Most of Voegelin's major work lay ahead, and twenty years after the abrupt departure from Vienna he returned to Munich, partly motivated by the hope of instilling "the spirit of American democracy" into Germany and of "injecting an element of international consciousness, and of democratic attitudes, into German political science."[34]

[34] Ibid., 116.

6

Yves R. Simon: a philosopher's quest for science and prudence

WALTER NICGORSKI

From a plentitude of early loves and political concerns, Yves Simon's call to philosophy emerged as dominant and defining for his life. He wrote some plays and poetry and at one point thought that he might devote himself to literary studies. At a later time, fascinated by the enterprise of modern empirical science and what it could do for humankind, he began down the path of medical studies. Entering his university years, he was engaged by political issues that lingered from the great divide of France's past, and then, ever more passionately so, by the struggles for genuine peace in the 1920s and '30s and a possible Fascist future for France and Europe. His Catholic family of republican convictions knew firsthand the sufferings of World War I, and his own life (1903–61) seemed marked by a special capacity to appreciate the concrete historical contingencies that must and should bear on specific moral and hence political decisions. It is not surprising that Simon was attracted to philosophy both as a way to understand the ingredients of good moral decisions and as the true and complete science, in the classic Aristotelian sense. Near the very end of his life, he appeared especially interested in protecting the sphere of practical judgment or prudence from both philosophy and social science. What direction he provided to politics was democratic in character; what direction to education, specifically education for political choices and leadership, was humanist, emphasizing historical and literary learning and the enrichment of direct human experience and cautioning against a curricular dominance of philosophy and theology.

Before he began his university studies early in 1922, Simon had already experienced the satisfaction of philosophical studies in his French schooling. As he entered higher studies and throughout his years before his 1938 departure to the United States, he wrote almost constantly for journals, magazines, and newspapers, and although political themes and issues were by no means his exclusive concern, they were regularly in evidence. On his arrival at the University of Notre Dame in 1938, it was not surprising that he got involved in a small circle of faculty members who were planning and supporting the launching of *The Review of Politics*. His mentor and lifelong friend, Jacques Maritain, writing on "integral humanism," was the author of the first article in the maiden issue of *The Review* in January 1939. Speaking in 1961 in praise of Maritain, Simon remarked that Maritain came relatively late in life, at the age of forty-five, to "political and related subjects."[1] Simon thus seemed aware of his difference from Maritain in this respect.

Yves Simon is sometimes thought to be a rather obscure philosopher, who came somehow, as if it all dropped out of the sky one day, to write a remarkable book on democratic theory. His *Philosophy of Democratic Government* (1951)[2] is particularly surprising to political scientists who suspect that the work of a Thomist must be largely deductive and heavily freighted with religious assumptions. They are wrong on all counts with respect to Simon. There is an "intimate" connection between his life and writings in his emphatic attention to human freedom, its exercise in moral choices, and the institutions that secure its practice.[3] His modern classic and so much else of his writing are made especially memorable and effective by his evident attention to common human experience.[4]

Robert Mulvaney notes that "every major writing of Simon devotes some attention to practical wisdom and its epistemological underpinnings."[5] Indeed, there seems a clear trajectory in Simon's life and work moving from

---

[1] Yves R. Simon, "Jacques Maritain," in *Jacques Maritain: Homage in Words and Pictures*, by John Howard Griffin and Yves R. Simon (Albany, NY: Magi Books, 1974), 9.

[2] *Philosophy of Democratic Government*, initially published in 1951 by the University of Chicago Press, has been available since 1993 at the University of Notre Dame Press. The Notre Dame edition incorporates a more detailed index and editorial corrections of earlier editions.

[3] Anthony O. Simon, editor's note, in *Acquaintance with the Absolute: The Philosophy of Yves R. Simon*, ed. Anthony O. Simon (New York: Fordham University Press, 1998), xiii. I am indebted to Anthony Simon, a son of Yves Simon and director of the Yves R. Simon Institute, not only for suggestions relevant to this chapter but also for his fruitful efforts over the years in seeing to publication and/or into translation much significant work of his father that had not appeared in his lifetime and in maintaining regularly the kind of complete bibliography that is available in the volume cited here.

[4] Notable is his rich treatment of the common good, including the "vivid examples" of the frustration in attaining the common good when a family's best planning of a holiday nonetheless results in disaster, and of the success of reaching the common good with the aid of an indefatigably uncompromising, single-minded but conscientious Latin teacher nearly fanatic in his attachment to the advancement of Latin (*Philosophy of Democratic Government*, 21–2, 45–6; the example of the family is richly elaborated for another purpose at 31–5). The singularly apt phrase "vivid examples" is that of James V. Schall, S.J., "Immanent in the Souls of Men," introduction to *Acquaintance with the Absolute*, 4.

[5] Robert J. Mulvaney, "Practical Wisdom in the Thought of Yves R. Simon," in *Acquaintance with the Absolute*, 148, 153.

(1) probing reflection on the specific political concerns of his youth and early adulthood, to (2) his early book on moral knowledge and its final chapter concerned explicitly with defending his use of examples drawn from political science in exhibiting "the noetic characteristics and method of moral philosophy,"[6] to (3) *Philosophy of Democratic Government* and the deep and expansive studies on authority and practical knowledge that follow it. It is important to note that this is a journey of the mind, of the inquirer, not one that leaves active politics behind. Simon's migration to the United States was but a new stage in his concern for a free and liberal France.[7] Nevertheless, his embrace of his new American homeland entailed a strong and ever developing critical awareness of its history, politics, and larger culture, as well as a sharing in the aspirations and challenges of American democracy. An advocate of democracy, he was thought by Leo Strauss to go too far in claiming a basis in the work of St. Thomas for the authority given the people in modern regimes; he clearly wrestled deeply with whether Thomism and in part Catholicism were obstacles rather than aids in defending genuine and hence healthy developments in liberal modernity.[8]

Yet Vukan Kuic is surely correct that Simon regarded himself as a philosopher.[9] Nonetheless, it is clear that the weight of his work thus far

---

[6] This book, his second in the year 1934, was *Critique de la connaissance morale* (Paris: Desclée de Brouwer, 1934). The quotation here from the last chapter is taken from the English translation by Ralph McInerny, *A Critique of Moral Knowledge* (New York: Fordham University Press, 2002), 75.

[7] Simon initially came to the United States for a year as a visiting professor at the University of Notre Dame, but he welcomed the opportunity to stay when free France fell.

[8] See Strauss's review of *Philosophy of Democratic Government* in Leo Strauss, *What Is Political Philosophy? and Other Essays* (Westport, CT: Greenwood Press, 1959), 306–11. Strauss strongly praised Simon's analysis of modern democracy, specifically *Philosophy of Democratic Government*, in my presence. Simon's concerns with the adequacy of Thomism and, to a degree, Catholicism in resisting Fascist authoritarianism come to the fore in correspondence between Simon and Maritain, especially during 1941; this is reviewed in John Hellman, "The Anti-Democratic Impulse in Catholicism: Jacques Maritain, Yves Simon, and Charles de Gaulle during World War II," *Journal of Church and State* 33, no. 3 (Summer 1991): 458–71. In the period between the intense days of early World War II and his writing *Philosophy of Democratic Government*, Simon gave more attention to the alleged and sometimes felt tensions between Thomism and Catholicism on the one hand and modern democracy on the other, for example in "The Doctrinal Issue between the Church and Democracy," in *The Catholic Church in World Affairs*, ed. Waldemar Gurian and M. A. Fitzsimons (Notre Dame, IN: University of Notre Dame Press, 1954), 87–114. A recent, fine interpretation of "the Thomist case for democracy" that Simon came to make in his work of the 1950s can be found in Jeanne Heffernan Schindler, "Democracy and Tradition: A Catholic Alternative to American Pragmatism," *Logos* 11, no. 2 (Spring 2008): 36–44.

[9] Vukan Kuic, *Yves R. Simon: Real Democracy* (Lanham, MD: Rowman & Littlefield, 1999), 1. As Anthony Simon observes, his father regarded himself as a "non-specialized philosopher by principle" (*Acquaintance with the Absolute*, ix). Yves Simon's range of philosophical interests is represented in the courses he offered as a member of the University of Chicago's Committee on Social Thought

made public and the attention he has drawn relate to practical philosophy, in an Aristotelian understanding that encompasses both moral and political philosophy. Simon seemed to care not so much about what he was called – political philosopher, moral philosopher, or simply philosopher – as about understanding what is philosophy, what are practical judgment and choice, and, accordingly, what that seemingly middle terrain is that might be called moral and/or political philosophy and what is its work. Such clarification of fundamental concepts and categories is an important dimension of his writings and is in part what he regarded as strictly philosophical work.

At the Sorbonne Simon studied social theorists of the nineteenth century, especially Pierre-Joseph Proudhon, for whom he had a singular enthusiasm. Proudhon, self-styled as an anarchist and sometimes described as a libertarian socialist, was interested in workers' organizations and opposed to centralized rather than federal political organizations. Simon was simultaneously drawn to Maritain and under his tutelage studied the philosophical-theological work of St. Thomas Aquinas at the Institut Catholique de Paris. Some years later, in an autobiographical reflection, Simon marveled that this "was surely the first time that a student of Proudhon happened to be a student of St. Thomas."[10] The keen interest in Proudhon and the social theorists appears wholly understandable for a bright young student concerned with the issue of economic justice as it arose in early twentieth-century Europe in the ravages and turmoil that followed World War I.[11] Such interest seemed simply to reflect a good republican citizen's concern with issues of the time. Yet how can we understand that which appears anomalous at this stage of his life: his deep commitment to studying philosophy in the mode of St. Thomas?

Simon's reflections on this period made during later stages of his life provide the basis for seeing how he understood his call to philosophy and the philosophical terrain that he marked out for his work.[12] In 1945, he recounted how, more than twenty years earlier, he first encountered

---

(1948–61), a list of which can be found in Yves Simon, *Work, Society, and Culture*, ed. Vukan Kuic (New York: Fordham University Press, 1971), xii.

[10] "Yves R. Simon," in *The Book of Catholic Authors*, ed. Walter Romig (Detroit: Walter Romig, 1945), 266.

[11] A detailed examination of these studies and their impact on Simon's later thinking is found in Ralph Nelson, "Freedom and Economic Organization in a Democracy," in *Freedom in the Modern World: Jacques Maritain, Yves R. Simon, Mortimer J. Adler*, ed. Michael D. Torre (Mishawaka, IN: American Maritain Association, 1980), 141–52.

[12] This chapter makes very little use of Simon's correspondence; a more extensive study of that will likely shed further light on his self-understanding and development as a philosopher. Relevant correspondence is now becoming available in a more accessible form, as evidenced by the recent

Maritain as a teacher of modern philosophy, taking courses under him on Descartes and Kant. He was drawn by Maritain "to love the truth that Maritain loved, and to feel anxious to know more about it." Conceding that he learned much about "methods of work and fields of research" from his teachers at the Sorbonne, Simon thought the overall teaching he received there was "unsystematic," best described "as a combination of positivism and idealistic relativism." He characterized his study of social theory at the Sorbonne as "practicing philosophy as a mere cultural exercise." He realized with satisfaction that he had turned to philosophy with higher expectations, "looking for a system of philosophical truth." It was yet another matter whether that system would be found in what he called "the newly rediscovered philosophy of St. Thomas."[13]

Simon's decision to move toward a rigorously argued philosophical system had much to do with the qualities of both Maritain and Thomas. For Simon, it was not only a move against the regnant practices of academic philosophers but also a means of overcoming what he realized was a personal obstacle. Even after his introduction to St. Thomas at the Institut, he felt deficient with respect to his background in mathematics and "scientific instruction." Setting aside his "reading a great deal in a random way," he committed himself to developing "the characteristics of the scientific mind. True to this resolution," he added, "I became increasingly eager for accuracy, exactness, and systematic orderliness in all fields of knowledge."[14]

Although Simon later confessed that Maritain's treatment of the relation between philosophy and experimental science was "an important reason why I followed [his] teaching . . . more than that of any other teacher," in time Simon came to think of his own "calling" as strictly philosophic, with the attendant "special guaranties of epistemological purity and logical rigor." This was in contrast to Maritain, who was seen truly to deserve the title of Christian philosopher by dint of treating "philosophical issues in the particular *state* that they assume by reason of their relation to Christian faith and theology."[15]

It will seem paradoxical to some that Simon's activity of nourishing "the characteristics of the scientific mind" cemented and developed his

appearance of Jacques Maritain and Yves Simon, *Correspondance*, vol. 1, *Les années françaises (1927–1940)*, ed. Florian Michel et al. (Tours: CLD, 2008).
[13] "Yves R. Simon," in *Book of Catholic Authors*, 264–6.
[14] Ibid., 267.
[15] Simon, "Jacques Maritain," 8–9, 14 (see also 11 for emphasis on how Maritain remains clear about and loyal to the philosophic calling).

attachment to St. Thomas. In his 1955 foreword to the collaborative translation of *The Material Logic of John of St. Thomas*, Simon conceded the
element of mystery "in religion, in metaphysics, in philosophy generally,
and in human affairs," but then lamented the "widespread aversion to scientific forms" in these very areas of learning. Again setting his philosophical
orientation against "literary" approaches to philosophy, he observed, "What
is lacking in our relation to mystery is neither earnestness nor abundance
of ideas, it is the rigor of the scientific spirit." What he sought concretely
and found present in St. Thomas and the best of Thomism was "clarity
in the statement of questions and principles, firmness in inference, rational
evidence of conclusions, appropriateness in prediction, integral preservation
of past developments, lucid order, and the unique defense against error that
rational forms alone can provide."[16]

In the initial publication in French of *Foresight and Knowledge* eleven years
earlier, Simon had urged scientists to appreciate that Thomists share their
"same spirit" and "belong to the same breed." The very terms by which
Thomists are at times ridiculed by other philosophers and elements of
"the cultured public" are the "mental traits" they "owe to the Aristotelian
school – the only school in which philosophical disciplines have been
brought to a degree of technical elaboration comparable to that which
accounts for the prestige of the exact sciences." Those "traits" for which
Simon here apologized with irony are "[our] perpetual criticism of the
meaning of words, these distinctions, this concern for precise definitions
and exhaustive divisions, for rigorous deductions and necessary arguments,
this horror of vague approximation."[17]

The kinship of philosophy with empirical science goes beyond style
of argument and inquiry or method. Thomists, Simon claimed, have a
conception of philosophy that "implies above all that philosophy is itself
a science or, to be more precise, that philosophic disciplines are each of
them a science."[18] Later in this work Simon returned to this theme and
specifically invoked metaphysics: "In our view, whoever wants to work
out a theory of the relations between philosophy and the sciences should
above all take note of the scientific character of philosophy and understand that metaphysics, which is the archetype of all philosophical thinking,

---

[16] Yves R. Simon, foreword to *The Material Logic of John of St. Thomas*, trans. Yves R. Simon, John J.
Glanville, and G. Donald Hollenhorst (Chicago: University of Chicago Press, 1955), xxii–xxiii.
[17] Yves R. Simon, *Foresight and Knowledge*, ed. Ralph Nelson and Anthony O. Simon (New York:
Fordham University Press, 1996), 4.
[18] Ibid.

is at the same time purely and simply the archetype of all scientific thinking."[19]

Simon emphasized that philosophical inquiry – from the moral/political to the ultimate metaphysical inquiry – often arises from the perplexities and issues in the practical realm.[20] He thus acknowledged the role of simple but direct wonder in moving inquiry and thought, but he also insisted on the commitment of true philosophy, as of science, to explanation that aspires to be demonstrative and productive of consensus.[21] First science, or philosophy, is at the level of abstraction that not only allows a grounding and defense of the concepts of moral and political philosophy but also locates the truths of empirical science in its comprehensive explanation. Simon provided some striking formulations that assist his readers in understanding this grand and significant set of relationships and how ultimate science, or metaphysics, can proceed. "Every positive scientist," he observed, "is on the wrong track when he uses a term whose meaning cannot be reduced to observable data. Every philosopher is on the wrong track who uses a term whose meaning cannot be reduced to being."[22] The analogy and the difference between the two kinds of facts, philosophical and empirical, were illustrated in Simon's conception of philosophy's responsibility to disengage scientific facts from their strictly scientific form.[23]

At the conclusion of a lecture given near the end of his life (although first published in 1988), the philosophical responsibility to abstract came again to the fore in Simon's reflection on the many ways of knowing: "The unintegrated multiplicity of disciplines and cognitions is in our time the heaviest burden of the human intellect. The greater simplicity that we so badly need is procured by formal abstraction, an intellectual operation relevant to serenity and to both theoretical and practical wisdom."[24]

---

[19] Ibid., 91.
[20] In *A Critique of Moral Knowledge*, Simon wrote: "A metaphysics of man's ultimate end is implied by every political concept. No doubt, the same idea of the ultimate end is compatible with different opinions on how the city should be organized" (80). See also ibid., 40, where the connection between moral science and metaphysics is made explicit.
[21] Yves Simon, *The Great Dialogue of Nature and Space*, ed. Gerald J. Dalcourt, rev. ed. (South Bend, IN: St. Augustine's Press, 2001), 21; Yves Simon, *Practical Knowledge*, ed. Robert J. Mulvaney (New York: Fordham University Press, 1991), 98–9; Yves Simon, "The Philosopher's Calling," in *Philosopher at Work: Essays by Yves R. Simon*, ed. Anthony O. Simon (Lanham, MD: Rowman & Littlefield, 1999), 4–5.
[22] Simon, *Foresight and Knowledge*, 76.
[23] Simon, *Great Dialogue*, 178; see also chapters 7 and 9.
[24] Yves R. Simon, "Philosophy, the Humanities and Education," *The New Scholasticism* 62, no. 4 (Autumn 1988): 471.

Thus far I have sketched Simon's understanding of the nature and object of philosophy, in fact of all science or rational learning. More important to this chapter is the subject side of philosophy, namely, the philosopher and his state of mind and soul. Here Simon was understandably more self-revealing, and we encounter more the existential tensions of living out the call to philosophy. At the close of his autobiographical essay, Simon called attention to the indissoluble unity of love for truth and the love for justice that must mark the soul of a genuine philosopher.[25] In his last public lecture, he used the dedication to truth and to justice as a characterization of Maritain's practice with abstract ideas and thus of the resources that Maritain, the man so critical in drawing him to philosophy, brought to bear on public and intellectual controversies.[26] Yet attributing the "love of truth" to an academic person, a scientist, or a philosopher is such a commonplace that the profound and unsettling challenge of living faithfully to such a love is easily slighted.

It is the force of the love of truth that drew Simon to respect all knowledge and modes of knowing and that pushed him on that metaphysical path sketched earlier toward the unity behind all the diverse experiences of humankind. The elevation of this drive reflected the distinctive human yearning for the fullness of truth and the conviction that both justice and charity will be served best when those called to find and communicate the truth live with vigorous fidelity to their vocation. It is not just on a grand scale that the devotion to the truth is to operate. Simon looked for this philosophic attitude in the treatment of practical issues of the day, even though he recognized that philosophers themselves at the point of practical choice may be among the most inept of citizens. Wary of "the flowery element of culture" that "makes for subjectivism, arbitrariness, and an attitude of frivolous aversion to nature and its laws," Simon pleaded that "the knowledge of truth, not the possession of culture, be our regulating ideal. And let us not doubt that, if truth is sought according to its own laws and to its own spirit, culture also will be attained."[27]

Simon's most moving and nuanced statement on devotion to the truth, in fact to a culture of truth, appeared as World War II had just wound down. He emphasized the connection between a culture of freedom and one of truth in the first chapter of *The Community of the Free*. "The spirit of

---

[25] "Yves R. Simon," 270.
[26] Simon, "Jacques Maritain," 13.
[27] Simon, "The Concept of Work," in *Philosopher at Work*, 18.

freedom," he wrote, "has no worse enemy than falsehood. The conquest of freedom in daily life implies above all else a daily fight against falsehood, a daily fight for truth."[28]

Simon then cautioned against underestimating how difficult a fight it is – for a community, for a single person, for a philosopher who is to be especially characterized by commitment to the truth:

Let us understand that it is hardly possible to ask of a man a harder sacrifice than this: for love of truth, he be ready to say No to what is thought and said every day by "his brothers and his fellows"; ready to discover the ravages of falsehood in the souls of those who are dear to him, and to continue to cherish their souls whilst he hates their lies; ready ceaselessly to unveil the lies of his own conscience.... If I adopt the attitude of saying No to all falsehoods, including those which are manufactured and propagated around me as well as those which I feel welling up in myself, I know that I am setting out into a fearsome solitude, into a desert country, without roads and without water. There my dearest companions will fail me. My habits, my tastes, my passions will abandon me. With no support but truth, I shall go forward, stripped and trembling.... Reflecting upon this program for life, we feel ourselves overwhelmed with agony. The real problem is now propounded; we must learn whether we love truth so much that we are willing to live with it, if need be, in agony, or whether we wish to avoid agony at all costs, even at the cost of truth.[29]

In other writings Simon noted special challenges a philosopher faced in sustaining a vocation of fidelity to the truth. In his stirring commitment to the truth at the end of his autobiographical essay, there is an indication of his early discouragement with what passed for philosophy and his consequent need to find saving encouragement in the enthusiasm and authenticity of his young students.[30] Elsewhere he drew attention both to how often even great philosophers go wrong and to the disagreements that plague philosophy.[31] A significant cause of bewilderment in philosophy, Simon wrote, is that success is never unquestioned.[32] Despite such difficulties, Simon held that consensus is possible in philosophy even if almost never seen. He argued that there are accidental rather than essential reasons for the disappointing pervasive disagreement among philosophers. He once enumerated the most important of these reasons as "(a) the inherent difficulty of philosophical

---

[28] Yves R. Simon, *The Community of the Free*, trans. Willard R. Trask, rev. ed. (Lanham, MD: University Press of America, 1984), 5.

[29] Simon, *Community of the Free*, 5–6. In the pages that follow, Simon showed the sensitivity and deftness in the service of the truth that allowed him to envision withholding truth and even using silence as means of serving truth in certain circumstances.

[30] "Yves R. Simon," 270.

[31] Simon, "The Philosopher's Calling," 1–2; "Philosophy, the Humanities and Education," 469.

[32] Simon, "The Philosopher's Calling," 3.

questions, (b) the influence of human, moral, and esthetic attitudes on the directions of philosophic thought, and (c) the strange fact that people who have no real understanding of philosophical issues can be successful as philosophy students and as writers in philosophy."[33]

Concluding his essay "To Be and To Know," Simon offered a psychological explanation for at least some of the troubled history of philosophy. Pointing out the subjective pressure for closure around a proposed explanation rather than openness to the complexity of reality and the fullness of being, Simon observed, "This accident [premature closure] happens, in particular, to the numerous persons who feel that the really important thing, especially in philosophy and religion, is not to know the truth, but to enjoy the bliss of the satisfied intellect."[34] So we might say that Simon does not hesitate "to call a spade a spade" in assessing the history and state of philosophy and the weaknesses of many who have taken the title of philosopher. Everywhere in his work, however, one finds evidence that in his regard for the complexities of concrete, contingency-ridden moments in human history, for the intricate depths of the human soul, and likely for the injunction of scripture against judging others, he made no ultimate judgments on the goodness of other human beings. He thus showed both honesty and courage – some might say folly; let us say, divine folly – in facing the frequently sad state of philosophy and in remaining faithful to the philosopher's defining call to the truth.

Simon spoke often of a philosopher's call and a philosopher's duty.[35] To respond well to that call, there is no substitute "for the fearless love of truth, for selflessness, fortitude, and humility."[36] This enumeration of requisite virtues for a philosopher appears in his 1958 address upon receiving the Aquinas Medal from the American Catholic Philosophical Association. Assuming that "some philosophers have access to demonstratively established truths," he cautioned that this is certainly "nothing to brag about, for access to rare truth is the most undeserved of all privileges. And yet they have to express their well-founded convictions with firmness and zeal." To so embrace this duty can appear as "insane pride," for one's tested philosophical convictions cannot be offered as mere "personal opinions," nor is

---

[33] Simon, "Philosophy, the Humanities and Education," 469.
[34] Simon, "To Be and To Know," in *Philosopher at Work*, 193.
[35] In "Jacques Maritain," 14, he presents Maritain as responding to his call rather than his choice in the sense of preference.
[36] Simon, "The Philosopher's Calling," 5.

one in the end to be governed by "mutually accepted opinion" and "good social manners." A philosopher's duty is to an "often solitary fight against learned and dignified persons, against Descartes and Spinoza and Berkeley... with the inescapable implication that he, the solitary fighter, knows better about the really important issues than most of the greatest among philosophical geniuses."[37]

From his understanding of genuine philosophy Simon sought to clarify the muddle in the general use of the word "ideology," a problem continuing to our present day.[38] For Simon ideology is what results when a would-be philosopher conforms too closely to the socially accepted opinion of any specific group, if not of the larger society. Not surprising in this student of social theories, Simon found the concept useful, as in "ideology of the working class." He understood ideology as a "system of ideas relative to subjects of philosophic interest... but which are held... in a particular society,... at a given period in its evolution, and... in answer to definite needs." Ideology thus entails an "interpretation of truth which is sociological, evolutionistic, and pragmatic." Most philosophic systems have ideological components, and most ideologies have a philosophic core. For example, John Locke's writings are riddled with ideological elements, Aristotle's teaching and Cartesianism are quite free of them, and Herbert Spencer's thought is "principally, if not entirely reducible to an ideology." Simon thought it very worthwhile in analysis "to go after the philosophic core of an ideology – that is, after the truth that is at variance with ideology precisely because it is independent of society, because it is independent of history, and, above all, because it is independent of human needs and aspirations."[39]

Despite philosophy's difficulties – from its seemingly endless contentiousness to its embeddedness so often in ideology – Simon found, beyond the high call of duty to the truth, certain deep satisfactions in living a philosophic life. In his autobiographical statement he indicated that he saw in philosophy, at least that of St. Thomas, the capacity for inspiration and thus for drawing one to a spiritual life.[40] As he closed his Aquinas Medal address he described how reaffirming of the call to philosophy are those times when philosophers break out of their solitude, in which their work must be largely

---

[37] Ibid.
[38] Simon, *Work, Society, and Culture*, 107–9.
[39] Ibid.
[40] "Yves R. Simon," 267; see also 264.

done, and find the joy of friendship born of successfully communicating their inspiration and love along with at least some particle of truth.[41]

Simon was acutely aware how rare are those moments, even for a genuine philosopher. Philosophy at its best – the study of it and the continuing inquiry in living the life of a philosopher – draws humans away from ordinary experiences and the moral and political problems associated with them. Even as he was becoming a philosopher, Simon lamented some of the effects of the process, and these concerns about philosophy's handicaps with respect to practical life constituted a very important theme in his philosophical work. In his autobiographical statement, Simon described his withdrawal for several years from "writing any magazine articles in order to concentrate upon his philosophical research" and his doctoral dissertation. With satisfaction, he noted that "once I had obtained my doctor's degree, it became possible for me to turn again to current events and . . . the burning problems of the day." Earlier he had taken a formal break from university studies, although he continued to study much each day. Reflecting on that period, he commented that "I now realize that this studious life was over-intellectual, gave too little a share to social and human experience." At another point he feared that his lack of experience and isolation would render his philosophical work unrealistic and sophistical.[42]

Near the end of his life and in that final lecture in praise of Maritain, Simon was saying much the same thing, only based on more experience – not only with such realities as the deteriorating international situation of the 1930s, the Spanish Civil War, and church–state issues in various nations of the West but also with philosophers and the life of philosophy. Simon complained that "political philosophers and theologians have a tendency to oversimplify things and to derive obnoxious satisfaction from the host of illusions that their lack of experience renders inevitable."[43] A little later in the lecture, he developed the perspective on contingencies and prudence that had already played an important role in *Philosophy of Democratic Government*.[44] Simon's analysis proceeded from the observations that the "factual situations," in which essential social and political realities exist, are marked by contingency and that in general "to assume that moral science

---

[41] Simon, "The Philosopher's Calling," 5–6.
[42] "Yves R. Simon," 269, 265, 267.
[43] Simon, "Jacques Maritain," 11.
[44] Robert J. Mulvaney adds, "[Simon's] message is a simple one: the traditional concept of practical wisdom has been lost in the past four centuries of Western experience. Its recovery is an urgent need in our individual and social lives" (Mulvaney, editor's note in *Practical Knowledge*, xii).

can deal with contingent matters without being supplemented by the virtue of prudence, is a silly illusion." We know from his other writings that Simon had empirical social science in mind as well as the philosophic sciences about which he was explicit here in defending the sphere of prudence or practical wisdom: "Prudence, as philosophers and theologians understand it, is a kind of wisdom so hard to get, to keep and to manage, that under a variety of names mankind is likely always to nurture *the ideal of science* which would suffice to trace our way in this world of contingency."[45] Once one realizes "that no scientific method will answer a question relative, in any way whatsoever, to contingent data, it soon becomes easy to understand that a philosopher, far from being able to answer *philosophically* the questions which puzzle his fellow citizens, may well be at a disadvantage and have particular reasons to remain silent." The disadvantage was, of course, the generally limited human experience that characterizes philosophers. In Simon's view, "a great deal of human experience is necessary" to acquire any kind of social and political prudence.[46]

Necessary as experience is, it is not a sufficient condition for prudence, in Simon's analysis. His definition of prudence in *Philosophy of Democratic Government*, where leadership is said "in the normal state of affairs" to belong to the prudent person,[47] draws our attention to another ingredient of practical wisdom. Setting prudence off once again against science, Simon defined it as "the fully determinate and unmistakably effective knowledge of the right use." He immediately added that prudence "is acquired, not principally by reading books and taking courses, but by practicing virtue."[48] Prudence appears to be both the fruit of the other basic virtues (temperance, courage, and justice) and their source, for they must be practiced by prudent choices to be realized.[49]

In Simon's analysis, there is another way that experience in itself is not usually sufficient for prudence. Having protected the sphere of practical choice from simple determination by science – including that most important science of sciences, philosophy – Simon endeavored in a number of his writings to articulate what connection there might be between philosophy and the world of practical choice and action. "Moral experience,"

---

[45] Simon, "Jacques Maritain," 12. The emphasis is mine.
[46] Ibid. Emphasis in the original.
[47] Simon, *Philosophy of Democratic Government*, 279.
[48] Ibid., 282–3.
[49] See Kuic, *Real Democracy*, 34–7 for an overall treatment of Simon's rejection of substitutes for the virtues as critical ingredients in practical wisdom.

he wrote on one occasion, "reveals the keenly felt need for investigation by an adequate moral philosophy."[50] Then, in *Philosophy of Democratic Government*, he made the same point with respect to macro-moral philosophy, namely, political philosophy. While discussing the phrase "government by the consent of the governed," Simon observed (in a manner reminiscent of Thucydides' observation on the partisan appropriation of key political concepts [III. 82]) that it has several meanings

which cannot be distinguished in political speeches or even in statements of principles. Such is the paradox of political notions considered in their sociological existence, for it is in a state of confusion that they are most active and produce their most important effects. About all the clarity that these subjects admit of will be procured *if instruments of clarification are available to whoever needs and cares to use them. To work out such instruments and see that they are kept in good order is what political philosophers are paid for.*[51]

In his last public lecture Simon was both more extensive and more specific about the political philosopher's responsibility when he described how he came to see that a prudent individual would sometimes need more than a "commonsense ability to handle 'abstract ideas.'" A good friend pointed out to Simon that his critique of Mussolini's invasion of Ethiopia, as any "defense of the public conscience against corruption by politicians and intellectuals," benefited from Simon's philosophical work on such ideas as "right, law, contract, community, authority, force, legal coercion, violence, autonomy and civilization."[52]

Simon concluded that however little we know about the physical universe, "it is less mysterious than the universe of morality." In morality, "the inclinations of just hearts" and "the traditions in which such inclinations are embodied" may suffice to lead to "fulfillment," meaning sound choice and action.[53] Moral philosophy, including political philosophy, might culminate in a general directive, and that form of practical wisdom is not yet the "ultimate practical wisdom" that is the action of the will fusing into the act itself. Here is where rules are applied in contingency-rich circumstances of each concrete individual considering a very specific action. Here is where

---

[50] Simon, *Practical Knowledge*, 96.
[51] Simon, *Philosophy of Democratic Government*, 190–1. Emphasis is mine.
[52] Simon, "Jacques Maritain," 12–13. The reference to Simon's writing on the invasion of Ethiopia is to a book that initially appeared in French in 1936 and has recently been republished: *The Ethiopian Campaign and French Political Thought*, ed. Anthony O. Simon, Robert Royal, and A. James McAdams (Notre Dame, IN: University of Notre Dame Press, 2009).
[53] Simon, *Practical Knowledge*, 96–7.

what Simon called "the problem of recognition" and saw pervading the moral sphere applies (e.g., given equality of opportunity as a desideratum, is this case before me one where the concept is applicable?).[54] Here too is ample space for the idiosyncratic and unpredictable aspects of the moral actor's experience to enter. So here, at the moment of affirming the command to act, at the moment of ultimate practical wisdom (the actual final test of prudence on a given occasion), there is plenty of space for mystery around the necessarily solitary individual actor. Simon wrote that "the incommunicability of the last [sc. last with respect to a specific action] practical judgment results from the affective and non-logical character of the act that determines this judgment."[55] In what follows he speculated on the reasons why we humans can reach what agreement we can in the practical realm; in other words, how our isolation with respect to practical matters is mitigated. Our communities need the structures of authority to find a way to overcome our solitude, singularity, and peculiarity and to act for the common good.[56]

Wrestling with the complexities of practical wisdom in the last stage of his life, Simon had come full circle from his initial youthful interest, rooted in political activism, about sound moral and political choice.[57] His journeys into the science of sciences led him to highlight the essential solitariness and mystery in philosophical work. So whether at the peak of our effort to understand reality or at the moment of deciding to act in this way rather than that, we humans are alone with our own history, dispositions, character, and set of experiences, including what is known from empirical science and the perspectives of technical experts. Such solitariness seems to complement and accentuate Simon's emphasis throughout his work on autonomy, liberty, and responsibility. In other words, freedom goes along with dedication and accountability to the truth.

That truth was a notably elusive one for Simon at the peak of inquiry and at the point of action. His basic attitude seemed ever to be one of calling us to respect reality and thus to resist forcing it wholly, let alone hastily and with an arrogant certainty, into our rational modes of explanation. Yet the drive for explanation, whether emanating from simple wonder or

---

[54] Simon, *Philosophy of Democratic Government*, 235 and throughout.
[55] Simon, *Practical Knowledge*, 24.
[56] Ibid., 40 n. 17.
[57] For some further elaboration of this and what follows in this essay, see especially Simon's exchange with Maritain in *Practical Knowledge*, 106–8 and Mulvaney's interpretive commentary on some aspects of the exchange in Mulvaney, "Practical Wisdom in the Thought of Yves R. Simon," 175.

from the need for guidance rooted in our need to direct and control human action and nature around us, is a distinctively human possession that joins us with others across cultures and ages. Finding the unity beneath the diversity of experience and of the various modes of knowing – in other words, abstracting – is the human way. Earlier in this chapter, Simon, writing from his position on the multidisciplinary Committee on Social Thought, was seen noting that "the unintegrated multiplicity of disciplines and cognitions" is the "heaviest" current "burden of the human intellect." In what immediately preceded this statement, he acknowledged the danger of over-simplification in seeking unity yet observed that it "should not blind us to the fact that the greatest scientific progress consisted in, or involved admirable simplifications."[58] Respecting reality is honoring the desire for truth and thus maintaining differences and hence distinctions where appropriate. This fundamental stance of respect for reality, of seeking to articulate difference while striving for simplicity and unity, seemed to capture the persistent philosophical attitude of Simon. He appeared confident that this tensional position promised good for humankind both in understanding and in action. This confidence is reflected in such pregnant observations as his crisp summation that "ontological optimism does not entail moral optimism." To which he quickly added, "it certainly does not entail moral pessimism either. It does not procure even a suspicion of what the ratio of good and evil" will be in the exercise of human freedom.[59] Later in his political classic, writing of the mix of good and evil in the institutions humans create, Simon observed that "the task of human wisdom is to find a principle capable of safeguarding the good and forestalling the evil." To that "significant platitude" he wished to join another: If that "principle is expected to work without a high ratio of failure, disappointment is bound to follow." Simon saw "two sorts of minds" that might and do arise to face the challenges of imperfect human practices and institutions: "those who accept with determination the prospect of never ending uncertainties, never ending trials and errors, incomplete successes, and new failures and those who decide that institutions causing so much trouble, opposing such obstacles to the reign of reason in society, entertaining in human history darkly mysterious regions, must disappear, regardless of the cost." The simple triumph of the latter mind, reflective of our human desire for

---

[58] Simon, "Philosophy, the Humanities and Education," 471.
[59] Simon, *Philosophy of Democratic Government*, 80.

rational direction and control, meant for Simon that "liberty is gone and death is coming."[60]

In his final public lecture, Simon spoke of philosophy specifically with respect to education. He rejected the tendency in some traditions to center training in the liberal arts on philosophy and observed that "on the college level it is man considered in the contingencies of his concrete existence who should be the main subject of liberal studies."[61] Accordingly he called for more attention to public affairs and to art, literature, and the spiritual life, favoring the humanists of the sixteenth century over the Scholastics when it was "a question of understanding man in the contingencies of history."[62] Yves Simon, who had rejected "literary" approaches to philosophy for system, rigor of demonstration, and assurance, seemed aware all along that the preparation for human action, for prudent human action, required more than the science of philosophy.

Suggestions for further reading

Kuic, Vukan. *Yves R. Simon: Real Democracy*. Lanham, MD: Rowman & Littlefield, 1999.
Simon, Yves R. *A General Theory of Authority*. Notre Dame, IN: University of Notre Dame Press, 1962.
———. *Philosophy of Democratic Government*. Notre Dame, IN: University of Notre Dame Press, 1993.

[60] Ibid., 138–9.
[61] Simon, "Jacques Maritain," 4.
[62] Ibid.

7

Hannah Arendt: from philosophy to politics

DANA R. VILLA

In the 1970s and 1980s, students of political theory invariably encountered the cliché that political theory and philosophy died sometime in the 1950s, only to be revived in 1971 by the publication of John Rawls's *A Theory of Justice*. One can be a great admirer of Rawls's work, as I am, and still be taken aback by the radical foreshortening of the history of political thought implied by this cliché. After all, the 1950s and early 1960s saw the publication of some of the most interesting – and enduring – works of political theory of the past sixty years or so.

A few landmarks will have to represent what was, in retrospect, a remarkably fertile period for political thought: Leo Strauss's *Natural Right and History* (1953), Eric Voegelin's *Order and History* (1956–7), Isaiah Berlin's *Four Essays on Liberty* (1969), Sheldon Wolin's *Politics and Vision* (1960), Jürgen Habermas's *Structural Transformation of the Public Sphere* (1963) and *Theory and Practice* (1966), C. B. Macpherson's *The Political Theory of Possessive Individualism* (1962), and Michael Oakeshott's *Rationalism and Politics* (1962). To this list must be added Hannah Arendt's major theoretical works: *The Origins of Totalitarianism* (1951), *The Human Condition* (1958), *On Revolution* (1963), and *Between Past and Future* (1968).

Merely glancing through this (admittedly selective) list of titles reveals a shared concern with history, reason, and freedom among an ideologically and methodologically diverse group of theorists. Perhaps more striking – and perhaps the central reason why these works are consigned to oblivion through the cliché cited earlier – is that all these works took a self-consciously textual and historical approach to the practice of political *theory*. For academic practitioners of analytic political *philosophy*, the historical or interpretive idiom was reason enough to dismiss many if not all of the works I mentioned. Indeed, from the point of view of many practitioners of normative analytic theory, nothing much *was* going on in political philosophy before the publication of Rawls's masterwork.

Of course, the passage of time has enabled us – and Rawls himself, in the later stages of his career[1] – to historicize *A Theory of Justice*. The collapse of Lyndon Johnson's Great Society and the unfortunate enduring legacy of Reaganism have meant that the enormous energy and inventiveness Rawls devoted to justifying the liberal democratic welfare state currently have more influence in Europe than in America. Indeed, when the later Rawls dispensed with the "difference principle," it signaled something more than a mere theoretical adjustment or scaling back. It was nothing less than an acknowledgment that the political terrain had irrevocably changed. The postwar liberal-Keynesian consensus no longer existed, and any mainstream political concern with social justice (in America, at least) died a slow death in the 1980s. "Power of the market" rhetoric and thinking trickled down to middle- and lower-middle-income citizens, the majority of whom now have a stake in the relentless pursuit of corporate profit and the expansion of "shareholder value."

It is not only the realignment of state and economy in what is usually termed a "neoliberal" fashion that has cast Rawlsianism in a peculiar historical light. It is also the return of many of the political and social problems – both at home and abroad – that once seemed on the verge of being consigned to the ash heap of history. Cultural differences, religious differences, and class differences; extraordinary gaps in wealth between developed and undeveloped countries; failed states and millions of "stateless persons"; proliferating wars and terrorism – all have combined to make a theory of justice focused on the welfare state look parochial, if not exactly quaint. Add to this list the decline of literacy, the decay of public-political space, and the absorption of political action and participation by fundraising, marketing, and lobbying, and one has a lengthy catalog of ills that clearly demand more capacious – and historically inflected – investigations into the nature, limits, and possibilities of politics.

I should state quite clearly that *none* of the "pre-Rawlsian" works I cited do the work of, or could take the place of, *A Theory of Justice*. When it comes to the question of social justice in liberal democracies, no serious discussion can occur *without* reference to Rawls. Nevertheless, it is useful to be reminded that the question of social justice is only one of many

---

[1] See John Rawls, *Political Liberalism* (New York: Columbia University Press, 1993).

confronting liberal democracies at the present time, even if one thinks – as I do – that it is a question that our politicians have, for the most part, shamefully ignored for the past thirty years. This "useful reminder" directs us to the multiple dimensions of the political world and to its historically shifting contours. Any of the works cited earlier can be read with profit when it comes to the question of this historical variability and to any attempt to come to grips with its peculiar characteristics in *our* age.

Perhaps unsurprisingly, I think Hannah Arendt's work is the most suggestive in this regard – *not* because it contains answers to our most immediate problems, but because it continually exemplifies the most important virtue of the political *theorist*: the imaginative capacity (born of deep learning and great intellectual ambition and daring) to take a large step *back* from the unthought presuppositions of our age. If for no other reason, Arendt's place in the canon of political theory is assured because none of the political thinkers of the past fifty to sixty years have so deeply and provocatively plumbed the question "What is the political?" as she did.

However much one may agree or disagree with Arendt's thinking, one must still be grateful for her strenuous effort to revive a question whose answer has, in the recent past, seemed either self-evident or irrelevant. To be sure, the answer Arendt gave to this question – the political as the speech and joint action of diverse equals in an institutionally articulated public space – has historical antecedents, most notably in the civic republican tradition. However, Arendt's version is distinctive enough and – from the standpoint of civic republicanism – "individualist" or diversity-centered enough to warrant a biographical overview of the experiences that both led her to embrace this tradition and also to radically depart from it.

Arendt was born in Hannover, Germany, in 1906 and grew up in Königsburg, East Prussia. The only child of Paul and Martha Arendt, secular Jews of a broadly social democratic bent, Arendt displayed an intellectual precociousness, learning ancient Greek as a child and reading the works of Kant and Kierkegaard as an adolescent. Despite her father's early death and the not entirely happy remarriage of her mother, Arendt excelled at the Luiseschule (although she was expelled for insubordination at age fifteen, following a teacher's insulting remark).[2] There followed several semesters

---

[2] See Elisabeth Young-Bruehl, *Hannah Arendt: For Love of the World* (New Haven: Yale University Press, 1982), 33–4.

as a special student at the University of Berlin (1922–3), where she studied classics and Christian theology, the latter with Romano Guardini. From there it was on to university study at Marburg, where – famously – she was the student (and lover) of Martin Heidegger during the period 1924–6. She left Marburg for a semester of study with Edmund Husserl before moving to Heidelberg to write her doctoral dissertation, *Der Liebesbegriffe bei Augustin* (*The concept of love in Augustine*), with Karl Jaspers in 1927–8.

As Arendt's biographer Elisabeth Young-Bruehl has noted, Arendt's university studies coincided with what were, relatively speaking, the most stable years of the Weimar Republic (1924–9).[3] She and other "resolute starvelings" such as Hans Jonas (her friend from these years) were free to pursue their philosophical vocation without the question of politics – or, more to the point, anti-Semitism – subsuming everything. Her philosophical education at the hands of Heidegger and Jaspers – the two leading lights of the new and revolutionary *Existenzphilosophie* – had an enduring impact, even if it was not quite so "determining" as some of Arendt's detractors would like us to assume.[4]

Here it is important to note that Arendt always assumed she would study philosophy; she was not drawn to it because it had suddenly become fashionable.[5] Arendt's vocation as a *political* thinker, however, was hardly in the cards during her university days. As she later acknowledged, this vocation was in large part a function of events in Germany in 1933 and later. This was a period during which she made a daring escape across the Czech border with her mother, emigrated to Paris, and – ultimately, via Marseilles and Lisbon – came to America in 1941 (she gained U.S. citizenship in 1951).

For Arendt, the implications of the Nazi ascendance in 1931–2 and eventual coming to power in 1933 were all too clear. In later years, she could be quite cutting with respect to those who hoped that life – and especially Jewish life – would somehow continue in a "normal" fashion. She could be even more cutting about those Germans who, although hardly convinced by Nazi ideological claims, nevertheless "coordinated" with the regime (for largely self-interested reasons) after 1933. Her sense of disillusionment with the academy and self-described "intellectuals" in the lead-up to the *Nazizeit* was severe. She never wanted to be associated with such people again.

---

[3] Ibid., 42.
[4] See, for example, Richard Wolin, *Heidegger's Children* (Princeton: Princeton University Press, 2001).
[5] See Hannah Arendt, "What Remains? The Language Remains: A Conversation with Gunter Gaus," in *Essays in Understanding, 1930–1954*, ed. Jerome Kohn (New York: Harcourt Brace, 1994), 9.

For obvious reasons, the case of Heidegger was more complicated. Like Jaspers, Arendt was painfully aware of both his human failings and his political idiocy, even going so far as to denounce his version of existential philosophy as a late excrescence of German Romanticism in her essay "What Is *Existenz* Philosophy?" (1947).[6] Later – in 1949, when she returned to Europe as the executive director of Jewish Cultural Reconstruction – she personally reconciled with Heidegger, whom she recognized, as did Jaspers, as one of the great philosophical minds of the twentieth century.[7]

Arendt's clarity about the significance of the Nazi rise to power was in no small part due to discussions she had with the German Zionist leader Kurt Blumenfeld. As Young-Bruehl's biography makes clear – and as the subsequently published Arendt–Blumenfeld correspondence bears out[8] – Arendt's political education really began with her experience as a German Jew in the early 1930s and through her contact with Blumenfeld. Although never a Zionist – she would, in later years, be quite critical of the tunnel vision of the movement[9] – she was anxious to *act* in some way against the enemies of her people and to let the world know what was happening to Jews in Germany in the period 1930–3.

When Blumenfeld suggested that Arendt could help Jews in Germany by collecting examples of anti-Semitic propaganda in the Prussian State Library and elsewhere, she jumped at the chance. Because she was not part of the Zionist organization, it was thought that Arendt could undertake this dangerous work with minimal risk to the group or its members. It was, indeed, a very dicey business, and Arendt was arrested by the German police for her activities. It was only owing to the kindness and credulity of the official in charge of her case, to whom she lied about everything, that she managed to be released from custody. She seized that moment in 1933 to escape from Germany, crossing the Czech border at night with her mother. Thus began Arendt's life as a "stateless person," a condition that would last for eighteen years.

---

[6] Hannah Arendt, "What Is *Existenz* Philosophy?" in *Essays in Understanding, 1930–1954*, 163–87.

[7] The personal relationship between Arendt and Heidegger is well covered in Young-Bruehl's biography. As to the philosophical relationship, see my study, *Arendt and Heidegger: The Fate of the Political* (Princeton: Princeton University Press, 1996).

[8] Hannah Arendt and Kurt Blumenfeld, "... *in keinem Besitz verwurzelt": Die Korrespondenz*, ed. Ingeborg Nordmann and Iris Pilling (Berlin: Rotbuch, 1995).

[9] See, for example, Arendt's comments in the previously unpublished manuscript "Anti-Semitism" (most likely composed in the late 1930s), in *The Jewish Writings*, ed. Jerome Kohn and Ron H. Feldman (New York: Schocken Books, 2007), 50–9. Of course, once the war began, Arendt was quite clear that the Zionist organization was the only true Jewish *political* organization and – as such – a key vehicle for active resistance to the Hitler regime. See her piece "*Ceterum Censeo*..." from *Aufbau*, December 26, 1941, in *The Jewish Writings*, 142–4.

There can be little doubt that both her Jewishness and her statelessness had a profound impact on Arendt's subsequent political thinking. Although a fierce opponent of *all* forms of tribal nationalism (and no friend of what we today call "identity politics"), Arendt was was convinced that, as she put it, "when one is attacked as a Jew one must defend oneself as a Jew."[10] Her repudiation of the fiction of assimilation – the central point she shared with the Zionists – took on theoretical flesh when (in part 1 of *The Origins of Totalitarianism*) she focused on the failure of European Jews to organize themselves as a *political* people. Organizing politically would have been much preferable to remaining a vulnerable minority dependent on state protection and the influence of a small set of Jewish plutocratic elites.

This particular strain in Arendt's writing has led some of her later critics – most notably Leon Wieseltier, the literary editor of *The New Republic* – to charge her with "blaming the victim." The recent publication of Arendt's collected Jewish writings should lay this particular canard – and the willful misreading on which it is based – to rest. The *Jewish Writings* amply demonstrate Arendt's fierce identification with her own people, and they underline the passionate intensity with which she preached political organization and self-reliance as the *sine qua non* of Jewish survival.[11]

The experience of statelessness – which included incarceration in a French concentration camp at Gurs for being an "enemy alien" in 1940[12] – had a similarly profound effect. It led Arendt to be deeply skeptical about moral-philanthropic declarations of universal "human rights" and human dignity. In the interwar period, such declarations proved entirely ineffectual. In response, Arendt focused on what she famously called (in *The Origins of Totalitarianism*) the "right to have rights": the right of every human being to be a member of *some* organized political community, to be a citizen with legal rights.[13]

The intensity of Arendt's focus on this basic right becomes more understandable when we remember that totalitarian and protototalitarian states abused the principle of sovereignty in order to denationalize entire populations, creating a refugee population in the millions (if not tens of millions) during the interwar period. No one wanted these "stateless" people – not

---

[10] This is the animating theme of the majority of the columns she wrote for *Aufbau*, with their insistent call for the creation of a Jewish army to take part in the fight against Hitler. See Hannah Arendt, "The Jewish Army – The Beginning of Jewish Politics?" in *Jewish Writings*, 136–9.

[11] See Arendt, *Jewish Writings*, 134–243.

[12] Young-Bruehl, *Hannah Arendt*, 153–5.

[13] Hannah Arendt, *The Origins of Totalitarianism* (New York: Harcourt Brace, 1973), 296–7.

their Central and Eastern European nation-states of origin, nor the Western parliamentary democracies to which they fled. In this regard, it is important to remember that concentration and internment camps were not a Nazi invention, but rather a pan-European phenomenon during the interwar years. Millions of Russian, Hungarian, Jewish, and other refugees appeared on the doorstep of various European nation-states, only to be treated as "superfluous" people – as people without a national "home" – who were (as a result) effectively right-less.

Arendt's own experience of statelessness – not to mention the narrowness of her escape from Germany in 1933 and from Europe in 1941 – led to a lifelong insistence on two basic principles. First, there was the overarching need to guarantee that a "nation" – an ethnic majority population – could never again be in a position where it could so easily overwhelm the "state" (the constitutional edifice of laws and institutions that protected citizens' rights). This is what happened between the wars, thanks in part to the rise of pan-Germanism and pan-Slavism. Second, there was the need to radically restrict both the idea and the practice of national sovereignty, most obviously through some type of federal apparatus (such as a European federation). *Only* by being guaranteed the "right to have rights" – that is, only by being guaranteed membership in a legally and constitutionally organized political entity – could the dignity of humankind be given concrete recognition and the "rights of Man" have a more than hortatory status.

These characteristically Arendtian views were to emerge later, during the writing of *The Origins of Totalitarianism* in the mid- to late 1940s. As a refugee in Paris in the 1930s, she was able to find employment with the Baroness Rothschild and worked extensively with Youth Aliyah, a Jewish social service organization that trained, fed, and clothed Jewish refugee youth, all in preparation for eventual settlement in Palestine.

This "hands-on" period of Arendt's life – mirrored, after the war, by her work for Jewish Cultural Reconstruction, in which capacity she helped save more than 1.5 million pieces of Judaica from a war-ravaged Europe – is frequently overlooked by American and Israeli Jews who were angered by *Eichmann in Jerusalem* (1963).[14] However praiseworthy (from a liberal point of view) her response to Gershom Scholem's charge that she lacked "*Ahabeth Israel*" may be,[15] there can be no doubt that Arendt was deeply

---

[14] Hannah Arendt, *Eichmann in Jerusalem: A Report on the Banality of Evil* (New York: Penguin Books, 1994).
[15] Arendt, *Jewish Writings*, 466–7.

committed to the Jewish people – to their survival, their political education and organization, and to their future.

Arendt – along with her second husband, the German leftist and auto-didact Heinrich Blücher, and her mother – arrived in New York in 1941. She went to work as a columnist for the German-language Jewish newspaper *Aufbau*. Her columns for the paper – under the heading "This Means You!" – manifest a passionate yet futile call for the creation of a "Jewish Army" to take the field with the Allies in the war against Hitler. The basic thought – undone by hard political realities, such as British imperial interests – was that political voice, power, and freedom would come to the Jewish people only if they showed themselves willing to fight under their own flag, against a common enemy. Reading these columns – collected in *The Jewish Writings* – one is struck by both their passionate intensity and their utterly atheoretical character. For obvious reasons, in the early 1940s Arendt was still far from linking her earlier philosophical vocation to the consideration of politics. The question of "what is to be done?" trumped the *thinking* of politics as such.

Things began to change when, in 1943, Arendt and her husband received confirmation of the darkest rumors from Europe concerning the fate of the Jews. Initially incredulous at reports of systematic extermination (Blücher tried to reassure her by insisting that the Nazis would never depart so radically from strategic and tactical imperatives, especially because they were now in a defensive posture), Arendt spent the next seven years engaged in an intensive effort to comprehend the *fact* of Auschwitz. Or, to put it more precisely, she began her "interminable dialogue" with the essence of totalitarianism, attempting to comprehend the set of political, cultural, and social factors that made concentration and extermination camps possible in the heart of civilized Europe. *The Origins of Totalitarianism* (1951) is the fruit of that effort. It is no exaggeration to state that almost everything Arendt says in that book was determined by the shock of the extermination and concentration camps and their "industrial production of corpses."[16]

Famously, Arendt viewed the concentration and extermination camps as "the central institutions of totalitarian government." She made this obser-vation *not* to underline the brutality of totalitarian rule but to direct her readers' attention to the utter novelty of totalitarian terror and totalitar-ian "politics." The totalitarians did not use terror in a strictly strategic or

---

[16] See Dana Villa, "Genealogies of Total Domination: Arendt, Adorno, and Auschwitz," *New German Critique*, no. 100 (Winter 2007): 1–44.

tactical fashion to contain or break resistance. Such an instrumental use of terror has been characteristic of tyrannical and authoritarian regimes from ancient times to our own. Rather, the totalitarians used terror "systematically," *after* their political opponents had been eliminated. Their goal was to realize an ideological "super-sense" of their respective movements, a goal that required *changing human nature* itself.

In Arendt's view, totalitarianism installed a new and radical form of *total* domination, one that eliminated the *space* between men and women, binding them together in an "iron band" of terror. The goal was to create "one man of gigantic dimensions" in place of plural individuals.[17] Deprived of any public or social space for free movement or discourse, stripped of the capacity for spontaneity through ideological conditioning and the ubiquitous threat and practice of terror, human beings would be reduced to sub-human "bundles of reflexes," much like Pavlov's dogs. Such creatures would be incapable of resistance. More to the point, they would no longer be a source of unpredictability and (thus) interference to the ostensibly "natural" forces determining – in a supposedly objective, "scientific" fashion – the destiny of the human species. For the Nazis, the terroristic immobilization of human beings would speed up the process of "natural" racial selection, culminating in the predestined hegemony of the Aryan race; for the Bolsheviks, it would accelerate the process of selection implicit in the idea of class struggle, bringing about the "inevitable" victory of the proletariat and the oblivion of "historically doomed" classes.

This, then, is the vision of totalitarianism that Arendt elicited from the camps, which she saw not as "anti-strategic" excrescences, but as crucial "laboratories" of total terror. It was in the camps that the most advanced "experiments" in changing human nature – in reducing unpredictable human beings to mere "bundles of reflexes" – were being carried out.[18] The dream of the totalitarians was to create an utterly determined and determinable world, one in which the "laws" of racial or historical selection would sweep through the passive, immobilized medium of human raw material. In this way, the ideologically specified "end" of History (understood as the process of class struggle) or Nature (understood as the process of racial selection) would be reached more quickly.

The striking element of Arendt's analysis of the camps in *The Origins of Totalitarianism* is its breathtaking dystopianism. Not only does she argue that

---

[17] Arendt, *Origins of Totalitarianism*, 466.
[18] Ibid., 455, 458–9.

the camps were the central – indeed, *defining* – institution of totalitarian rule but also that they were, in principle and (to a degree) in practice, *successful* in their project of changing human nature. This is perhaps the most shocking claim in the entirety of *The Origins of Totalitarianism*, one that goes against many religious and metaphysical ideas about human nature.[19] However, anyone who has read either Primo Levi's descriptions of the all-but-dead *Müsselmanner* in Auschwitz, or David Rousset's descriptions in *Les jours de notre mort*, will have to acknowledge at least a portion of this "success." Drawing on eyewitness accounts such as Levi's and Rousset's, Arendt's theoretical point is that there is nothing *in us*, no untouchable spiritual or metaphysical core, that can prevent human beings from being literally *dehumanized*, turned into mere examples of the animal species, humankind.[20]

The Origins of Totalitarianism not only put totalitarianism on the map as a *theoretical* concept but it also made Arendt world famous. It also created the unfortunate but still lingering image of her as first and foremost a Cold Warrior. This image greatly impeded her reception in the generally *marxisant* intellectual cultures of postwar France and Italy, where her work has gained a sympathetic hearing only recently. On the plus side, the early recognition of *Origins* as a masterpiece of theory and analysis, combined with its virtual bestseller status, enabled Arendt to devote the rest of her life to thinking, writing, and part-time teaching. A series of visiting professorships at Princeton, Berkeley, and – perhaps most famously – the University of Chicago (1964–7) were more or less the direct result of the enormous success of the totalitarianism book.

In these days of the academic professionalization of "the life of the mind," it is striking to recall that Arendt was only offered a full-time professorship – in the Graduate Faculty at the New School – relatively late in life (1967). However ambivalent she might have been about the academy, her return to university life (even if only as a "visitor") enabled Arendt to deepen her understanding of the nature and limits of Western political thought. For although totalitarianism was, on one level, a repudiation of everything the Western tradition of political and philosophical thought stood for, it was, on another level, the exaggerated and pathological manifestation of some of this tradition's most deeply rooted prejudices.

[19] See, for example, the exchange between Arendt and Voegelin on *The Origins of Totalitarianism* in *Review of Politics* 15, no. 1 (January 1953), 68–85.
[20] Arendt, *Origins of Totalitarianism*, 441. See my essay "Terror and Radical Evil," in *Politics, Philosophy, Terror* (Princeton: Princeton University Press, 2001), 1–32.

Foremost among these prejudices was the oblivion or effacement of the basic political phenomenon of *human plurality*. For Arendt, human plurality – the "fact that men, not Man, live on the earth and inhabit the world" – was *the* fundamental constitutive condition of politics and political relations. And politics, for Arendt, was not a relation of rule or domination, the activity of administration, or the state's tending of the economic "life process" of society. Rather – and this is something her encounter with the pure *antipolitics* of totalitarianism made clear to her – it was the activity of debate, deliberation, and decision exercised by plural and diverse civic equals in a legally and institutionally articulated public space.

Of course, it is easy to comprehend the totalitarian *negation* of the basic fact of human plurality. It is somewhat more difficult to grasp the ways in which *the Western tradition of political philosophy*, from its beginning in Plato to its "end" in the thought of Karl Marx, consistently undermined or bracketed human plurality (and diverse, talkative civic equality) through a series of misleading metaphors. From the Platonic analogy between the structure of the soul and that of the "just" polity, to Aristotle's insistence on "natural" relations of hierarchy, to Hobbes's and Rousseau's doctrines of a unitary sovereign will (whether monarchical or popular), to, finally, the Marxian idea of a society without class divisions that has "overcome" politics – again and again, the tradition effaces the *sine qua non* of authentic politics: the discursive relations of *plural* equals.

It was the depth of this antipolitical prejudice against plurality that Arendt discovered as she began research on her follow-up to *The Origins of Totalitarianism*. A study of the prototototalitarian elements in the thought of Karl Marx – funded by an award from the Guggenheim Foundation in 1952 – was to have shored up what Arendt (and many of her critics) considered the weaker side of *Origins*, namely, its analysis of Soviet communism. Her engagement with Marx's thought led her – I almost want to write "inevitably" – back to a depth reading of the tradition, the better to understand the roots of an idea of political community from which plurality, in all its richness, had been expunged. The ultimate fruit of that labor was *The Human Condition* (1958), a book that in many respects is Arendt's theoretical *summa*. Most often cited for its distinctions between labor, work, and action and its emphasis on the public realm, the book contains a penetrating and never equaled critique of the tradition – a critique that, as I have already suggested, reached back to Plato and Aristotle and forward to liberalism, Marxism, and our increasingly technological society, one from which genuine politics is rapidly disappearing.

It is hard to overstate the influence of *The Human Condition*, even though some (e.g., Isaiah Berlin) have tried to dismiss it.[21] More or less singlehandedly, the book rescued the ideas of the public realm and a noninstrumental form of praxis from oblivion. It is impossible to conceive the early- and middle-period work of Jürgen Habermas, or Sheldon Wolin's *Politics and Vision*, or even J. G. A. Pocock's *The Machiavellian Moment*, without it. In broader and less academic terms, the book's "retrieval" of political action as a form of joint action or "acting together" had a significant impact on both the American civil rights and antiwar movements. More recently, through the work of Jonathan Schell and others, its themes of earth- and world-alienation have influenced not only the antinuclear movement but environmental activists as well.[22]

Yet despite its influence, *The Human Condition* remains, more than fifty years after its publication, an untimely book. It was untimely in the late fifties and early sixties insofar as it questioned the impulses driving an increasingly scientific and technological civilization. It is untimely now because its central notions of an institutionally articulated public space and a *civic* form of plurality sit uneasily with our current fixation on interest- and identity-group politics. Finally, it is untimely insofar as it suggests – in a manner parallel to but radically different from Hegel's *Phenomenology of Spirit* – that the concrete reality of freedom is to be found in action with others in the public realm, and *not* in the spheres of consumer choice, "self-fashioning," intimate relations, or withdrawal from the world.

Of course, Arendt's idea of *public* freedom has a long and distinguished pedigree in Western political thought, going back to the Greek polis and to the republican city-states of Renaissance Italy. She illuminated this pedigree in her next major theoretical work, *On Revolution* (1963). If, as is generally acknowledged, *The Human Condition* is Arendt's most "Heideggerian" book, *On Revolution* is her most unabashedly republican. In it she comes to terms not only with a tradition of political discourse stretching back to Montesquieu, Harrington, Machiavelli, Cicero, and (ultimately) Aristotle;

---

[21] See Isaiah Berlin and Ramin Jahanbegloo, *Conversations with Isaiah Berlin* (New York: Scribners, 1992). Berlin's lack of regard for Arendt might, at first glance, appear to be a function of an analytic philosopher's disdain for a more "Continental," dense, and occasionally aphoristic form of writing. In fact, as Jeremy Waldron has recently pointed out, Berlin's own prose is hardly the most disciplined or "rigorous," at least from an analytic point of view. The real source of Berlin's dismissal was, unsurprisingly, political. Berlin was an intimate of many establishment figures in Israeli politics and the Zionist movement, and he had little regard for those – like Arendt – who were critical of either. Academic vanity also played a role.

[22] See Jonathan Schell, *The Fate of the Earth* (New York: Picador, 1982).

she also comes to terms with the two main competing interpretations of the modern revolutionary tradition, namely, Marxism and liberalism.[23]

Using a broadly comparative method (one focusing on the French and American Revolutions), Arendt argues that the pathos of the modern revolutionary tradition derives from its most basic and defining act: the *founding* of a *new space of public freedom*, a founding that occurs through the creation of a new (constitutional and republican) form of government. However, Arendt claims, the central importance of political *foundation* – of starting a new "story" through the creation of a new "space of freedom" – has been covered over by the Jacobin-Marxist obsession with the question of poverty (the "Social Question") and by the liberal reduction of constitutional government to the "essential" purpose of protecting civil rights and individual freedoms. Breathing new life into what many had considered a moribund theoretical tradition, *On Revolution* paved the way for a civic republican renewal in Anglo-American thought. This renewal is manifest in works as diverse as Pocock's *Machiavellian Moment*, Michael Sandel's *Democracy's Discontent*, and Bernard Bailyn and Gordon Woods's influential reinterpretations of the history of the American Revolution.

When it appeared in 1963 *On Revolution* was completely overshadowed by another book Arendt published that year: *Eichmann in Jerusalem*. This work – which grew out of her trial reportage for *The New Yorker* in 1961 – has been the single most enduring source of antipathy toward Arendt, in both academic and nonacademic circles. To understand this antipathy, one has to go back to the campaign by a variety of Jewish organizations in the United States to prevent the book's publication.[24] *Eichmann in Jerusalem*, it was claimed, exonerated the "monster" and blamed the victims. That this is nothing short of a libel is clear to anyone who has actually read the book. However, the possibility of deciding for oneself was precisely what the campaign sought to eliminate.

What Arendt did do – in eight pages in the middle of a 300-page book – was to bring up the topic of the *Judenräte*, their relations with the Nazis, and their activities during the Holocaust. Needless to say, Arendt does not blame the members of the "Jewish Councils" – which the Nazis set up to administer the ghettos they created in Poland and elsewhere – for the extermination of European Jewry. The Nazis and their various European

---

[23] See Albrecht Wellmer's important essay "Arendt on Revolution," in *The Cambridge Companion to Hannah Arendt*, ed. Dana Villa (New York: Cambridge University Press, 2001), 220–41.

[24] See Elisabeth Young-Bruehl's detailed account in *Hannah Arendt: For Love of the World*, 347–62.

allies and fellow travelers did that. And Eichmann – as Arendt repeatedly emphasizes in the book that supposedly "exonerates" him – zealously and efficiently carried out his duties as "transport czar" for the Final Solution.[25]

In Arendt's opinion, what some of the "elites" who made up the *Judenräte* did was to betray their people through administrative fulfillment of many Nazi requests – for example, drawing up lists of property holdings slated for confiscation, as well as lists of members of the community suitable for shipment to the East and so-called special treatment. Hyperbolically, Arendt claimed that, without this administrative complicity in organizational matters, fewer than half of the six million European Jews who were eventually slaughtered would have met their fate. Of course, there is no way of knowing how many Jews might have been saved had a consistent policy of noncompliance been in place. Suffice it to say that individuals such as Chaim Rumkowski – the self-styled "King of the Jews" in Lodz, Poland – remain problematic even for scholars such as Isaiah Trunk, whose massive work *Judenrät* was written precisely to dispute Arendt's charge of (limited) elite complicity.[26]

The "Eichmann Controversy" – which lasted for years in the 1960s – took a tremendous toll on Arendt. As she insisted time and again in her own defense, in the Eichmann book she was a "trial reporter" and nothing more. Indeed, her portrait of Eichmann – as an "ordinary" man in the worst sense of the word – was confirmed by many who attended the trial. They, like Arendt, expected to see a devil – or at least an ideological fanatic and Jew hater – in the dock. Instead they encountered an ordinary and none-too-bright midlevel bureaucrat, one given to self-pity and officialese.

In this regard, *Eichmann in Jerusalem* deflated the narrative that the lead prosecutor, Israeli Attorney General Gideon Hausner, struggled so mightily to put in place. Hausner framed Eichmann as the "architect" of the Final Solution. This he most clearly was not, as both the trial and subsequent scholarship have made entirely clear. The fact that Eichmann was not the "mastermind" he was presented as did not stop Arendt from insisting that he did, in fact, deserve the death penalty for the crimes against humanity he had committed. She was quite clear about that. As to the tangled question of whether Arendt and others were deceived by Eichmann's "nonideological" self-presentation – for that to be cleared up, Yad Vashem, the Israeli

---

[25] See my essay "Conscience, the Banality of Evil, and the Idea of a Representative Perpetrator," in *Politics, Philosophy, Terror*, 33–61.
[26] See Isaiah Trunk, *Judenrät* (Lincoln: University of Nebraska Press, 1996).

Holocaust Museum and Archive, will have to publish the 3,000-page transcript of Eichmann's interrogation (which Arendt read in preparation for her book). Then and only then will scholars be in a position to assess the extent of his anti-Semitism and its role as a motive for his activities.

Of course, it is entirely possible that Arendt got Eichmann's specific motivation – or, more precisely, his *lack* of a motive – wrong. Nevertheless, the concept that occurred to her when she was confronted by Eichmann in the flesh – the famous "banality of evil" – remains crucial for understanding how it is that thousands of normal people, neither fanatical nor hate filled, are able to make themselves available for what the political theorist George Kateb has called "evil as policy."[27]

Events such as the genocide in Rwanda or 9/11 incline us to a traditional or theological view, one that sees hatred, fanaticism, and sheer wickedness as defining characteristics of most if not all evil in the world. Nevertheless, the fact remains that tens of millions of victims were sent to their graves in the twentieth century, more often than not by men and women who lacked ideological fervor, racial hatred, or even what Kant would call an "evil will." This is not to say that fanatics, sadists, and racists were *not* involved in these massacres. However, *state* terror – evil as policy – does not depend on such individuals, who always constitute a relative minority in the actual apparatuses of death. Such massive undertakings as the rationalized extermination of European Jewry or the creation of the Soviet gulag could never have been carried out were it not for the involvement of thousands of ordinary men and women. Which is to say that *all* state-initiated terror requires people who obey the laws, follow orders, and do their jobs – no matter how merciless the job in question might be.

The Eichmann controversy generated Arendt's most enduring and vociferous critics. More than a few would later seize on the revelation of Arendt's youthful relationship with the "Nazi" Heidegger to question both her moral bearings and her intellectual integrity. This revelation was made – in detail – in Young-Bruehl's 1982 biography (some seven years after Arendt's death at age sixty-nine). However, it was only with the publication of Elsbieta Ettinger's psychologizing *Hannah Arendt/Martin Heidegger* in 1995 that the "Hannah Arendt scandal" occurred. To be sure, Ettinger had no particular ax to grind and clearly identified with Arendt at some level. Somehow, she gained permission to view the Arendt–Heidegger correspondence,

---

[27] See George Kateb, "On Political Evil," in *The Inner Ocean: Individualism and Democratic Culture* (Ithaca: Cornell University Press, 1994), 199–221.

which had previously been off-limits to scholars (it was finally published, in German, in 1998 and in English translation in 2003).[28] On the basis of this perusal, Ettinger was able to claim that Arendt not only forgave and reconciled with Heidegger after the war but also recommenced their liaison.

The notion of "sleeping with the enemy" was too much for many, even though we have no confirmation that a romantic relationship was restarted. More to the point – and something those who blame Arendt for her personal connection to Heidegger tend to forget – Heidegger was obviously *not* a Nazi in 1924–6. His public role in the regime – as Rektor of Freiburg – lasted nine months, even though he retained his Nazi Party membership until 1945. Of course, his politics throughout the period was hypernationalist, xenophobic, and antimodernist to the core. However, the idea that his call for a return to a pre-Socratic "first beginning" somehow provided the Nazis with important ideological fodder is, of course, absurd. After 1933, he withdrew from any public involvement with a movement that had let him know – early and clearly – that his thinking did not sufficiently toe the party line.[29]

Needless to say, individual readers are entirely within their rights if they choose to blame Arendt for reestablishing contact with Heidegger in 1949 or for accepting (more than a little naively) his version of events and of his motivations during the Nazi years.[30] What cannot be done – at least legitimately – is to reduce the complicated structure of Arendt's political thought to the woolly-headed musings of a "left" Heideggerian disciple. True, like Heidegger, Arendt worried a lot about the political implications of modern science and technology. Also like Heidegger, she focused attention on the "initiatory" dimensions of political action, its character as a "radical beginning." However, the fact remains that she was a firm believer in constitutionalism, federalism, equal civil and political rights, and an inclusive public sphere. She was also a staunch opponent of *all* forms of tribal nationalism and of the general political legacy of German Romanticism (a legacy she viewed Heidegger as fatally imbibing). These points are

---

[28] Hannah Arendt and Martin Heidegger, *Letters, 1925–1975*, ed. Ursula Ludz, trans. Andrew Shields (New York: Harcourt, 2003).

[29] For a record of Heidegger's political activities during the Nazi period, see Hugo Otto, *Martin Heidegger: A Political Life*, trans. Allan Blunden (New York: Basic Books, 1993). For a balanced view of the nature and background of his political thought (such as it was), see Otto Pöggeler's essay "Heidegger's Political Self-Understanding," in *The Heidegger Controversy: A Critical Reader*, ed. Richard Wolin (Cambridge, MA: MIT Press, 1992), 198–244.

[30] See Hannah Arendt, "Martin Heidegger at 80," in *Heidegger and Modern Philosophy*, ed. Michael Murray (New Haven: Yale University Press, 1978).

lost on Arendt's contemporary academic critics, who – on the basis of the Eichmann book and the liaison with Heidegger – portray her as confused, irrationalist, and (as the old saying goes) "bad for the Jews."

All of this, however, is to jump ahead to recent polemics. In the late sixties and early seventies, Arendt was one of America's most recognizable, forceful, and – the Eichmann book notwithstanding – respected public intellectuals. The essays contained in the collection *Crises of the Republic* (1972) attest to her fierce commitment to the American ideal and to her intense worries about the country's future. Unlike elitist critics of American democracy (to whom she is sometimes falsely compared), Arendt urged greater governmental transparency and broader public attention and political participation. The revival of citizenship and the "preservation and augmentation" of the public space of freedom opened by the U.S. Constitution were her persistent themes. Her opposition to "elite" critics who think that we somehow suffer from *too much* democracy is readily apparent.

At the time of her death – from a heart attack while entertaining friends in her New York apartment – Arendt was working on the third part of *The Life of the Mind*. The first two volumes – on thinking and willing, respectively – were finished, albeit in rough form. The third, on judging, was scarcely begun.

As many a commentator has noted, Arendt's death robbed us of what would have been a highly original analysis of a faculty too often identified with the mechanical activity of subsuming a particular thing, event, or person under a pregiven concept, or "universal." Like Hans-Georg Gadamer – but working out of a Kantian rather than an Aristotelian tradition – Arendt thought that particulars and universals actually "co-determined" one another and that the faculty of judgment was most its own, *not* when reading events, people, or things back into familiar categories, but rather when it spontaneously did justice to their novelty and unprecedented quality through the creation of a *new* concept.[31] As she herself states in the introduction to *The Life of the Mind*, the "banality of evil" was just such an instance of judgment's reflective exercise, its *ascent* from a concrete particular – Eichmann – to a new and spontaneously generated concept. The "banality of evil" captured a new but increasingly widespread phenomenon characteristic of twentieth-century life: political evil on a massive scale,

---

[31] For an extended comparison of Gadamer and Arendt, as well as a nuanced appreciation of Arendt's debt to Kant's third *Critique*, see Ronald Beiner, *Political Judgment* (Chicago: University of Chicago Press, 1984).

committed without the presence of wickedness or, indeed, any particular motive on the part of the perpetrators.[32]

In the years immediately preceding her death, Arendt won many awards, including the Danish Sonning Prize for Contributions to European Civilization. She was invited to give the Gifford Lectures at Aberdeen University in 1973 and 1974, suffering a first serious heart attack at the beginning of the second series. Her status as an intellectual celebrity, well established at the time of her death, has in recent years given way to a widespread recognition of the canonical status of her work. It can truthfully be said that she is the first woman to gain admission to the Western canon of political thought. Of course, some would argue with this assessment, preferring to see her as an exemplar of the lack of rigor that analytic philosophers associate with so-called Continental figures. Thus, despite the fact that her work is discussed, written on, and taught in virtually *all* fields in the humanities today, she remains a fugitive presence in all but a few American philosophy departments.

The verdict of some analytic philosophers notwithstanding, interest in Arendt is currently at an all-time high. As her centenary in 2006 demonstrated – with conferences and celebrations in France, Italy, Germany, Brazil, Turkey, Israel, Sweden, Japan, America, and elsewhere – the extent of her influence is now *world*wide. Of course, no one can say whether her reputation will wax or wane in the decades to come. What one can say is that she was the single figure in a luminous gallery of émigré intellectuals who made the public realm and the political significance of human plurality her enduring theme. Transcending the context of totalitarian horror that gave birth to it, Arendt's political theory reminds citizens of the contemporary world that the meaning of politics is not power, wealth, or virtue. As she puts it simply in the unfinished *Introduction into Politics*, "the meaning of politics is *freedom*."[33]

---

[32] Hannah Arendt, *The Life of the Mind*, vol. 1, *Thinking* (New York: Harcourt, 1978), 3–4.
[33] Hannah Arendt, "Introduction *into* Politics," in *The Promise of Politics*, ed. Jerome Kohn (New York: Schocken Books, 2005), 108.

Part III

The revival of liberal political philosophy

8

Friedrich Hayek on the nature of social order and law

ERIC MACK

The standing of F. A. Hayek (1899–1992) as one of the most important social and legal theorists of the twentieth century rests largely on the depth and insight of his challenge to two presumptions that dominated most twentieth-century social and legal thought. The first is the presumption that rational and beneficial *social order* must be intentionally planned or designed order; the second is that *law* must be the (intentional) command of an authority that, as the source of law, cannot itself be subject to law. This chapter presents the crucial elements of Hayek's challenge to these commonly held presumptions. Combined with an appreciation of the alternative conceptions of social order and law that Hayek offers, the recognition of the nature, pervasiveness, and falsity of these commonly held presumptions supports a radical and illuminating transformation in our understanding of the nature and value of social, economic, and legal order.

Any more extensive discussion of Hayek than is possible in this chapter would explore the connections between Hayek's "scientific" investigations of the nature of social order and law and his various attempts to restate the case for the fundamental values or principles of liberal individualism. The two most sustained and important attempts at such a vindication are Hayek's defense of individual liberty in *The Constitution of Liberty* and his defense of fundamental rules of just conduct in *Law, Legislation and Liberty*.[1] Any exploration of these defenses would have to examine the extent to which Hayek succumbs to, manages to circumvent, or unknowingly challenges another central presupposition of twentieth-century thought: that there is a radical divide between "factual" or "scientific" judgments and normative judgments, such that no normative judgments can ever be grounded in

---

[1] F. A. Hayek, *The Constitution of Liberty* (Chicago: University of Chicago Press, 1960); Hayek, *Law, Legislation and Liberty* (henceforward LLL), 3 vols. (Chicago: University of Chicago Press, 1973–9).

"factual" or "scientific" judgments. Such an exploration would also have to examine whether Hayek's critique of the "rationalism" that he associates with misguided conceptions of social order and law leaves room for any *rational* grounding of the liberal individualist social world that Hayek labeled "the Great Society." A more extensive discussion of Hayek would examine the nature, justification, and limits of his "antirationalism," or his "critical" or "evolutionary" rationalism,[2] and also the nature and validity of Hayek's critique of "social justice." Although we must forgo these investigations in this chapter, by focusing on Hayek's conception of the nature of social order and law, we can attend to what is most central and distinctive in his philosophical thought and what Hayek believed yields a renewed appreciation and endorsement of the values or norms at the base of the Great Society.

Two conceptions of order

A great deal of Hayek's work in social and legal philosophy from the late 1930s through his final work, *The Fatal Conceit*, can and should be seen as an expansion and generalization of his contribution during the mid-1930s to the debate about the rationality of central economic planning.[3] Advocates of such planning always appeal to the idea that the only alternative to economic disorder is comprehensive economic planning. Under such planning some central authority draws up an inventory of all the nation's economic resources, surveys all the different combinations of ways in which these resources might be put to use, identifies the best comprehensive combination of resource allocations and uses, and issues and enforces all the commands necessary to direct each economic agent in the performance of his or her assigned task within that best comprehensive allocation and use of resources. Rational economic order will exist only to the extent that information about all available resources is gathered up and conveyed to the organizing central authority that, in light of that information and guided

---

[2] Hayek's antirationalism appears in his early essay "Individualism: True and False" (1944), in *Individualism and Economic Order* (Chicago: University of Chicago Press, 1948), 1–32. It is less prominent in his important earlier essay "Freedom and the Economic System" (1939), in *The Collected Works of F. A. Hayek*, vol. 10, *Socialism and War* (Chicago: University of Chicago Press, 1997), 189–211; in *The Road to Serfdom* (Chicago: University of Chicago Press, 1944); and in *Constitution of Liberty*. It reemerges strongly in *Law, Legislation and Liberty* and is even more pronounced in *The Fatal Conceit* (*Collected Works*, vol. 2 [Chicago: University of Chicago Press, 1988]).

[3] See the three essays on socialist calculation that are reprinted in *Individualism and Economic Order*, 119–208.

by some measure of the common good, will draw up and enforce such a central plan. The basic appeal of any such scheme reflects a surprisingly pervasive disposition among human beings to believe that order must be the product of organization, that systems cannot be self-ordering but must be ordered by some external organizer. Order cannot be endogenous; it must be exogenous.

Is such rational socialist calculation possible? Hayek's economic mentor, Ludwig von Mises (1881–1973), provided a remarkably elegant argument against the possibility of rational socialist planning.[4] How can planners know which prospective inputs ought to be devoted to which prospective outputs (many of which outputs would be possible inputs for further possible outputs)? Roughly, the answer is that the planner should select the array of allocations of inputs to outputs such that the ultimate value of the outputs most exceeds the value of the inputs. However, Mises and subsequently Hayek pointed out that the planner can act in accordance with this answer only if he or she knows the market values – that is, the market prices – of all the relevant inputs and outputs. For only market prices encapsulate otherwise totally dispersed information about the scarcity of and the demand for the priced resources. For example, only the knowledge of market values reveals the irrationality of devoting all of society's titanium to the production of license plates. However, because the institution of central planning *eliminates* market prices, that institution makes rational central planning impossible. Hayek added to this Misesian critique by emphasizing the existence of another batch of crucial information beyond what would be encapsulated in market prices, were markets to be allowed to operate. This is the highly local and often only tacitly grasped information that is scattered among individuals and not yet reflected in market prices (even supposing that market prices are allowed to emerge). This scattered information and the effective right of individuals to act on it are essential to beneficial economic innovation. Yet this information is also necessarily unavailable to the central planner, and even if it were available, the central planner would have to forbid individuals from acting on it.

Hence, rational economic order cannot be designed and exogenously imposed. Yet is nondesigned, endogenous, self-organizing rational economic order possible? Hayek endorses the understanding of Adam Smith (1723–90) that economic order arises out of particular economic agents deploying their personal resources in pursuit of their separate ends and on

---

[4] See especially Mises's *Socialism* (1922), trans. J. Kahane (Indianapolis, IN: Liberty Fund, 1981).

the basis of their own inventory of knowledge, including their knowledge about others' preferences, resources, and likely actions. Order arises not through the imposition of any overall plan but rather through the ongoing mutual adjustment of elements that make up the order to their local and changing circumstances. Without any particular individual or authority intending it, an economic order arises by "invisible hand" processes. The order that results from such processes is, in the language of Smith's contemporary Adam Ferguson (1723–1816), "the result of human actions, but not of human design."[5] Within such a *spontaneous* economic order, individuals advance their private ends through production activities, trade, or the formation of new forms of property or economic relationships that move resources from low-value to high-value uses; hence, the economic rationality of the overall spontaneous economic order.

Economic order is not the only sort of emergent, nondesigned order. Other highly salient examples include the order that obtains among the elements that make up any particular living organism and among those that make up an ecological system. There was a time at which most people thought that such complex orders had to be the products of an exogenous designing intelligence and, indeed, that such orders were the primary evidence for the existence of such an intelligence. These design arguments for the existence of God have been dethroned by our understanding of biological orders as grown, emergent, unintended orders.

Nondesigned, emergent economic and biological orders are concrete and factual in the sense that their coordinated elements are particular observable entities; for example, human activities, material resources, biological organs, and colonies of this or that species. However, Hayek, following Ferguson and Carl Menger (1840–1921),[6] also emphasizes the existence of more abstract evolved and unintended orders. The elements that make up these more abstract orders are norms or patterns of conduct. Two outstanding examples of such abstract orders are money and language. As has been the case with concrete economic and biological orders, people have been strongly disposed to think that abstract orders such as money and language must be the product of design. Money and language must have been invented by some *very smart* individual or been intentionally instituted through some agreement among brainy individuals. Surely, the thought

---

[5] Adam Ferguson, *An Essay on the History of Civil Society* (London, 1767), 187.
[6] See Carl Menger, *Principles of Economics* (1872), trans. B. F. Hoselitz and J. Dingwall (New York: New York University Press, 1981).

goes, such beneficial order can no more be the product of chance than can the striking coordination of the parts of the human eye. Yet Hayek argues that such beneficial abstract orders are no more the product of intelligent design than are beneficial emergent concrete orders. Just as no aspiring central planner could have the information needed to design a concrete rational economic order, no individual or committee could have had the extraordinary innovative genius to think up money or language. Such abstract orders arise neither by intentional design nor by chance, but rather by an evolutionary process of primarily cultural mutation, modification, and selection. Abstract orders of norms or patterns of conduct emerge and survive insofar as they facilitate – in ways normally not appreciated by their beneficiaries – the formation of advantageous and more concrete orders.

According to Hayek, morality is also an abstract order of norms that is a product of human action but not of human design. A subset of these norms and compliance with them are especially crucial to the formation of mutually advantageous spontaneous concrete orders. These "rules of just conduct" are general negative prohibitions – which will take somewhat different forms at different times and in different places – against interference with individuals' chosen deployment of their persons, talents, energy, and (legitimately acquired) possessions and against violation of persons' valid contractual claims. A unifying feature of these norms is that others' compliance with them constitutes one's freedom. For, according to Hayek, an individual's freedom consists in not being precluded from "us[ing] his own knowledge for his purposes" (LLL 1:56), and each of these norms prohibits a way of precluding individuals from using their knowledge for their own respective purposes. Recall here Hayek's emphasis on the fact that the knowledge needed for successful action is radically scattered among individuals. It follows that only in a realm of freedom in which individuals are allowed to act on their own particular insights and preferences will the possibilities for successful action be maximized. In *The Constitution of Liberty* Hayek suggests that this freedom is to be respected because coercion is in itself evil; yet he argues more extensively that this freedom is to be respected because of its beneficial consequences. In any case, we should not think that the norms that constitute freedom have been adopted because people understood the fruitfulness of freedom. Rather, where such norms have been allowed to develop, they have emerged and taken hold because general compliance with them has facilitated successful human action and interaction, and hence the societies in which they have emerged and taken hold have had greater fitness for survival. Just as concrete spontaneous economic order has what Robert Nozick calls an "invisible-hand explanation,"[7] so too does the abstract order of morality and, more specifically, the rules of just conduct.

In contrast to other moral norms, these rules of just conduct are understood to be eligible for *coercive* enforcement.[8] People's settled expectations that others and they themselves will be required to abide by the rules of just conduct (as they have developed within their respective societies) are a necessary condition for the sort of private-property, free-market economic order that Hayek takes to be the rational alternative to central economic planning. Indeed, the settled expectation that the rules of just conduct will be complied with is the crucial precondition for the development and advancement of that complex of spontaneous concrete social orders that add up to the ever evolving, dynamic, pluralist Great Society. The more particular social and economic institutions and relationships that make up the Great Society emerge only insofar as that society's background norms – especially the rules of just conduct as they have been articulated in that society's history – are respected and known to be respected.

According to Hayek, there is no common end or set of commensurable ends that all individuals and, hence, society as a whole ought to serve. Human beings have come to have many different sorts of life-defining ends, and there is no way of ranking alternative concatenations of this diversity of ends. Or, if there is a way of achieving such rankings, we are ignorant of it.[9] Thus, the deepest error of central planners is that they believe that they can identify the common end or set of commensurable ends that their plan should aim to maximize. The Great Society is not itself planned, and like other spontaneous orders, it has no determinate purpose *of its own*: "A Great Society has nothing to do with, and is in fact irreconcilable with 'solidarity' in the true sense of unitedness in the pursuit of known common goals" (LLL 2:111). However, general compliance with such a society's rules of just conduct and the many avenues for the attainment of personal ends that arise within such a society provide individuals with unprecedented opportunities to plan their own lives.

Nevertheless, Hayek does *not* maintain that all beneficial human order is emergent and unintended. Rather, he holds that there is a vital

---

[7] Robert Nozick, *Anarchy, State, and Utopia* (New York: Basic Books, 1974), 18–22.
[8] Hayek repeatedly claims that only coercion that is directed against coercion is justifiable. Yet he also claims that coercion is justifiable whenever it is in accordance with general rules.
[9] Hayek's assertion of this pluralism of incommensurable ends is most explicit in "Freedom and the Economic System."

place for intentionally created, designed orders – that is, "organizations" – within the larger, encompassing, spontaneous order that is the Great Society. Firms, unions, churches, teams, and armies are just a sampling of such organizations. Such organizations have determinate purposes – for instance, profit maximization, increased remuneration, salvation, championships, and the utter destruction of the enemy – that are shared by the individuals who join them. Within any such organization, individuals are expected to proceed in accordance with its program for the attainment of its respective purpose; they are expected to recognize and abide by that organization's plan. The Hayekian free society is richly layered with such intentional communities and the various networks that they form – precisely because individuals are free to choose their own array of associations on the basis of their own diverse knowledge and preferences.

As Hayek sees it, the modern "rationalist" belief that society itself must and should be designed is only one of the two main enemies of the open, pluralist, and voluntarist society that he favors. The other main enemy is our premodern – indeed, tribal – disposition to want to be members of intense communities of shared values and to insist that all others whom we encounter pay allegiance to those specific values and serve those communities. According to Hayek, the great psychological challenge for individuals within modern liberal societies is to reap the rewards of participation in particular combinations of these communities of shared values while appreciating that it is the protection of everyone against the legal imposition of any set of substantive values that makes possible this rich array of available communities of shared values.

One rather special organization *within* spontaneous society is government. As an organization, government has a purpose or set of (putatively) compatible purposes. For Hayek, not surprisingly, the primary purpose of government is the clarifying articulation and the enforcement of the rules of just conduct. Hayek also frequently assigns to government the roles of (1) producing (or financing the production of) those public goods that would not be provided via voluntary market transactions and (2) providing a social safety net for "some unfortunate minorities, the weak or those unable to provide for themselves" (LLL 1:141–2). However, we should note that Hayek believes that some of the goods commonly thought to require governmental provision really can be (better) provided privately,[10] and he is

---

[10] See Hayek's endorsement of the private provision of money in *Denationalisation of Money*, rev. ed. (London: Institute for Economic Affairs, 1990).

concerned that within the dynamic of democratic politics the call for the provision of that safety net will open "the floodgates" to a redistributive state that advances the interests of some ruling political coalition at the expense of all other members of society (LLL 2:140). Without resolving the question of precisely how much government Hayek favors or should favor, it is clear that for him government ought to be a particular organization *within society* with specific, narrowly defined, purposes. Whom, then, may government direct for the sake of those purposes? The Hayekian answer is that, in a free society, government will have certain means for achieving its ends. These means will include (to a certain extent) those individuals who have become members of that organization, but "these means do not include the private citizen" (1:133).

Two conceptions of law

According to Hayek, there are two fundamentally divergent conceptions of law: the command conception and the coordinating norm conception. Even though many theorists have argued that it is simply a conceptual truth that law is the command of the (divine or temporal) sovereign, it is important to see that this command conception of law is also the natural accompaniment of the design conception of rational social order. If one subscribes to this understanding of rational social order, one must hold that there is some determinate end that the order is supposed to serve and that the elements within the order must be organized exogenously for that end best to be served. As we have already seen, the designer of that social order will have the task of surveying all the resources (economic and otherwise) within the society, determining which concatenations of which uses of these resources will best advance the (supposed) purpose of that society, and issuing directives to all the other members of society about how they should deploy themselves and particular nonhuman resources so that the conjunction of their actions maximally achieves that society's (supposed) purpose. Individuals who receive these directions will not generally see how the actions respectively required of them will contribute to that end, because they will only have their separate fragments of information, not the synoptic vision of the whole that the designer is imagined to possess. In addition, they are likely to be more concerned with their private purposes than with the attainment of the radiant societal goal to which the designer is devoted. Thus, it cannot be left up to the recipients of these directives to decide whether they will comply with them. Instead, the directives must be understood as placing those individuals under a legal duty to carry them out simply because they have been issued by the "sovereign" authority.[11] Citizens will be understood to have a duty to comply with the positive law – that is, the law posited by political authority – simply because it has been posited. The commands of this authority themselves provide citizens with reasons for compliance.

Law, then, is understood as the expressed will of some authority that is backed by threats of punishment for noncompliance. Because the agency that expresses and coercively enforces this will is itself the source of law, that agency cannot itself be subject to law. Nothing that this agency wills and enforces can be contrary to law; everything that it wills and enforces is law. There can be no genuine legal constraints on this law-creating authority. As this doctrine was put in the seventeenth century, first comes the king, then comes the law. Indeed, when this view was articulated in the seventeenth century in service of the authority of absolute monarchs, it was often said that somewhat general and written laws came to be issued by monarchs simply because they had become too busy to direct in detail all the activities of their subjects. On this view of law, when judges seek to find and apply the law in particular cases, what they are really trying to do is to ascertain and enforce the will of the monarch whose lieutenants they are.

Because not even the most avid advocate of designed social order believes on reflection that the social engineer will be able to gather up all the relevant detailed local information that individuals will have, the advocate of such an order will envision a central plan that leaves some room for the agent on the scene to adjust action to his or her knowledge of the local facts. The brigade commander directs the platoon lieutenant to capture Pork Chop Hill. The platoon lieutenant then incorporates some of his local knowledge (about, for instance, the strengths of his squads) into his commands to his various squad commanders. The squad commanders employ further (and yet more local) information in their commands to the squad members. And so on. Similarly, the factory manager in a planned economy is directed to produce 5,000 pairs of boots with the material that others are directed to supply to him. The manager incorporates local information into his more specific directives to his foremen, and so on. (Whatever success central plans seem to enjoy will often be the product of enterprising individuals exercising discretion well beyond its planned limits.) Nevertheless, even if the societal plan is adjusted to the fact that the subjects of its directives must have some

---

[11] Some hold to this view of law while embracing the fantasy that the true sovereign is the People.

discretion in their choice of how to carry out their assigned tasks, the plan must take the form of assigning varying sets of more or less specific tasks to individuals. The law of the designed social order must be an enormous set of different task assignments that individuals are commanded to carry out. (Among the tasks assigned to nearly everyone will be that of not preventing others from carrying out their assigned tasks.)

Against this command conception, Hayek maintains that law in its most fundamental sense precedes and is conceptually independent of governing authority; law in this sense is historically antecedent to legislation. Law in its essence is a set of norms general compliance with which makes social order among a group of individuals (or families or clans) possible. Or, to differentiate law from the totality of such norms, one can say that law in its most fundamental sense is the subset of those rules that function in part through the expectation and acceptance of their coercive enforcement. Law is the set of norms that people – perhaps only dimly – perceive must be abided by in their interactions with their societal fellows if the social order they are nested within and its benefits are to be maintained. People find themselves in social orders in which such rules are complied with and are generally perceived as necessary to their beneficial interaction precisely because no social order can survive without the existence of such compliance and perception. If such norms and perceptions of them do not emerge, neither does social order.

Although at some point specific members of the evolved society may be assigned the task of enforcing these norms when necessary, the norms themselves are not, and ought not to be seen to be, the results of any societal member's will or design. Though legislation may further codify these norms, the norms themselves and their prescriptive force are not the product of legislation. Indeed, it is because these norms are in fact a product of unintended cultural evolution and not any agent's will that they have often been perceived to be permanent, God-given laws that are akin to unbreachable laws of nature.

Hayek's argument for the priority of law over willed legislation is both historical and conceptual. What we are strongly inclined to think of as law in fact existed long before legislation, that is, the explicit positing of enforceable rules. Generally, the role of established political authority was, and was perceived to be, the enforcement of preexisting and mostly only tacitly grasped law. Chronologically, first comes law, and then comes the king. Moreover, Hayek argues that command doctrines of law (and similar forms of legal positivism) need the notion of *lawful authority* to differentiate between lawful and obligating commands and the dictates of the highway robber. However, lawful authority can only be understood as authority that expresses and enforces rules that merit expression and enforcement in virtue of their coordinating function. It is this (often not appreciated) coordinating function that gives prescriptive force to the rules and that makes an authority that expresses and enforces them lawful. We can distinguish lawful authority from the highway robber only on the basis of the lawful content or quality of the rules that they are respectively prepared to enforce. Aspiring authorities can constitute themselves as lawful only by enforcing the law that exists independently of their will. Hence, conceptually, first comes the law; then comes the king.

Seventeenth-century opponents of the command conception and, especially, its implication that the king must be above the law often offered an argument that combines Hayek's chronological and conceptual points. The argument turned on the ubiquity of coronation oaths. At least in many European countries, a legal condition of becoming a lawful monarch was taking the established coronation oath. In the absence of this legal rule, which was not itself established by the will of any monarch, no one could become a lawful monarch. Moreover, the aspiring monarch had to swear to uphold the law of the land, that is, a body of legal norms that themselves were neither of his making nor within his authority to abrogate.

Of course, this is to return to Hayek's view that law − or at least a certain type of law − is an *emergent* abstract order. This sort of order arises among groups of people because of the benefits it confers on them and characteristically not because people understand how or even that the order serves their interests. Such law continually evolves as people stumble upon advantageous articulations, modifications, or extensions of their existing law. For Hayek, the primary vehicle for these evolutionary transformations is the dispute-resolution efforts of elders and judges, who must in changing social and economic circumstances continually find and apply the rules that underlie people's reasonable expectations about others' conduct and extend or refine those rules in ways that facilitate emerging forms of cooperation for mutual advantage. Societies increase their likelihood of surviving and of being imitated as more and more of their members are free to interact and transact with one another (and with members of other societies) on the basis of their own perceptions and values. This freedom for individuals to employ their own knowledge singly or jointly in pursuit of their own purposes develops as the basic norms of a society move from rules that direct individuals to some shared (for instance, tribal) end to rules that merely place everyone under negative duties not to interfere with other people's doing as they see fit with themselves or their possessions.

This attenuation of enforceable norms from rules that require individuals to promote certain substantive ends to rules that merely require noninterference with others is necessary to bring more and more individuals with increasingly diverse ends of their own into interlocking networks of cooperative interaction. Under this sort of attenuation of legally enforced rules, everyone is subject to and protected by the same legal rules (LLL 2:88–9). Moreover, the duty of judges is to find and enforce these general coordinating norms rather than the will of any supralegal sovereign. Hence, the elusive ideal of the rule of law is satisfied. In contrast, bodies of legal rules that conform to the command conception of law necessarily assign to different people different (and unpredictably changing) legal duties and immunities, and a judge's search for this law amounts to an attempt to identify and enforce the sovereign's will.

Hayek emphasizes that these general norms of just conduct are "purpose-independent" in the sense that they do not exist for the sake of advancing any determinate "societal" end; they exist merely to facilitate individuals' pursuit of their own chosen ends. A crucial question that cannot be explored here is whether this facilitation of persons' separate ends provides a ("rationalist") justification for these purpose-independent norms even though the norms are (at least for the most part) not the product of any intention to provide this facilitation.[12]

Of course, Hayek is not saying that there is no proper or useful place for law in the sense of directives or assignments of required tasks. Law as directives is essential for the operation of organizations – for instance, firms, churches, and teams – through which individuals advance many of their diverse ends. Also recall that for Hayek government itself is a useful organization *within society* with special purposes of its own, chief among these being the further articulation and enforcement of the rules of just conduct. Thus, the various levels and components of government operate by issuing directives of various degrees of specificity *to the members of those governmental organizations*. Government employees are to carry out those instructions. Yet it is a grave and destructive error to infer that lawfulness on

---

[12] See Eric Mack, "Hayek on Justice and the Order of Actions," in *The Cambridge Companion to Hayek*, ed. Edward Feser (Cambridge: Cambridge University Press, 2006), 259–86.

the part of members of society at large consists in *carrying out* governmental instructions. Rather, lawfulness in its most fundamental sense consists in all members of society and all the organizations they form – including government – acting *in compliance with the constraints of* freedom-instituting rules of just conduct.

9
Michael Oakeshott: the philosophical skeptic in an impatient age

TIMOTHY FULLER

Michael Oakeshott was born on December 11, 1901, in Kent, England, and died December 19, 1990, at his cottage in the village of Acton on the Dorset coast. He distinguished himself as an undergraduate at Gonville & Caius College, Cambridge, and then as a fellow of the college and lecturer in history. From the 1920s he remained at Cambridge, except for service in the British army in World War II, until the late 1940s. Thereafter he spent a brief period in Oxford before appointment as professor of political science at the London School of Economics and Political Science (LSE) in 1951. There he taught in and convened the Government Department, introducing the MSc in the History of Political Thought. This one-year degree program attracted students from many parts of the world, especially Canada and the United States. Although he officially retired in 1968, Oakeshott continued to participate in the fall term of the program, presenting papers in its general seminar until 1980.

Oakeshott was an extraordinary teacher and lecturer, enjoying exchanges with students that faculty half his age could not match. In old age he never forgot what it was to be young. He was charmed by the exuberance of undergraduates as they were charmed by him. The period from the 1950s to the 1980s was a fertile period for the study of political theory in the Government Department at LSE. Oakeshott had attracted an illustrious group of scholars and teachers: John Charvet, Maurice Cranston, Elie Kedourie, Wolfgang von Leyden, Kenneth Minogue, Robert Orr, and others.

Trained in modern history and an admirer of such greats as Frederick Maitland, Oakeshott was devoted to the study of political thought. In his Cambridge lectures in the 1930s he examined the history of political thought. The distinguished medievalist Brian Tierney and the great Locke scholar Peter Laslett have related to me their vivid recollections as undergraduates of his lectures even after fifty or more years. His notebooks, which go back to the early 1920s, show that he studied the works of Plato and Aristotle with care. A philosopher more than a historian, at times he said he was neither. He ranked thinkers according to the degree to which they escaped preoccupation with merely practical issues of the moment. He was deeply interested in the study of politics but not attracted to political activism. In his celebrated introduction to Hobbes's *Leviathan*,[1] he singled out Plato, Hobbes, and Hegel as exemplary thinkers and wrote of three great moments: Plato exemplified the tradition of "reason and nature," Hobbes that of "will and artifice," and Hegel that of the "rational will." These thinkers examined politics as the intersection of time and eternity – they were interested in understanding the character of politics and the human condition as such while being alert to the pressing contingencies of their time and place.

In essays that he wrote on the nature of philosophy and political philosophy in the 1930s and 1940s, Oakeshott insisted on the open-endedness of thought, referring to philosophy as "radically subversive" questioning that shuns ideology and political advocacy.[2] By "subversive" he did not mean the attempt to revolutionize regimes or public policy. He meant rather that the aspiration of the philosopher is to grasp experience as a whole without an ulterior motive other than to understand better what one already understands in part. For such an inquirer political allegiances will be weak: Philosophy is not the carrying on of politics by other means. Philosophers may be deeply interested in what is to be learned by examining political life, but ultimately their inquiry carries them beyond politics as they come to realize that interminable incoherencies unavoidably arise in politics. If their vocation is to pursue wisdom or, as Oakeshott put it, to understand better what they already understand in part, then they must accept the implication of that pursuit.

He spells these ideas out in his first major book, *Experience and Its Modes* (1933).[3] This remarkable work, which remains in print to this day, established him as an important and original philosophic voice. In it Oakeshott

---

[1] Michael Oakeshott, introduction to *Leviathan*, by Thomas Hobbes, ed. Michael Oakeshott, Blackwell's Political Texts (Oxford: Blackwell, 1946). I refer to this version because when Oakeshott published a collection of his Hobbes essays in 1975, *Hobbes on Civil Association*, he revised the original introduction substantially. Comparison of the two versions is instructive for those who wish to follow Oakeshott's thinking on Hobbes.

[2] Michael Oakeshott, *Religion, Politics and the Moral Life*, ed. Timothy Fuller (London: Yale University Press, 1993).

[3] Full bibliographical information for this and other important works by Oakeshott can be found in the reading list at the end of this chapter.

acknowledges the influence of Hegel's *Phenomenology of Spirit* and F. H. Bradley's *Appearance and Reality*. *Experience and Its Modes* is ostensibly in the tradition of British Hegelianism, but readers will see that it is the work of a most creative mind that has absorbed and digested much, making it his own, and offering thoughts distinctive of the author.

The gist of his argument is this: The distinction between "the world" and our "experience of the world" is untenable. The world and our experience of it are interrelated so tightly that efforts to treat them as separable fail. The world and our interpretation of the world are a single world of our experience. The world is a whole and is a world of thought. We have no access to anything that is not in our thought. We invent various modes for interpreting experience. We try to comprehend experience as a whole through varying, partial interpretations that fasten on some features of experience as if they were sufficient to explain the whole.

In 1933 Oakeshott expounded three prominent modes of experience: science, history, and practice. He admitted that there could be many modes and that these three were not exhaustive, but he thought they were both prominent and sufficiently developed for careful analysis. Science makes sense of the world by interpreting all experience in terms of stable, quantitative relationships that are fully transparent (a world understood *sub specie quantitatis*); history makes sense of the world by treating all experience as past experience (a world understood *sub specie praeterito*); and practice – which includes both politics and religion – understands the world as the tension between "what is" and "what ought to be" or *sub specie voluntatis*, a world defined by will and desire.

Each mode attempts to make sense out of experience as a whole from the point of view of its own assumptions or postulates. Each achieves coherence to its own satisfaction only by discounting those elements of experience that would pose difficult, intolerable contradictions. Thus the philosopher's investigation does not "correct" a mode's deficiencies of abstraction by amalgamation with other modes, because doing so will only multiply the contradictions. The aspiration to encounter experience as a whole requires abandoning allegiance to any mode to seek the whole unmodified; every mode in identifiable ways abstracts from the whole. Abstraction is explaining the whole of experience through the partiality of a particular mode. It is not the philosopher's task to "improve" a mode, but rather the philosopher must depart from these abstractions in quest of the "whole unmodified."

The use of one mode to explain the others creates categorical irrelevancies. History may offer a history of science, but it is not an alternative to scientific investigation. Politics tries to draw lessons from history, but uses past events to confirm perspectives or positions we already hold; we invoke historical examples to justify or to undermine current political ambitions. This "practical past" is not the "historian's past." Historians can describe political decisions in the context of the complex of conditions in which they were made, but politicians have to make decisions here and now, pursuing the intimations of their situation and overlooking the inconvenient features of past experience. Studying the past "for its own sake" constrains or even paralyzes practical judgment. Nor can science and politics be integrated.

However, there is much talk about the "politics of science" or the politics of historical research, as we also talk of the "science of politics." Thus Oakeshott eventually arrived at his notion of the "conversation of mankind," which he worked out in the 1950s in a small book, *The Voice of Poetry in the Conversation of Mankind* (1959).[4] If there is no hierarchy of modes, their practitioners nevertheless might talk to each other, even stumbling onto the vocation of the philosopher to seek the whole. Oakeshott thought conversation the most human thing, that which distinguishes us from other creatures. Universities are the "places of learning" where the conversation can be celebrated as an end in itself.

How does this notion affect his concept of political philosophy? For Oakeshott, philosophy is "radically subversive" questioning. Political philosophy is the philosophic investigation of politics, examining the character of political life without political attachments. To use political philosophy to supply intellectual support for political positions or policies is to abandon the philosopher's task for the politician's task, or for ideology. The political philosopher is neither a would-be philosopher-king nor a policy scientist.

That no mode of experience is, philosophically speaking, privileged over any other may seem odd because the practical life is so dominant and intrusive. One is tempted to think that practical life is the foundation from which all the other modes must spring. Oakeshott did not think this. Understandably, intrusiveness is confused with priority. Because there are numerous modes that offer to explain our experience, the choice of a mode is a choice to understand in a certain way. Philosophy itself is not a mode. Rather, philosophy is critical of "arrests in experience" that every mode instantiates. The statements that we "ought" to look at the world scientifically or historically or that we "ought" to take the view that

---

[4] Michael Oakeshott, *The Voice of Poetry in the Conversation of Mankind* (London: Bowes and Bowes, 1959). This work is reprinted in *Rationalism in Politics and Other Essays*.

everything is politics are exhortations prompted by the recognition that one need not exalt one or another of these.

The philosopher in principle chooses none of these alternatives, and thus, qua philosopher, he or she does not examine politics as if it were the key to experience as a whole, even if it is highly revealing of humanity when engaged in to pursue "imagined and wished-for satisfactions" and to resolve the interminable tension between "what is" and "what ought to be."

Yet Oakeshott was mindful of the politics of his time and place. In *The Social and Political Doctrines of Contemporary Europe* (1939) – comprising documents and commentary on liberalism, Catholicism, communism, Fascism, and National Socialism – he called the latter three the "modern authoritarian doctrines":

To the Liberal and the Catholic mind alike the notion that men can authoritatively plan and impose a way of life upon a society appears to be a piece of pretentious ignorance; it can be entertained only by men who have no respect for human beings and are willing to make them the means to the realization of their own ambitions.[5]

From 1947 to 1960, Oakeshott wrote a series of remarkable essays, many of which he collected and published in 1962 under the title *Rationalism in Politics and Other Essays*. The title essay, "Rationalism in Politics" – together with essays titled "Rational Conduct," "Political Education," "The Political Economy of Freedom," and "On Being Conservative" – constitutes a powerful critique of ideological politics, of the attempt to model the social sciences on the physical sciences, and of the disregard of traditional wisdom and insight in the belief that a kind of Baconian/Cartesian methodology could free us from reliance on our traditions.

Ideological politics asserts an independently premeditated (abstractly idealistic) program for guiding our decision making toward a suppositious perfection or end state. Calling himself a "skeptic who would do better if only he knew how," Oakeshott famously commented that in politics we set sail on a boundless and bottomless sea and its principal task is to keep the ship afloat. By this Oakeshott did not mean that life has no meaning or there is reason to despair, although some of his critics asserted this, one even calling him a "lonely nihilist." Oakeshott saw that meaning may be found elsewhere than in politics – more likely in religion, art, poetry, or

---

[5] Michael Oakeshott, *Social and Political Doctrines of Contemporary Europe* (Cambridge: Cambridge University Press, 1939), xxii.

philosophy. Oakeshott was avowedly Augustinian in this respect. Ideological politics asserts that political action is the source of meaning rather than a means to provide the background conditions for us to seek our meaning in more promising ways.

Oakeshott was skeptical of the pretensions of politics and spoke of politics as a "necessary evil." He was at the same time reserved in speaking of transcendence even though he had a lifelong interest in religion. He looked for the poetic in the midst of the quotidian experience. Politics – attending to the arrangements of a set of people brought together by choice and chance – is an instrument in maintaining equilibrium but not something in which to put one's faith. He was a skeptical conservative, not a "movement conservative." To him, to be conservative is to look for the possibilities of enjoyment in the present moment. He invoked Augustine, Pascal, Montaigne, Hobbes, and Hume. He was not an enthusiast for Burke or Russell Kirk, nor was he anything like a neoconservative. In early essays from the 1920s, Oakeshott wrote explicitly about the religious character as living in the present.[6] He later wrote explicitly about the tension between the "politics of skepticism" and the "politics of faith" ("faith" here meaning political faith of the ideological/utopian sort) in his posthumously published *The Politics of Faith and the Politics of Scepticism* (1996; probably written circa 1950–52).

In the idealist philosophical tradition from which he began, Oakeshott dismissed dualistic versions of experience, specifically the duality of worldliness and other-worldliness. He spoke rather of different motives of self-understanding in a single world of experience. To reject worldliness is to reject the current confusions and preoccupations that distract one from the effort to penetrate the mystery of life without imagining that mystery can be explained away. To be religious meant to him to live so far as possible without anxiety about past actions or future uncertainties. To be distracted by what has been or by what we imagine may come to pass is to lose the religious understanding of life, and it also promotes susceptibility both to ideology and to using the powers of government to "pursue perfection as the crow flies." Oakeshott saw that longing for an orderly world is likely, through excess and concentrated power, to turn ideologies into recipes for graveyards. He said that the philosopher might have a heavenly home but is in no hurry to get there. This assertion may be taken in two ways: First,

---

[6] See Oakeshott, *Religion, Politics and the Moral Life.*

there is no point in "hurrying" because there is no plan, program, map, or shortcut to speed one on the way; second, the enjoyment and careful exploration of the present possibilities are ruined if one is preoccupied with the sense that one ought always to be somewhere else than where one is.

Among Oakeshott's favorite biblical stories was the Tower of Babel. He wrote two essays with this title. The first, written in the 1940s, appeared in *Rationalism in Politics*; the second appeared in *On History and Other Essays* (1983). In both, Oakeshott shows that this tale provides a permanent insight into our incessant proclivity to storm the heavenly kingdom and occupy it. The disaster that follows is eventually forgotten in new attempts to succeed where all before us have failed. Modern rationalism and the preoccupation with technology that goes with it are our versions of this primordial experience.

Yet Oakeshott was more than a mere skeptic. His positive political theory appears in *On Human Conduct* (1975), his magnum opus. Oakeshott described *On Human Conduct* as a set of three essays. Readers will see that the three essays, in fact, constitute a tightly structured, systematic effort to summarize Oakeshott's political philosophy. The first essay is "On the Theoretical Understanding of Human Conduct," the second is "On the Civil Condition," and the third is "On the Character of a Modern European State." This structure corresponds to the structure of Hobbes's political philosophy, the political philosopher on whom Oakeshott published more than on any other. The first essay explores what it means to be human; the second, how human beings of the sort he describes interact in the civil condition; and he concludes with a historical essay on the achievement of the modern European state as the structure most suited to human beings who understand themselves as individuals trying to come to terms with each other under modern conditions.

What is a human being? Oakeshott addressed this question most systematically in *On Human Conduct*, but he considered this question also in his essays on liberal education (most of which are collected in *The Voice of Liberal Learning* [1989]). For Oakeshott, human beings are individual agents learning to become something in terms of their self-understanding. We are, he said, "in ourselves what we are for ourselves." "Conduct" is not "behavior," where behavior is understood as exhibitions and emissions determined by and emanating from underlying processes that allow us no choice. We must seek to understand ourselves and the world we inhabit, and we remain active in this endeavor from birth to death, responding to the world in terms of how we understand ourselves and the circumstances in which we must operate.

Oakeshott was a radical individualist. Every human being is an essay in self-understanding; every human being thinks and interprets and responds to the world. Freedom, Oakeshott thought, is "intelligent response." We are not autonomous, because we are constrained by a preexisting world into which we are inserted, a world of goings-on that emerged and developed long before us and will likely go on long after us. We cannot live without this background inheritance – whether we like or do not like it – because we have to learn everything, and we need to start somewhere. Yet what we acquire from this inheritance does not determine how we appropriate it and respond to it. Every human action is an "intelligent response," in which we are neither autonomous nor predetermined. Of course, Oakeshott does not mean that every human action is sensible or successful, but that every action for good or ill is the response of a being reasoning about a situation, pursuing imagined and wished-for outcomes, avoiding what is thought to be undesirable or dangerous. All human beings, no matter how bizarre their actions, are agents in this sense.

Oakeshott understands the civil condition in terms of such beings. He replaces the familiar term "civil society" with the term "civil association." Oakeshott's Hobbes (and his Hume) qualified his Hegel: Individuals associate but do not compose a "society," which, for Oakeshott, is an abstraction obscuring the fact that individuals do not cease to be individuals even when they wish to escape the ordeal of consciousness. A human being is *homo inter homines*, a self among other selves, inescapably a "for itself." "Civil association" acknowledges individuality and points to the question of what formal structures may be appropriate to a set of human beings associating with each other in this way. The structure includes the rule of law and the exercise of authority by those authorized and recognized among the associates.

In the third essay, on the origins of the modern European state, Oakeshott argues that political authority based on consent is a European achievement emerging from a long process of trial, error, and accommodation, a history representing the gradual transformation of the authority relationship from command and obedience to acknowledgment and consent. The theory of the social contract is a summary statement of what in the seventeenth and eighteenth centuries it was believed Europeans had already achieved in the transition from the medieval to the modern world, including the identification of individuality and involving a new concept of authority and of the state as the organizing principle in modern politics. If in antiquity the central object of investigation was the polis, the central object in modern times is the state. The theory of the social contract, which offers an explanation of the modern European state, comes at the end of a long historical development that it did not initiate.

However, a revolutionary implication in contract theory is lurking in the demand that existing regimes must be continually re-formed to con-form to the shape some imagine they would have if they had originated in a pure contract in which all residual alternative forms of human relationship are also transformed. One need only think of John Rawls's work to see this implication. Contract theory is thus a sophisticated argument criticizing both the past and the present in terms of a model for an imagined and wished-for future. It is philosophizing to change, not only to explain or describe, the prevailing order. Like Hume, Oakeshott is a political skeptic about a world suffused by the ideological deformation of philosophy and is, in this sense, a skeptical conservative. Oakeshott offers not a prudential argument that it is better for us to be cautious, nor is it an argument that what is older is better than what is newer. There may have been a romantic streak in Oakeshott – there certainly was an attraction to the poetic – but there is nothing romantic in his arguments. Against the universalism of our time, Oakeshott did not think the universal could replace the local, or the abstract the concrete.

Politics is important to us because it is intrusive and unavoidable, an intractable feature of human existence. It is interminable because it must try to make the temporal manageable. Politics is the very emblem of temporality unable to extricate itself from temporality's endlessness. The reconciliation of "what is" with "what ought to be" will forever elude us. Oakeshott's critique focused not so much on specific beliefs, programs, or actions as on what he thought to be a pervasive and mistaken modern understanding of the function of reason in practical life: to imagine perfection and to gather the power necessary to put it into practice. To him this understanding contradicts the character of civil association.

A civil association is a set of people bound together by a recognized authority and rule of law. However, being "an authority" is not being "in authority." Officeholders who are "in authority" govern not by claims to special knowledge or insight but because they have been acknowledged to have a right to exercise the office of authority through which they establish law for all and adjudicate disputes impartially. They have authority because they are recognized to have it.

In the modern state, the holders of an office of authority are authorized by those whom they govern to make rules to which those associated within the bounds of a given territory are expected to subscribe. They are expected to subscribe because the laws emanate from those whom they have entrusted with the task to make them. Both the makers of law and the subscribers to the law can understand the basic purpose of law; reasons can be given for the particular laws that are made. This does not preclude argument about the merits of the laws, but such argument occurs within a structure acknowledging that they are authoritative.

The authority is exercised in respect of individuals who are civilly associated. Such rules as may proceed from that authority are not intended to transform or override individuality or to define for individuals who they are "for themselves." A large proportion of their activities will consist in private, voluntary transactions facilitated by the rule of law. Typically, in civil association there will be incessant arguments over the scope of the government's powers.

There is an alternative image of the modern state that sees it as a joint enterprise to achieve a common goal within a "community" transcending civil association, in which the governors are understood to be managing a productive enterprise and citizens are seen as role players in a cooperative effort to achieve a common final end: In this view the state does not preside over an association but rather a corporation, or what might be called the administrative/regulatory bureaucratic state. Oakeshott thought that these alternatives, civil association and the managerial enterprise association, constituted a continuing dialectic in modern European – and North American – history, explaining a good deal about why modern politics carries on as it does. Modern politics has long been an argument between those who are skeptical of the power of governments to reconstruct and perfect social life and those with faith in our power to do exactly that. In our time the rationalist voice of the politics of faith seems dominant. Yet Oakeshott hoped that, even if modern rationalism is not in retreat, its pretensions, which will always be prey to disillusion, might be restrained by the continuing presence of the skeptical voice. In terms of his own understanding of political philosophy, he could not, qua political philosopher, simply prescribe one of the alternatives, but he could show reasons for thinking carefully. Philosophically speaking, he had to remain skeptical even of his skepticism. There is no doubt, however, as to what direction his own inclinations tend. As he said in "Political Education" (1951), his inaugural address at the University of London,

Political philosophy cannot be expected to increase our ability to be successful in political activity. It will not help us to distinguish between good and bad political projects; it has no power to guide or to direct us in the enterprise of pursuing the intimations of our tradition. But the patient analysis of the general ideas which have come to be connected with political activity – ideas such as nature, artifice, reason, will, law, authority, obligation, etc. – in so far as it succeeds in removing some of the crookedness from our thinking and leads to a more economical use of concepts, is an activity neither to be overrated nor despised. But it must be understood as an explanatory, not a practical, activity, and if we pursue it, we may only hope to be less often cheated by ambiguous statement and irrelevant argument.[7]

Many students of political philosophy will argue that this constrained role is too limiting. It may be useful to remember, however, that the modesty of his refusal to lionize political activity is reminiscent of the Socratic admonition that the beginning of wisdom lies in "not knowing" what everyone around one claims to know. It is also a means to avoid opposing one "rationalism" with another.

On Human Conduct (1975) not only summarizes his political philosophy but is also Oakeshott's philosophic valedictory, in which he expresses the serenity of one who, inspired by Socrates and Montaigne, is learning how to die:

Philosophic reflection is recognized here as the adventure of one who seeks to understand in other terms what he already understands and in which the understanding sought (itself unavoidably conditional) is a disclosure of the conditions of the understanding enjoyed and not a substitute for it. Its most appropriate expression is an essay where the character of the utterance (a traveller's tale) matches the character of the engagement, an intellectual adventure which has a course to follow but no destination. A philosophical essay leaves much to the reader, often saying too little for fear of saying too much; its attention is concentrated, but it does not stay to cross all the ts of the argument; its mood is cautious without being defensive; it is personal but never merely "subjective"; it does not dissemble the conditionality of the conclusions it throws up and although it may enlighten it does not instruct. It is, in short, a well-considered intellectual adventure recollected in tranquility.[8]

---

[7] Michael Oakeshott, "Political Education," in *Rationalism in Politics and Other Essays*, rev. ed. (Indianapolis: Liberty Fund, 1991), 132. This was Oakeshott's inaugural address as professor at the London School of Economics in 1951.

[8] Oakeshott, *On Human Conduct* (Oxford: Clarendon, 1975), vii.

One of Oakeshott's favorite stories was of the Chinese wheelwright who was unable, at age seventy, to turn over his craft to his son because his son could not get the hang of it. Generalizing from his son's failure to learn more than the abstract rules of the craft, the wheelwright remarked to his duke, who was reading the works of the sages, that books are the "lees and scum of bygone men." "All that was worth handing on," the wheelwright said, "died with them; the rest they put into their books."[9] I suppose Oakeshott was also thinking of the Platonic Socrates who refused to write philosophy down. We recall, however, that Plato devised a method of writing it down without writing it down. I think Oakeshott's intent was along those lines: In the lees and scum there may linger something of the essence that is a blessing in disguise. In his preference for the essay, he locates himself in a line of British authors (not to mention Montaigne and Pascal) extending from Bacon to Hume to Macaulay to John Stuart Mill. His voice is his own, distinguishing himself as a most worthy conversational entrant in the great conversation of humankind in which they, and he, continue to speak to us.

Suggestions for further reading

Oakeshott's writings are extensive and much has been published in recent years. The following are fundamental expressions of his thought.

Experience and Its Modes. Cambridge: Cambridge University Press, 1933.

Hobbes on Civil Association. Berkeley: University of California Press, 1975. New edition with foreword by Paul Franco. Indianapolis: Liberty Fund, 2000.

Introduction to *Leviathan*, by Thomas Hobbes, edited by Michael Oakeshott. Blackwell's Political Texts. Oxford: Blackwell, 1946.

Morality and Politics of Modern Europe: The Harvard Lectures. Edited by Shirley Letwin. London: Yale University Press, 1993.

On History and Other Essays. Berkeley: University of California Press, 1975. New edition with foreword by Timothy Fuller. Indianapolis: Liberty Fund, 1999.

On Human Conduct. Oxford: Clarendon Press, 1975.

The Politics of Faith and the Politics of Scepticism. Edited with an introduction by Timothy Fuller. London: Yale University Press, 1996.

Rationalism in Politics and Other Essays. New York: Basic Books, 1962. New and expanded edition. Indianapolis: Liberty Fund, 1991.

Religion, Politics and the Moral Life. Edited by Timothy Fuller. London: Yale University Press, 1993.

---

[9] Oakeshott's account of this story from Chuang Tzu is found in the title essay of *Rationalism in Politics*, 14.

10

Moral pluralism and liberal democracy: Isaiah Berlin's heterodox liberalism

WILLIAM GALSTON

When the definitive history of political theory in the twentieth century is written, Isaiah Berlin will take his place as one of the most distinguished representatives of the liberal tradition. His was an unorthodox liberalism in both substance and method, and during an era dominated by John Rawls, Berlin's distinctive merits were eclipsed. Today they are becoming more visible. Berlin was less systematic than Rawls, but he reflected more deeply on fundamental alternatives to liberalism and to the Enlightenment outlook that forms liberalism's customary backdrop. He wrestled more explicitly with the tension between universalism and particular attachments in the liberal tradition and in human affairs. And although in later years Rawls reconfigured – some believe disfigured – his theory to accommodate the "fact of pluralism," Berlin went farther, not only in explaining this fact but also in assessing its value.

Berlin was born in Riga, Latvia, in 1909, the only child of a prosperous merchant and an adoring mother. In 1916 the family moved to Petrograd, where they remained until 1920, when rising political instability and pressure from the new Bolshevik regime sparked their removal to London, where Berlin spent the next eight years. He attended Oxford from 1928 until 1931, spent a year as a tutor at New College, Oxford, and was then elected a fellow of All Souls' College, his intellectual home for decades. He quickly became the center of a philosophic circle that included A. J. Ayer, the enfant terrible of logical positivism; the redoubtable ordinary-language philosopher John Austin; and his student/critic Stuart Hampshire. At Oxford he began to develop the dense network of social, intellectual, and political relationships that was to characterize the remainder of his life.

For Berlin as for so many others, World War II proved transformative. Starting in 1941, he analyzed American politics and public opinion, first for the British Information Services in New York and then for the Foreign

Office, working out of the British Embassy in Washington. His weekly reports circulated officially to a select group that included Prime Minister Churchill and unofficially in a *samizdat* version to friends and senior civil servants.

Immediately after the end of the war, Berlin visited Moscow and had a series of momentous encounters with Russian literary figures, including Boris Pasternak and the poet Anna Akhmatova. The atmosphere of pervasive fear he encountered helped propel him into liberal anticommunist circles and accelerated the development of what became characteristic theses – the critique of historical determinism and materialism and the defense of the liberal conception of freedom. In 1958 he delivered the famous "Two Concepts of Liberty" as his inaugural lecture as Chichele Professor of Social and Political Theory at Oxford. In 1966, he became the founder and first principal of Oxford's Wolfson College, a role he discharged with panache for nearly a decade. During the last two decades of Berlin's life, Henry Hardy's tireless editorial efforts dispelled the belief that Berlin had talked incessantly but written little, as monographs and essay collections appeared in rapid succession. He died, loved and lauded, on November 5, 1997.[1]

General outlook

Reflecting on his life, Berlin once remarked that he had been formed by three traditions – British, Russian, and Jewish. From his life and education in Britain he absorbed not only a respect for decency, civility, and toleration of differences but also his adopted land's characteristic empiricism. From Russia – and especially from nineteenth-century figures such as Herzen and Turgenev – he drew his complex liberalism, focused on individual liberty and opposed to every kind of determinism. His Jewish upbringing sensitized him to the importance of communal ties. His Judaism was communal rather than creedal, his Zionism instinctive rather than ideological.

His outlook may be summed up in balanced antitheses. To begin, he embraced empiricism but not scientism.[2] He rejected the logical positivists' reduction of meaning to verification and deductive inference; for him philosophy consisted of those "queer questions" that neither can settle.[3]

---

[1] The best single source for Berlin's life is Michael Ignatieff, *Isaiah Berlin* (New York: Henry Holt, 1998).

[2] Steven Lukes, "An Unfashionable Fox," in *The Legacy of Isaiah Berlin*, ed. Mark Lilla, Ronald Dworkin, and Robert B. Silvers (New York: New York Review of Books, 2001), 54.

[3] George Crowder, *Isaiah Berlin: Liberty and Pluralism* (Cambridge: Polity, 2004), 192.

His empiricism extended to moral matters. He stressed the importance of fidelity to moral experience; the point of moral philosophy was to explain, not explain away, phenomena such as rational regret for the loss of value inherent in even the most defensible moral choices.[4]

Another key antithesis: Berlin noted and celebrated cultural variety, but without adopting a full-blown social constructionism. On complex, perhaps even contradictory grounds, he believed in a minimalist but substantive conception of human nature that delimited the range of possible variation among human lives.[5] In matters of religion, finally, he was a Humean skeptic but not an atheist, and he regarded the Enlightenment's idolatry of secular reason as callow. "Stone-dry atheists," he once remarked, "don't understand what men live by."[6]

Approach to political theory

Berlin thought of himself as (although not only as) a political theorist, and he espoused a distinctive conception of political theory. At the beginning of his most famous essay, mentioned earlier, he endorsed the view that political theory is a "branch of moral philosophy" because it "starts from the discovery, or application, of moral notions in the sphere of political relations."[7] This proposition contains an explicit ambiguity, the elucidation of which makes a considerable difference. If political theorists simply *apply* exogenous morality to politics, we have a quasi-Kantian picture in which "all politics must bend its knee before the right." Yet if theorists *discover* moral principles by examining politics as a distinctive sphere of human activity, then political theory may well have a distinctive, although still recognizably moral, content that cannot be derived from nonpolitical morality. It appears that Berlin intended both meanings. On the one hand, we take into politics an understanding of liberty as central to human being and human agency. On the other hand, the practice of politics raises unique questions about the scope of liberty. Obedience and coercion are, he claimed, the "central question" of politics, but they are hardly the central question of individual morality.

---

[4] Aileen Kelly, "A Revolutionary without Fanaticism," in *The Legacy of Isaiah Berlin*, 63; Thomas Nagel, "Pluralism and Coherence," in *The Legacy of Isaiah Berlin*, 65; Crowder, *Isaiah Berlin*, 130–1.
[5] Crowder, *Isaiah Berlin*, 55.
[6] Ignatieff, *Isaiah Berlin*, 294.
[7] Isaiah Berlin, "Two Concepts of Liberty," in *Four Essays on Liberty* (London: Oxford University Press, 1969), 120.

However understood, Berlin's practice reflected the proposition that morality is central to political theory. He was far more interested in the ends of politics – ways of life constituted by distinct conceptions of what is right, good, or important – than in the means of politics – constitutions, institutions, and public policy. Consistent with this approach, his liberalism was a general orientation, not a precise theory of justice or anything else. He would have been skeptical about designating any single value *tout court* as the "first virtue of social institutions."[8]

Because morality was central, political theory could not avoid the imprecision inherent in moral argument. However useful they might be in other fields of inquiry, Berlin warned against the application of abstract logical structures and minute analysis to politics. There can be no "unity of method" in philosophy. The method should be suited to the subject, not imposed on it. The subject matter of politics is unstable and mutable, and its concepts are blurry edged. In this respect, although not in many others, Berlin's approach was Aristotelian. Had it been presented to him, he would have endorsed Aristotle's dictum that "it is the mark of an educated mind to expect that amount of exactness in each sphere which the nature of the particular subject admits" (*Nicomachean Ethics* 1094b23).

Berlin believed in the power of political ideas to change the world. Although he was hardly blind to the influence of our circumstances on our conceptions, he was a relentless critic of what he dubbed "vulgar historical materialism." Ideas, he insisted, are anything but epiphenomenal. They are at the heart of what makes us human, and they reflect our primordial liberty to shape (and reshape) our lives. If so, theorizing about politics is not purely contemplative but represents a form of political action. At least in the case of politics, Berlin could not have accepted Ludwig Wittgenstein's claim that philosophy "leaves everything as it is."[9] (For his part, Wittgenstein might have regarded this feature of political theory as sufficient evidence that it was not and could not be philosophical.)

Berlin's liberalism

In calling the limits of permissible coercion and mandatory obedience the central question of politics, Berlin fell squarely within the classical liberal tradition. The answer that he proposed for that question rested on premises

---

[8] As John Rawls famously did for justice in *A Theory of Justice.*
[9] Ludwig Wittgenstein, *Philosophical Investigations*, sec. 124.

more widely accepted in the nineteenth century than in the twentieth. In "Two Concepts of Liberty," he distinguished between negative and positive liberty, noncoercion and self-mastery, identifying the former with liberalism and the latter with political doctrines that evolved in antiliberal directions. "The fundamental sense of freedom," he declared, "is freedom from chains, from imprisonment, from enslavement by others. The rest is extension of this sense, or else metaphor."[10] So understood, freedom is negative because the prisoner need not have an affirmative conception of what he would do if unchained; he resists confinement as evil in itself, not only because it thwarts the achievement of this or that goal. In an essay on Hegel, Berlin insisted that "the essence of liberty has always lain in the ability to choose as you wish to choose, because you wish so to choose, uncoerced, unbullied, not swallowed up in some vast system. . . . That is true freedom, and without it there is neither freedom of any kind, nor even the illusion of it."[11]

Berlin was at pains to decouple the definition of negative liberty from actual desires an individual may have; to purge oneself of unattainable desires may conduce to greater happiness or security but not, he thought, to greater liberty. Freedom is not the absence of frustration, but rather the "absence of obstacles to *possible* choices and activities." The issue is not whether I wish to walk through a door, but whether it is open.[12] When the jailer unlocks the cell and tells the prisoner that he is free to go, he enjoys negative freedom, whether or not he wishes to leave. Berlin distinguished as well between the freedom to do something and the ability to do it. I lack the physical capacity to run a four-minute mile, but it would be absurd to say, on that account, that I am unfree to do so. I lack the material resources to stage a hostile takeover of a large corporation, but I am not unfree to do that either. Inability becomes unfreedom when it results from human arrangements that are designed to preclude, or have the foreseeable result of precluding, certain choices. (Whether poverty amounts to unfreedom depends on the best account of the causes of poverty in specific circumstances.)

Berlin was not entirely hostile to positive liberty, understood as self-mastery. He understood that inner subjection to desire, addiction, ignorance, delusion, or weakness of will could be experienced as a constraint – indeed, just as constraining as subjection to any external force. Berlin's fear was that any distinction between a higher and lower self, between the rational self

[10] Berlin, *Four Essays*, lvi.
[11] Isaiah Berlin, *Freedom and Its Betrayal: Six Enemies of Human Liberty*, ed. Henry Hardy (Princeton: Princeton University Press, 2003), 103–4.
[12] Berlin, *Four Essays*, xxxix.

and unreasoning desire, between true and false consciousness, would open the door for some groups to dominate others. Sympathetic critics have wondered whether this slippery slope points to a necessary relationship between concept and outcome, or rather to historical contingency. Positive liberty, they object, need not deny individualism or promote coercion. In addition, is it reasonable to describe persons in the grip of psychosis as "free," even if they have not been institutionalized? Human freedom tacitly includes some conception of normal human agency, which has internal as well as external preconditions.[13]

Berlin understood the force of these objections. In part, his thesis was empirical and political rather than conceptual or philosophical. The perversion of the notion of positive liberty into its opposite, he wrote, "has for a long while been one of the most familiar and depressing phenomena of our time. For whatever reason or cause, the notion of 'negative' liberty . . . has not historically been twisted by its theorists as often or effectively into anything so darkly metaphysical or socially sinister as its 'positive' counterpart." As a practical matter, then, it was more pressing to expose and oppose the aberrations of the latter.[14]

Yet Berlin's defense of negative liberty was more than tactical, because it went to the heart of his conception of humanity. As he wrote in a terse profession of faith,

The central thought of common thought and speech seems to me to be that freedom is the principal characteristic that distinguishes man from all that is non-human; that there are degrees of freedom, degrees constituted by the absence of obstacles to the exercise of choice; the choice being regarded as not itself determined by antecedent conditions, at least not as being wholly so determined. It may be that common sense is mistaken in this matter, as in others; but the onus of refutation is on those who disagree.[15]

However, it is suggestive that in this passage Berlin moves seamlessly from freedom as the absence of external obstacles to the exercise of choice to the choice itself as free in a more internal and metaphysical sense. Although he approvingly cited Hobbes and Bentham, he could not follow them all the way.

---

[13] Crowder, *Isaiah Berlin*, 84–6.
[14] Berlin, *Four Essays*, xlvii.
[15] Isaiah Berlin, "From Hope and Fear Set Free," in *The Proper Study of Mankind*, ed. Henry Hardy and Roger Hausheer (New York: Farrar, Straus and Giroux, 1998), 109.

By giving pride of place to negative liberty, Berlin aligned himself against communism and with the liberal tradition. Yet in other respects Berlin's liberalism was anything but orthodox. Liberalism is usually (and not unjustly) linked to the Enlightenment, and Berlin once declared that "fundamentally I am a liberal rationalist. The values of the Enlightenment... are deeply sympathetic to me."[16] However, he departed nonetheless from the Enlightenment in several crucial respects.

In the first place, as Avishai Margalit has observed, "though Berlin was a great believer in the morality of liberalism, he never trusted its psychology, especially not that which derived from the psychology of the Enlightenment, which he found downright silly."[17] He found the standard liberal psychology – self-interest trammeled by reason and a sense of justice – woefully inadequate. We must, he thought, bring psychological complexity – the passions and emotions, the evil and destructive side of human motives, even the unconscious – to bear on the theory and practice of politics.

Although Berlin was a staunch defender of individual liberty, he was uncomfortable as well about what he saw as the Enlightenment's excessive individualism. He thought that human beings have a natural desire to divide into affinity groups, and he cautioned against underestimating the force of the simple desire to belong. Group-oriented particularism, he argued, is not antithetical to liberalism. Far from being an oxymoron, "liberal nationalism" denotes a viable form of contemporary politics. Berlin was both a Zionist and a liberal, and he saw no necessary contradiction between them.

Nor could Berlin accept the ahistorical thrust of Enlightenment-based liberalism. Not only is history a powerful force in human affairs but it also partly constitutes what being human means in particular communities and epochs. This is not to say that human existence is historical through and through, but it is to caution against the easy belief that the aspect of our humanity that endures, unchanged, is more important than what is mutable.

Finally, Berlin spent decades arguing against the hopeful thesis, which many Enlightenment thinkers embraced, that the goods of human life are compatible with one another or tend to become so over time. The things that we value are plural and inharmonious, a brute fact that history is powerless to rectify. Liberalism is not, cannot be, about universal harmony. If the great liberal dream of "perpetual peace" is to be achieved, it is not

---

[16] Quoted in Crowder, *Isaiah Berlin*, 98.
[17] Avishai Margalit, "The Crooked Timber of Nationalism," in *The Legacy of Isaiah Berlin*, 151.

through the convergence of the human species on the same concepts and values, but rather through the effective management of enduring differences.

The belief in universal harmony was one aspect of what Berlin saw as the Enlightenment's excessive faith in the power of reason, which shaded over into a rationalism that could and often did undermine liberty, and equality and tolerance as well. If what is truly good for human beings can be known with certainty, then those who possess that knowledge can claim authority over those who do not. If the human good is everywhere and always the same, then moral truth and human diversity stand opposed, and truth-based authority may seek to repress the error that diversity represents. Although Enlightenment thinkers criticized what they regarded as the obscurantism of the Catholic Church, they were anything but united in opposition to secular political despotism. The famous *Encyclopédie* of Diderot and d'Alembert praised the rule of the mandarin class in China, and Voltaire bluntly stated the underlying rationale: "The people are cattle, and what they need is a yoke, a goad and fodder." It is fair to observe, as Mark Lilla does, that major Enlightenment figures such as Mendelssohn and Lessing advocated tolerance for other cultures and religions.[18] Nonetheless, Berlin was not wrong to discern a link between rationalism and the homogenizing use of political authority.

The sources of Berlin's heterodoxy

Berlin saw dangers to liberty, not only in dogmatic rationalism but also in the reaction – the Counter-Enlightenment – that it sparked, and he devoted decades to studying the leading representatives of that movement. In so doing, he exemplified the liberal mind at its best – open, undogmatic, willing to consider even the deepest challenges to one's beliefs and hopes. As Michael Ignatieff put it, "Berlin was the only liberal thinker of real consequence to take the trouble to enter the mental worlds of liberalism's sworn enemies."[19]

Of all the "enemies of human liberty," it was perhaps the Catholic monarchist Savoyard Joseph de Maistre who most influenced Berlin's political outlook. Maistre inveighed against the Enlightenment and what he took to be its logical consequence, the Great Terror into which the French Revolution had descended. The root of the disaster, he argued, was a blindly optimistic

---

[18] Mark Lilla, *The Legacy of Isaiah Berlin*, 68.
[19] Ignatieff, *Isaiah Berlin*, 249.

view of the human species. Human beings are neither rational nor good. On the contrary (Berlin's summary), "Man is by nature vicious, wicked, cowardly, and bad. What the Roman Church says, what Christianity says, about original guilt, original sin, is the truest psychological insight into human nature. Left alone, human beings will tear each other to pieces."[20] Humanity is not set apart from the rest of nature, which is the arena of ceaseless competition, brutality, and killing. Neither reason nor a voluntary social contract can protect human beings from one another, only authority backed by coercion – authority whose sources and claims cannot withstand rational scrutiny but which is nonetheless necessary and justified by the destructive irrationality that it restrains.

It is hard to imagine a starker antithesis to the tolerant civility Berlin preached and practiced. Nonetheless, Berlin prized Maistre as the prophet of, and guide to, the kinds of forces that will always threaten human liberty. The characteristic vice of liberalism is a shallow optimism, the belief that economic and social contrivances can eliminate, or permanently override, the darker aspects of our nature. A deeper and more sustainable liberalism must construct its domestic institutions and conduct its foreign relations with these harsher realities firmly in view. Liberal orders that do not understand this will be startled, perhaps overwhelmed, by new forms of antiliberalism. That is one reason why Berlin insisted that liberty needed its critics as well as its supporters and why the defenders of liberalism must study their adversaries even more carefully than their friends.

In Berlin's account of nineteenth-century intellectual history, the Counter-Enlightenment critique of reason laid the foundation for the Romantic movement and for nationalism. Romanticism emphasizes the power of the human will to create reality, especially the will of the rare creative genius. In turn, nationalism is the collective manifestation of the romantic will.[21] Individuals belong to particular and separate cultural groups, united by shared understandings and a common language, organized organically rather than mechanically. Nationalism not only provides a political home for these groups but also makes their freedom and unity supreme values. The nation becomes the primary focus of personal identification, its interests serve as the basis of moral justification, and its goals may be promoted by force. Despite the defeat of the most extreme manifestations of nationalism – Fascism and Nazism – during the twentieth century,

---

[20] Berlin, *Freedom and Its Betrayal*, 141.
[21] Crowder, *Isaiah Berlin*, 105–7.

nationalism persists as a long-term, perhaps permanent, feature of the human condition.

Nationalism makes most liberals uncomfortable, and for good reason. Liberalism tends toward universalism, prizes reason, and strives for peace; nationalism rests on particularism, promotes unreasonable group self-preference, and tends toward war. Berlin nonetheless saw no outright contradiction between liberalism and nationalism. He had some sympathy for Maistre's notorious denunciation of liberal universalism: "In the course of my life, I have seen Frenchmen, Italians, Russians. . . . But as for man, I declare that I have never met him in my life; if he exists, he is unknown to me."[22] Human beings gain identity through particularity; what we have in common does not define us, at least not fully enough so that we can recognize ourselves.

Understood organically, cultural groups can be antithetical to individual liberty, a fact of which Berlin was painfully aware. If individuals are conceived as "parts," it is natural to regard them as inferior in dignity to the "whole." Yet this conception pointed not to the intrinsic evil of cultural groupings, but rather to the need for political limits on the power of groups to coerce their members. As Michael Walzer suggests, Berlin advocated "liberal nationalism" as the best way of combining particular attachments and general principles in the political realm. This form of nationalism embodies a measure of equality and reciprocity, endorsing self-determination not only for one's own group but for others as well. It is no more oxymoronic than are parents who wish the best for their children while accepting a framework of common rules for grading and college admissions.[23]

For both Walzer and Berlin, liberals who seek to expunge group attachments from politics are doomed to disappointment because these attachments are deeply rooted in our moral emotions. We all want a sense of belonging and a place (like "home") where we are accepted for what we are. More than that, we all want self-determination and an end to the sense of humiliation that living under another's boot evokes. We all want to feel normal and live normally, which in modernity requires state structures that express cultural identities or at least allow for such expression. Berlin's lifelong Zionism reflected these emotions and expressed his conviction that within limits they were both honorable and conducive to human flourishing.

[22] Quoted in Berlin, *Freedom and Its Betrayal*, 144.
[23] Michael Walzer, "Liberalism, Nationalism, Reform," in *The Legacy of Isaiah Berlin*; also Crowder, *Isaiah Berlin*, 41.

It was from Johann Gottfried Herder, above all, that Berlin derived his understanding of cultural identity and its importance. Summarizing Herder, Berlin declared that the right life for human beings is to live in "natural units" constituted by common cultures whose language expresses the group's collective experience.[24] To imitate other cultures is to live artificially, unnaturally. Each culture has its own center of gravity, its own principles and norms; each has its own unique merits; each must be judged in its own terms, not those of other cultures. We should not grade cultures, but rather understand and celebrate each one as a distinctive manifestation of the human spirit.

Berlin's emphasis on cultural diversity was rooted not only in the thought of Counter-Enlightenment figures such as Herder but also in his study of Giambattista Vico, the eccentric eighteenth-century Neapolitan writer whose reputation Berlin did much to revive. Vico revolted against Descartes' belief in the unity of scientific method, which he argued was inapplicable outside a limited sphere. The natural sciences could describe mechanical phenomena clearly and precisely, from the "outside." Yet the human sciences required us to understand their subject matter from the inside, because human conduct is intentional and purposive. Entering imaginatively into the interior lives of others is essential. To do this, we must learn how to interpret linguistic and cultural signs. In addition, we must not assume that others are just like us beneath the skin. Human beings think and act differently in different historical epochs, and we cannot hope to understand them unless we take history seriously. History is not a tale told by an idiot, full of sound and fury, signifying nothing. Rather, as Berlin put it, Vico conceived of history as "stages in the pursuit of an intelligible purpose – man's effort to understand himself and his world, to realize his capacities in it."[25] The nature and capacities of the human species must be understood genetically as well as statically, and what changes from one epoch to the next is at least as important as what does not.

Through Berlin's interpretation, which has not gone undisputed, Vico becomes the forerunner of the progressive historicism of Hegel and Marx. Yet Berlin did not accept the idea of progress, and he did not see history as teleological. In this respect, he opted for Herder's nonprogressive pluralism. Herder emphasized not the superiority of later over earlier epochs,

---

[24] Isaiah Berlin, *Three Critics of the Enlightenment: Vico, Hamann, Herder*, ed. Henry Hardy (Princeton: Princeton University Press, 2000), 186.
[25] Ibid., 55.

but rather cultural variety, and his understanding of culture was organic rather than mechanical. Each culture is an ensemble of beliefs and practices in complex relation to one another, balanced against one another like a Calder mobile. We cannot construct our individual plans of life by breaking different cultures into their atomic parts and engaging in existential *bricolage*. However much we may admire Achilles, the Homeric virtues are inextricably linked to the brutality of a warrior society. Plutarch's *Lives* may move us, but even George Washington, America's greatest public classicist, had to refract the Roman virtues through the prism of an individualist and egalitarian society.

Value pluralism

Berlin's determination to understand cultures and their characteristic thinkers on their own terms has given rise to the suspicion that he was a relativist. He was not. He distinguished between pluralism, which he espoused, and relativism, which he repudiated. The grounds on which he did so were varied, complex, and sometimes opaque. To follow his thought in this matter, I must now lay out his theory of value pluralism, one of the contributions to modern moral and political thought for which he is best known.

Berlin argued against what he called moral monism – the view that "all ethical questions have a single correct answer, and that all these answers can be derived from a single coherent moral system."[26] His opposition was in part practical: He was convinced that monistic claims had helped bolster modern tyrannies. It was in part historical, derived from his study of different cultures and thinkers, above all Machiavelli. It was also empirical. He insisted that ordinary experience reveals the reality of deep moral conflicts rooted not in confusion but rather in the clash of worthy goods, and he refused to sacrifice the phenomena of moral life to the demands of theoretical coherence.

Berlin denied that there is a single highest value, that there is a single metric by which all values can be ranked, and that the many goods and principles we regard as worthy form a harmonious whole. Berlin was no subjectivist in moral matters; he believed that fundamental values spoke to objective features of the human species and the circumstances in which we are placed. Yet the things we rightly value are multiple, incommensurable,

---

[26] Crowder, *Isaiah Berlin*, 127.

and in conflict with one another. In practice (and often in theory), to realize one value is to subordinate another. And this is true not just in individual lives: Cultures and moral codes constitute clashing ensembles of goods and principles. Pagan antiquity represented one moral outlook, Christianity another. There is much to be said for magnanimous pride and also for reverent humility, for an ethics that gives pride of place to citizenship and for one that focuses on the well-being of the soul. However, they cannot be made to cohere with one another; we must choose between them.

This necessity has led some interpreters to regard Berlin as an existentialist, advocating (or at least resigned to) radical ungrounded choice, the moral equivalent of a leap of faith. Although Berlin offers some verbal ammunition for this view, it seems inconsistent with the main thrust of his thought. At various junctures he gestures toward a form of moral particularism. Even if we cannot choose among abstract moral concepts, we can make reasoned choices among goods and principles in particular circumstances when we are well acquainted with the facts of the case. In context, reasonable observers open to fact and argument will be able to agree that one option sacrifices too much along one dimension of value compared to what is gained along another and that the alternative course of action represents a better balance among competing but worthy claims.

Still, there are countervailing currents in Berlin's moral theory. At various points he invokes the language of human dignity, inviolable rights, and minimal freedoms that we must not trade off against other goods. There is, he insisted, a common human horizon of basic categories in terms of which we understand human experience and the human species. It is these categories that enable us to communicate, however imperfectly, across lines of cultural difference and also to render moral judgments. Indeed, Berlin insisted, the possibility of human understanding, communication, and judgment "depends upon the existence of some common values, and not on a common 'factual' world alone." There is empirical madness, and also moral madness: "Those who are out of touch with the external world are described as abnormal, and, in extreme cases, insane. But so also – and this is the point – are those who wander too far from the common public world of values.... Acceptance of common values (at any rate some irreducible minimum of them) enters into our conception of a normal human being."[27] This is the commonsense core of doctrines of natural law and universal rights, and the reason why we speak with confidence of the

---

[27] Berlin, *Four Essays on Liberty*, xxxi.

summum malum – the great evils of the human condition – even though we cannot specify a universally binding *summum bonum*. We need not be able to rank human communities and cultures from top to bottom to reach the judgment that Hitler's Germany was beyond the human pale.

We might then depict Berlin's view of the moral universe as an indistinct space divided by a horizontal line – universality below the line, pluralism above. If so, the real argument concerns the location of the line. Berlin does not seem to have regarded forms of government as falling below the line. For example, he could imagine relatively decent and rights-regarding autocracies, as well as populist democracies that systematically invade the private sphere.[28] Similarly, although liberty and decency require an economic minimum, they do not dictate socialism or even social democracy. (Berlin's own inclinations were moderately center-left; Ignatieff characterizes him – plausibly – as a liberal social democrat.) In Berlin's view, the matters reserved, not to theory but to individual or collective choice, were those that defined the key differences among human beings and communities – a zone of indeterminacy wide enough to rule out most forms of paternalism and cultural condescension without placing manifest evil beyond the scope of moral condemnation.

Berlin's value pluralism has come in for its share of criticism. Proponents of monistic moral theories – Kantian, utilitarian, and others – are not persuaded that rigor and coherence should yield to moral intuitions, however strongly felt. Although regret may be the emotional concomitant of much moral choice, it is not ipso facto "rational." Ronald Dworkin argues that Berlin was too quick to diagnose a clash of basic values: Before we conclude that liberty and equality conflict, we should do our best to construct the most attractive conceptions of those values, a process in which integrity among values is itself a value.[29] Bernard Williams retorts on Berlin's behalf that not all moral (or legal) questions have single right answers and that recognizing this fact helps us take politics seriously as the best way of dealing with pluralism and also of treating our fellow citizens with respect as the bearers of views different from, but not necessarily inferior to, our own.[30] It is always sensible, Charles Taylor suggests, to look for ways to relax the tension among basic goods or at least to achieve tradeoffs and balance among them at a higher level.[31] Berlin would have regarded this

[28] Ibid., lvii.
[29] Ronald Dworkin, "Do Liberal Values Conflict?" in *The Legacy of Isaiah Berlin*, 126–7, 132.
[30] Bernard Williams, "Liberalism and Loss," in *The Legacy of Isaiah Berlin*, 102.
[31] Charles Taylor, "Plurality of Goods," in *The Legacy of Isaiah Berlin*, 118.

suggestion, I believe, as a friendly amendment, but easier to state in theory than to realize in practice.

Berlin was a value pluralist in morals and a liberal in politics, a conjunction that has given rise to a burgeoning literature. At one end of the continuum stands John Gray, who argues that Berlin's pluralism rules out liberalism as a universally valid account of political ideals; liberalism is at most one among many acceptable political options, the choiceworthiness of which depends on local circumstances rather than on general features of morality or human existence.[32] At the other end is George Crowder, who argues that Berlin's pluralism leads not just to liberalism but also to Enlightenment liberalism that gives pride of place to the value of personal autonomy.[33] My own view is that value pluralism functions as a principle of estoppel in moral and political argument, defeating claims that one way of life above the line is unequivocally preferable to others above the line, and that the space for individual and political choice remaining once we have ruled out such claims is roughly congruent with the liberty that liberalism seeks to defend.[34] This argument is unlikely to end any time soon, but for those theorists and citizens who regard pluralist morality and liberal politics as the most plausible points of departure, it is an important and inescapable zone of contention.[35]

Conclusion: Berlin's enduring contribution to moral and political thought

Although much of what made Berlin so distinctive was rooted in his personal biography and circumstances, he made contributions to moral and political thought that future scholars are likely to ponder, and some to emulate. His characteristic mode of analysis fused history and philosophy, at once making history philosophical and philosophy historical. His lively sense of time and place never overrode the larger significance of the great minds whose thought he traced. He exercised to a remarkable degree what one of

---

[32] John Gray, *Isaiah Berlin* (Princeton: Princeton University Press, 1996), chap. 6.

[33] Crowder, *Isaiah Berlin*, chap. 6; and Crowder, *Liberalism and Value Pluralism* (London: Continuum, 2002), part 3.

[34] William A. Galston, *Liberal Pluralism* (New York: Cambridge University Press, 2002), chap. 5.

[35] For a parallel controversy concerning the relation between value pluralism and the truth claims of religion, see William A. Galston, "Must Value Pluralism and Religious Belief Collide?"; Michael Jinkins, "Pluralism and Religious Faith"; and Henry Hardy, "Taking Pluralism Seriously," all in *The One and the Many: Reading Isaiah Berlin*, ed. George Crowder and Henry Hardy (Amherst, NY: Prometheus Books, 2007).

his intellectual heroes, Giambattista Vico, called *fantasia* – the capacity for entering into and imaginatively reconstructing the thoughts of individuals very different from ourselves, living in cultures whose basic premises may seem odd and even repellent.

Turning from method to substance, Berlin's clarification of the differing dimensions of liberty and their practical consequences has often been criticized but never dismissed. His distinction between monism and pluralism retraces what Plato called the ancient quarrel between philosophy and poetry. Berlin dared to suggest that philosophical inquiry itself may vindicate the poetic focus on conflict and mystery rather than the "philosophical" presumption of harmony and intelligibility. And although the great totalitarian movements of the twentieth century have receded into history, Berlin showed why the totalitarian temptation is an enduring feature of the human mind. Judge Learned Hand once commented that "the spirit of liberty is the spirit which is not too sure that it is right." Berlin agreed, but with the caveat that living with uncertainty is difficult and uncomfortable, a hard-won achievement for both individuals and communities that we must never take for granted.

Suggestions for further reading

Berlin, Isaiah. *Four Essays on Liberty*. London: Oxford University Press, 1969.
———. *Freedom and Its Betrayal: Six Enemies of Human Liberty*. Edited by Henry Hardy. Princeton: Princeton University Press, 2003.
Crowder, George. *Isaiah Berlin: Liberty and Pluralism*. Cambridge: Polity, 2004.
Lilla, Mark, Ronald Dworkin, and Robert B. Silvers, eds. *The Legacy of Isaiah Berlin*. New York: New York Review of Books, 2001.

11

H. L. A. Hart: a twentieth-century Oxford political philosopher

JOHN M. FINNIS

Hart's life

Herbert Hart was born in 1907, a son of prosperous tailors in the north of England. From the age of eleven he went to boarding school in the south, but after some years was schooled close to home at an excellent grammar school where he finished as head prefect, regarded by the headmaster as a head boy of unsurpassed loyalty and capacity. By competitive scholarship examination he proceeded to New College, one of the University of Oxford's oldest and best colleges, where he studied Greek, Latin, ancient history, and philosophy, with brilliant success.

Passing the bar exams in late 1930, Hart joined commercial chambers in Lincoln's Inn where he practiced with notable success, especially in tax matters. Although he had joined the Inns of Court Regiment early in his career at the bar, and participated enthusiastically in stag hunting and like pursuits, his political views, always liberal, moved decisively left during the mid-1930s even before he became associated in 1936 with Jenifer Williams, who had been a member of the Communist Party since 1934. But, as she later wrote of Hart (whom she married in late 1941), "he was strongly opposed to communism both as theory and practice."[1]

In June 1940, Hart joined MI5, the intelligence organization dedicated to counterespionage in Britain. There he worked until the end of the war on counterespionage, the dissemination of disinformation to the enemy, and the processing of results of MI6's ultrasecret deciphering of the German codes; he was regarded within MI5 as outstandingly able, reliable, and acute, and he patriotically maintained the mandated secrecy about these activities down to the end of his life.

---

[1] Jenifer Hart, *Ask Me No More: An Autobiography* (London: Peter Halban, 1998), 72.

At war's end, Hart returned not to the bar but to New College, as a fellow and tutor in philosophy. It was hoped and expected that he would maintain the antiempiricist tradition of his Platonist tutor H. W. B. Joseph, but he soon gravitated to the modern-minded opposition, the circle of philosophers who under J. L. Austin's leadership pursued a way of thinking philosophically that Hart like others was content to call linguistic, or sometimes analytical. Still, in 1952, immediately before his election to the chair of Jurisprudence, he was lecturing on legal and political theories in Plato.

Hart's inaugural lecture in 1953 laid out an agenda for an analytical jurisprudence informed by linguistic philosophy, which he presented as practiced if not inaugurated by Jeremy Bentham. Nevertheless, as we shall see, his master work, *The Concept of Law* (1961), is not in its deep structure either linguistic or analytical. Nor does Hart's best-known book, *Law, Liberty and Morality* (1963), owe anything to fashions in philosophical methodology.

In 1968, the year his *Essays on Punishment and Responsibility* appeared and six years before retirement age, Hart left the chair of Jurisprudence and the university (though not the family house in central Oxford), feeling he had said all he had to say.[2] He worked for the next five years on editing and commenting in essay form on Bentham's accounts of law, rights, powers, and legal language, and he continued the quasi-governmental work he had begun in 1966 as a member of the Monopolies Commission. He returned formally to the university as Principal of Brasenose College, 1973–78, and thereafter until his death in December 1992 was granted a room for work in University College. A principal scholarly concern of his in these late years was preparing a response to some main critics of *The Concept of Law*; the fruits of this work – a response to his successor in the chair, Ronald Dworkin – appeared posthumously in 1994, edited by Hart's closest jurisprudential successor, Joseph Raz, as the postscript to that book's second edition.

Not long after his seventieth birthday, Hart wrote, "[L]oss of the belief that [moral judgment and argument] are backed by something more than human attitudes or policies is, and will continue to be, for many as profound as the loss of belief in God."[3] That he had rejected belief in God at some early stage of his life is clear from the exceedingly intimate (and philosophically informed) biography published in 2004.[4] In retrospect at least, everything suggests that he also lacked the other belief, that moral judgments can be

---

[2] Nicola Lacey, *A Life of H. L. A. Hart: The Nightmare and the Noble Dream* (Oxford: Oxford University Press, 2004), 289.

[3] H. L. A. Hart, "Morality and Reality," *New York Review of Books*, March 9, 1978, p. 35.

[4] Lacey, *A Life*.

really true. Yet his activities as a philosopher, teacher, mentor, colleague, and friend – like his performance of wartime duties in defense of his country, his fidelity to his family, and his devoted care for their disabled youngest child – amply display a morally demanding range of virtues.

The political philosophy in Hart's theory of law

Hart's significance can be understood only when his work is measured against conceptions of political philosophy that were dominant in Oxford in the years between his postwar return and the publication of *The Concept of Law*. Although these conceptions might be divided, like Hart's own philosophical formation, between the prelinguistic and the linguistic, they had much in common. As Eric Voegelin emphasizes in his mordant survey "The Oxford Political Philosophers,"[5] written in the summer of 1952, a contemporary prelinguistic Oxford political philosopher as methodologically informed and representative as A. D. Lindsay held that political theory transcends the description of institutions by being a study of the "operative ideals" which, as beliefs of citizens, sustain their respective states in existence. This conception makes political theory essentially a history of ideas, with some sorting, arranging, and axiomatizing in the mode (as Voegelin observes) of theology, which takes its principles not from philosophical considerations but as givens, *dogmata*. Lindsay's concession that there remains a question about the "absolute worth" of operative ideals is fleeting: "[T]he primary business of the political theorist" remains the understanding of *actually operative* ideals; "political theory, then, is concerned with fact."[6]

What then of the linguistic-philosophical approach becoming dominant in Oxford around 1950? It was approvingly summarized, toward the end of its dominance, by Anthony Quinton, in his introduction to a book of readings in political philosophy: the great works in political philosophy (or, synonymously, political thought or theory), from Plato and Aristotle to Marx and Mill, consist of (1) "factual or descriptive accounts of political institutions and activities" (political science), (2) "recommendations about the ideal ends that political activity should pursue and about the way political institutions should be designed in order to serve those ends" (ideology), and only to "a small, though commonly crucial extent" (3) "conceptual reasonings," the kind of reasonings now known to be the only properly

---

[5] Eric Voegelin, "The Oxford Political Philosophers," *Philosophical Quarterly* 3, no. 11 (1953): 108.
[6] A. D. Lindsay, *The Modern Democratic State* (Oxford: Oxford University Press, 1943), 45; cf. 37–8, 47.

philosophical activity, namely, "classifying and analyzing the terms, statements and arguments of the substantive, first-order disciplines" or modes of thought, which are "concerned with some aspect or region of the world" – unlike philosophy, which is "conceptual and critical, concerned with *them* [sc. those substantive, first-order modes of thought] rather than with the reality they investigate."[7]

What makes reasoning conceptual or analytical? How might such reasoning add anything to descriptions of the institutions found in historically given societies and "recommendations" of "ideals"? These questions are left in shadow by Quinton and indeed by the whole school of philosophers whose self-understanding Quinton was articulating. Hart too, while framing much of *The Concept of Law* in terms of "analysis" of "concepts," says little to make explicit what counts as conceptual or analytical or what counts as success in such analysis.[8] But what he proposed as the fruits of his philosophical work in that book, and the arguments deployed to yield them, together made clear that political philosophy could and can still be pursued in a way that is simply not envisaged in Quinton's triad (institutional description, ideological recommendation, conceptual analysis). Moreover, that way is continuous with main parts of the tradition of political philosophizing which the triad so mischaracterizes.

Hart's preface to *The Concept of Law* speaks of "the political philosophy of this book." This seems to point to two of the book's theses or themes. The first is *articulated* firmly in terms of analysis of concepts. Hart says that by "referring" to "manifestations" of "the internal point of view" – that is, "the view of those who do not merely record and predict behaviour conforming to rules, but *use* the rules as standards for the appraisal of their own and others' behaviour" – we can provide an "analysis" that dissipates "the obscurity which still lingers about [the concepts (which bestride both law and political theory) of the state, of authority, and of an official]." For though some manifestations of the internal point of view – those under "the simple regime of primary rules" – are "most elementary," the "range of what is said and done from the internal point of view is much

---

[7] A. M. Quinton, ed., *Political Philosophy*, Oxford Readings in Philosophy (London: Oxford University Press, 1967), 1.

[8] He quotes approvingly J. L. Austin, leader of the Oxford school of ordinary-language, "analytical" philosophy: "[A] sharpened awareness of words [can be used] to sharpen our perception of the phenomena" (H. L. A. Hart, *The Concept of Law*, 2nd ed. [Oxford: Oxford University Press, 1994], preface). Here "perception" is an evasive word for understanding, and "phenomena" for reality, or truths.

extended and diversified" with "the addition... of secondary rules," an addition that brings with it "a whole set of new concepts... legislation, jurisdiction, validity, and, generally, of legal powers, private and public." Thus "the combination of primary rules of obligation with the secondary rules of recognition, change and adjudication" is not only the heart of a legal system but also "a most powerful tool for the analysis of much that has puzzled both the jurist and the political theorist."[9]

What matters here is not the various technical problems that commentators have identified in details of this analysis.[10] Rather, it is the argumentation employed by Hart to show that the distinctions marked by his new technical terms – internal and external points of view, primary and secondary rules – are distinctions not just in legal thought or political theory but also in the social reality that he often prefers to call "social phenomena" – reality that, if it does not exist (as it does in our here and now), can in favorable circumstances be deliberately and reasonably brought into being, as state, law, legal system, courts, legislatures, and so forth. For Hart's argumentation asserts that alternative "general" accounts of law failed to recognize both the variety of ways in which rules of law *function* and, more fundamentally, the variety of *functions* served, or possessed, by social rules and legal systems and by the main components of legal systems.

Therefore the two fundamental ways in which rules function as guides to behavior are by imposing obligations and conferring powers. Yet if a theorist like Kelsen denies that this duality of normative functioning is fundamental, Hart refutes him by pointing to the different functions served by the two types of rule. *Obligation-imposing* rules guide both the uncooperative (by threatening them with sanctions) and those who are willing to cooperate if only they are told what is required of them.[11] *Power-conferring* rules, understood "from the point of view of those [private persons] who exercise them," confer on private citizens the "huge and distinctive amenity" of being "private legislator[s]," "made competent to determine the course of the law within the sphere of [their] contracts, trusts, wills, and other structures of rights and duties which [they are thereby] enabled to build." The introduction into society of rules conferring *public* powers such as legislative or judicial powers to make authoritative enactments and orders

---

[9] Hart, *Concept of Law*, 98–9.
[10] Thus, as Joseph Raz showed, not all secondary rules are power conferring, and not all power-conferring rules are secondary (Raz, "The Functions of Law," in *The Authority of Law* [Oxford: Oxford University Press, 1979], 178–9).
[11] Hart, *Concept of Law*, 39–40.

"is a *step forward* as important to society as the invention of the wheel."[12] The difference in normative types (ways of functioning) is grounded on the differences in social function – that is, on the different *reasons for valuing them* – which make exercise of powers "a form of *purposive activity* utterly different from performance of duty or submission to coercive control."[13]

Although Hart loyally continues to speak of this argumentation as "giv[ing] some . . . analysis of what is involved in the assertion that rules of these two types exist,"[14] it is clear that what is going on in his explanation of "the features of law," and in his claim that his explanation has superior "explanatory power," is not merely linguistic or conceptual.[15] Rather, it is an acknowledgment, or reminder, or disclosure of certain aspects of the human condition as it really is. His later reflections on the grounding of the concept(s) of "need and function" enable us to be more precise: In Hart's own self-understanding, appeals to function are "ways of *simultaneously describing and appraising* things by reference to the contribution they make"[16] to a "proper end of human activity."[17]

Hart articulates these later reflections in relation to the second of the two theses or themes he thought made a contribution to political philosophy: his discussion, in *The Concept of Law*'s chapter "Law and Morals," of what he calls "the minimum content of natural law."[18] The section bearing this title – which might equally well have been "The Minimum Content of Positive Law"[19] – argues vigorously, though with many signs of anxiety, that we should reject "the positivist thesis that 'law may have any content.'" Besides definitions of words and "ordinary statements of fact," there is "a third category of statements: those the truth of which is contingent on human beings and the world they live in retaining the salient characteristics which they have."[20] More precisely, such contingently *universal* truths include statements about what Hart calls "natural necessity," by which, in this precise context, he means the *rational* necessity yielded by the

---

[12] Ibid., 41–2 (emphasis added).
[13] Ibid., 41 (emphases added).
[14] Ibid., 81.
[15] Ibid.
[16] Ibid., 192.
[17] Ibid., 191 (emphasis added).
[18] Ibid., 193.
[19] For the conclusions it reaches at ibid., 199, concern the "indispensable features of municipal law." See also the phrase "what content a legal system must have" in H. L. A. Hart, "Positivism and the Separation of Law and Morals" (1958), in *Essays in Jurisprudence and Philosophy* (Oxford: Oxford University Press, 1983), 81.
[20] Hart, *Concept of Law*, 199–200.

conjunction of a universal human "aim" and various natural facts or "truisms"; such truisms include that human beings are approximately equal to each other in strength and vulnerability; are limited in their "altruism," understanding, and strength of will; and are subject to scarcity of resources and the need for a division of labor to exploit them.[21] Given the common or universal wish to continue in existence ("survive") and the truisms about vulnerability, "what reason demands is *voluntary* co-operation in a *coercive* system."[22]

Hart's anxiety about this head-on challenge, not only to Kelsenian legal positivism but also to the reigning assumptions (such as Quinton's or Lindsay's) about method in political philosophy, is manifested in the immediately preceding, preparatory pages. On the one hand, he shows here that even after Aristotelian principles of cosmology and physics have been expelled, we cannot sensibly talk about or adequately understand human beings without having a "teleological view." He instances, for example, our talk of natural "human *needs* which it is *good* to satisfy"[23] and of "the *functions* of bodily organs"[24] – all the talk that makes possible our talk of harm and injury. He sketches, albeit without unambiguous endorsement or repudiation, a more developed version of this teleology of human existence and nature: "a condition of biological maturity and developed physical powers" that "also includes, as its distinctively human element, a development and excellence of mind and character manifested in thought and conduct."[25]

On the other hand, just at this point he shrinks back, declaring that "what makes sense of this mode of thought and expression is . . . the tacit assumption that the proper end of human activity is survival, and this rests on the simple contingent fact that most men most of the time wish to continue in existence."[26] This drastically limited conception of "the proper end of human activity" he ascribes to Hobbes and Hume, whose "modest" or "humble" conception of human ends should be preferred to the "more complex and debatable" conceptions of Aristotle or Aquinas. Hart gives no sign, in this book, of noticing that survival is quite inadequate as an aim or end in accounting for the developed "excellences of mind and character."

[21] Ibid., 194–7.
[22] Ibid., 198.
[23] Ibid., 190 (Hart's emphases).
[24] Ibid., 191 (Hart's emphasis).
[25] Ibid., 190.
[26] Ibid., 191.

The inadequacy goes further, because the desire to survive does not begin to account for the fundamental elements in his concept of law: the secondary rules introduced (as his first theme or thesis made clear) to remedy the defects – the social problems – that plague a society governed only by "social morality's" prelegal "primary rules."

Hart soon tacitly acknowledged this inadequacy. Writing the following year about "social morality," not as temporally prelegal but as the standards acknowledged, over and above the law, even in legally ordered societies, he articulated universal values, virtues, and standards, still on a purportedly Hobbesian basis but now with an adjusted rationale:

[A]ll social moralities... make provision in some degree for such universal values as individual freedom, safety of life, and protection from deliberately inflicted harm.... Secondly, ... the spirit or attitude which characterizes the practice of a social morality is something of very great value and indeed quite vital for men to foster and preserve in any society. For in the practice of any social morality there are necessarily involved what may be called *formal* values as distinct from the *material* values of its particular rules or content. In moral relationships with others the individual sees questions of conduct from an impersonal point of view and applies general rules impartially to himself and to others; he is made aware of and takes account of the wants, expectations, and reactions of others; he exerts self-discipline and control in adapting his conduct to a system of reciprocal claims. These are universal virtues and indeed constitute the specifically moral attitude to conduct.... We have only to conduct the Hobbesian experiment of imagining these virtues totally absent to see that they are vital for the conduct of any cooperative form of human life and any successful personal life.[27]

Cooperation and social rules therefore have a rationale going well beyond survival: a successful personal life. John Rawls in *A Theory of Justice* (1971) elaborates that kind of rationale in the "thin theory of the good" – the range of "primary goods" that are good for each one of us because they are needed, "*whatever else one wants.*"[28] Hart himself had said a little more about his adjusted rationale in 1967: If law "is to be of any value as an instrument for the realization of human purposes, it must contain rules concerning the basic conditions of social life.... Without the protections and advantages that such rules supply, men would be grossly hampered in the pursuit of any aims."[29] Such rules are provided for by social morality, but only in ways that "leave open to dispute too many questions concerning the precise

---

[27] H. L. A. Hart, *Law, Liberty and Morality* (London: Oxford University Press, 1963), 70–1.
[28] John Rawls, *A Theory of Justice* (Cambridge, MA: Harvard University Press, 1971), 396–407, 433–4.
[29] H. L. A. Hart, "Problems of the Philosophy of Law" (1967), in *Essays in Jurisprudence and Philosophy*, 112.

scope and form of its restraints." Hence the human need for law, for a legal system that performs functions of the type indicated in the first theme of Hart's account: the union of primary (mostly duty-imposing) and secondary (mostly power-conferring) rules.[30]

Both Hart and Rawls thus broke the bounds of political philosophy as conceived by many in their philosophical circle. They went beyond describing institutions and beyond generalizations about historically given institutions, to offer not recommendations of ideals, but sober accounts of what human persons and groups *need* and *rationally* desire, and of states of affairs and arrangements that are *universally* valuable (good) for beings with the nature we have. To that extent they rejoined the enterprise launched by Plato and Aristotle, though professing to admit only what would be admitted by a Hobbes who openly derided the "old moral philosophers" for their talk of what is intrinsically and most completely and constitutively good for human persons.[31]

There is truth in John Gardner's remark that Hart and Rawls (with some others unnamed) "together revived political philosophy (and helped to shape as well as capture the distinctive liberalism of the 1960s) by asserting political philosophy's relative autonomy from the rest of moral philosophy."[32] Insofar as Hart's political philosophy was embedded in a philosophy of law, one might say more precisely that his attempt was to do political philosophy even if there is *no* moral philosophy. Still, Hart's late-period work also shows the extent to which he was willing to admit, at least by implication, that the asserted autonomy of political from moral philosophy was unsustainable. For against Rawls, Mill, Nozick, and Dworkin, he objected that attempts to ground *basic individual rights or liberties* on arguments of utility, or on the separateness of persons or their claims to equal respect, or on hypothesized choices by self-interested but partially ignorant parties in an original position are all foredoomed: "[A] theory of basic individual rights must rest on a specific conception of the human person and of what is needed for the exercise and development of distinctive human powers."[33] And such a theory of rights "is urgently called for."[34]

---

[30] Ibid., 114.
[31] Hobbes, *Leviathan*, chap. 11.
[32] John Gardner, introduction to *Punishment and Responsibility: Essays in the Philosophy of Law*, by H. L. A. Hart, 2nd ed. (Oxford: Oxford University Press, 2008), xlviii–xlix.
[33] Hart, introduction to *Essays in Jurisprudence and Philosophy*, 17.
[34] Hart, "Utilitarianism and Natural Rights" (1979), in *Essays in Jurisprudence and Philosophy*, 196. This double-edged formula hints at Hart's deep skepticism about our capacity to make rational judgments (or "theories") about such matters.

Hart's liberalism

Hart's biographer says, credibly, that *Law, Liberty and Morality* (1963) "stands, over 40 years after its publication, as the resounding late twentieth-century statement of principled liberal social policy. Its ideas continue to echo in both political and intellectual debates."[35] Its key thesis she identifies accurately enough: "[D]emocratic states are not entitled to enforce moral standards for their own sake: the mere belief that, say, certain kinds of sexual activity are immoral is not enough to justify their prohibition."[36] She remains as innocent as Hart of the profound ambiguities that make his book's resounding success in shaping debate and policy a dismaying triumph of confusion and error.

Law, Liberty and Morality opens with a misstatement of English law, an error that points directly to the entire book's misidentification of the political-philosophical issues at stake:

The Suicide Act 1961, though it may directly affect the lives of few people, is something of a landmark in our legal history. It is the first Act of Parliament for at least a century to *remove altogether* the penalties of the criminal law from a *practice* both clearly condemned by conventional Christian morality and punishable by law.[37]

But though the individual, private act of committing or attempting to commit suicide ceased to be a crime, the 1961 statute rigorously confirmed, indeed strengthened, the criminal law's penalties and prohibitions *against any social* practice *of suicide* – against any and every kind of public assistance, advice, promotion, or facilitation of it.[38]

Hart went on:

Many hope that the Suicide Act may be followed by further measures of reform, and that certain forms of abortion, homosexual behaviour between consenting adults in private, and certain forms of euthanasia will cease to be criminal offences; for they think that here, as in the case of suicide, the misery caused directly and indirectly by legal punishment outweighs any conceivable harm these practices may do.[39]

---

[35] Lacey, *A Life*, 7.

[36] Ibid., 6–7.

[37] Hart, *Law, Liberty and Morality*, preface (emphases added). This prefatory page, like its successor in 1981 (see n. 41), is not included in the American editions.

[38] Suicide Act 1961, s. 2, imposes imprisonment for up to fourteen years for any counseling (advising), procuring, or assisting in advance of or in the act of suicide; and any attempt to provide such advice or assistance is a serious offense under the general law of criminal attempts.

[39] Hart, *Law, Liberty and Morality*, preface.

In all these matters, the structure of the issue at stake was fundamentally the same and was wholly overlooked by Hart. The issue was and is as follows: Supposing that the truly *private acts* of an adult individual or set of consenting adults should and/or did cease to be criminal offenses, what should be the policy of the law and of society's other governing institutions (e.g., public education) in relation to the *public promotion or facilitation* of such acts? After all, in many states outside the Anglo-American world a sharp distinction of principle was and is drawn between *private* and *public*, a distinction well grounded in the philosophical-theological tradition.

However, these serious deficiencies in Hart's handling of the legal issues are overshadowed by his mishandling of his principal theoretical topic, the idea of *enforcing morality as such*. "Is the fact that certain conduct is by common standards immoral sufficient to justify making that conduct punishable by law? Is it morally permissible to enforce morality as such? Ought immorality as such to be a crime? To this question..."[40] Here we should interject. The tradition of political philosophy flowing from Plato and Aristotle would have answered as follows: "This question" is not one, but at least two. For the fact that conduct is "by common standards immoral" is never sufficient justification for punishing it; common moral standards notoriously may be more or less immoral. And if "morality as such" means, as Hart presumes, the same as common moral standards qua common, the same reply applies. Yet if "(im)morality as such" refers (as it should) to what critical morality rightly judges (im)moral, then the tradition divides between (a) the Platonist-Aristotelian stream that "paternalistically" authorizes penalizing immoral acts for the sake of the character of those who do or would otherwise engage in them and (b) the Thomist tradition authorizing penalization only when the act has a public character and jeopardizes public order or public morality or the rights of others.

Hart, alas, did not envisage either of those responses,[41] but plunged off in another direction, suggested to him by the ruminations of an English judge

---

[40] Ibid., 4.

[41] In 1967, revisiting the debate, Hart begins by reporting (at last) what he calls "the classical position," corresponding to the Platonist-Aristotelian as sketched earlier; he ignores the Thomist position and says he will have nothing to say about the classical. (The same paragraph confirms his unawareness of the mainstream Christian [and Thomist] position that the strict requirements of revealed morality are *also* natural – that is, accessible – under favorable epistemic conditions, by reason unaided by revelation.) See Hart, "Social Solidarity and the Enforcement of Morality," in *Essays in Jurisprudence and Philosophy*, 248. See also section 3 of Hart's preface to the 1981 reprint of *Law, Liberty and Morality* (Oxford: Oxford University Press, 1981), ix–x, confirming that in the second and third of his three versions of the question, he was and is speaking of "morality as such" (and "immorality as such") as judged "by common standards," that is, of positive not critical morality.

of no philosophic formation, Patrick Devlin. Having pointed to the pertinent distinction between critical and positive morality, Hart summarized the question his book tackles: "[O]ur question is one of critical morality about the legal enforcement of positive morality."[42] That was indeed Devlin's artless question. Yet it was a question that no one ought to take very seriously,[43] because when one is deliberating about the moral and the immoral, "positive morality" is never determinative. Positive morality, as such, is nothing other than the set of opinions held, in fact, by a group of persons concerning right and wrong actions, dispositions, and so forth. Such opinions, as facts about that group's beliefs, can never settle for the deliberating person what he or she *should* judge to be right or wrong.

In Hart's own terminology, the central case of morality understood from *the internal point of view* is *critical*, that is, justified, morality.[44] Conscientiously deliberating persons are deliberating about what they should count as *reasons* for action, and the bare fact that others count something a reason does not make it a reason (although it may be persuasive as ground for some evidentiary presumption that those other persons have some good reason for their belief). Indeed, one is scarcely thinking morally unless one considers that one's deliberated judgment could be morally right even if no one else now agrees with it.

Hart's exclusive focus on positive morality cut the debate off from the main political-philosophic tradition, and from reason. It generated a casual presumption that those who uphold a group's morality have no moral reasons for doing so or that no one need inquire what those moral reasons might

---

[42] Hart, *Law, Liberty and Morality*, 20.

[43] I am setting aside, as secondary, unfruitfully vague, and lacking in evidence, the question (one of fact) debated by Hart and Devlin: Will the noncriminalization of strongly held moral opinions lead people who hold them to crumble in their allegiance to society and/or their own morality?

[44] Note that in *Concept of Law*'s set-piece discussion (168–84) of morality, Hart was clearly failing to grasp that even the adherents to a widely or universally accepted morality will each, at least in the central case, be adhering to it not because the others do but because they each consider it right, that is, consider it justified by its successful articulation of the requirements of the well-being, dignity, honor, excellence, etc., of persons and groups. This serious failure in Hart's analysis was pointed out by Ronald Dworkin in 1972, who described what I have called the critical internal point of view in such a case as a "consensus of *independent conviction*" (as opposed to a consensus of convention, in which the general conformity of the group is counted by the individual members as the, or a, reason for their acceptance of it) (Dworkin, "The Model of Rules II," in *Taking Rights Seriously* [Cambridge, MA: Harvard University Press, 1972], 53). In the posthumously published postscript to *The Concept of Law*, Hart conceded all this, admitting that the book had not provided "a sound explanation of morality, either individual or social" (*Concept of Law*, 255–6). He had in fact been aware of this error, which he recognized as "large," since 1980 at the latest; see Lacey, *A Life*, 335–6.

be.[45] This pernicious presumption has a first manifestation in Hart's never examined assumptions that "deviations from conventional sexual morality such as homosexuality afford the clearest examples of offences which do not harm others"[46] and that "sexual morals [are obviously] determined... by variable tastes and conventions."[47] But – to take up the issue on which Hart chose to focus – those who actually judge homosexual acts, *like other nonmarital sex acts*, immoral, although they might grant that the private homosexual sex acts of two already morally corrupt adults in private do no harm, can argue with force that predisposing children to approve of adult homosexual sex acts, and to be disposed to engage in them when of age, is gravely and unjustly harmful to the child and to society; it is harmful because it involves the child and eventually perhaps society in a gross misunderstanding of the contribution sex acts have to make – and of the act-descriptive conditions without which such acts cannot make that contribution – to marriage as the indubitably most favorable and fairest milieu for the procreation and upbringing of children and for the lifelong fulfillment of the married persons themselves.[48]

Hart and skepticism

If the misconceived and sterile "Hart-Devlin debate" and Hart's plausible success in it had a large and long-lasting social impact, that would suggest a decay going wider than just in the practice of political philosophy.[49]

---

[45] The recent counterpart to this resultant of Hart's mistake is Dworkin's: Ronald Dworkin, *A Matter of Principle* (Cambridge, MA: Harvard University Press, 1985), 67–8, 368.

[46] Hart, *Law, Liberty and Morality*, preface.

[47] Ibid., 73.

[48] See John Finnis, *Philosophy of Law* (Oxford: Oxford University Press, 2011), 135–8; John Finnis, *Human Rights and Common Good* (Oxford: Oxford University Press, 2011), 317–33.

[49] The climax of the lectures on knowledge and the Good in Plato's *Republic*, given in Hart's first years as a student by his tutor and friend H. W. B. Joseph and published, without comment or commentary, by Hart in 1948, is Joseph's conclusion about the point of the allegory of the Cave (*Rep.* 514a–517a): that what we need is not just intellectual formation from inevitable ignorance, but conversion "from a plight into which we ought not to have come" but have come through the "evil training" of social institutions; although leaving people free to develop "naturally," without such institutions, would only allow other pressures to distort and block sound judgment, it is in fact "the pressure of lies that acts on us in States as they now are; and only by a hard struggle can a man reach, and only in the face of obloquy and opposition from those whom it disturbs can he teach, the truth" (H. W. B. Joseph, *Knowledge and the Good in Plato's "Republic,"* ed. H. L. A. Hart [Oxford: Oxford University Press, 1948], 43–4). It was not Hart's fate to have to face much obloquy on account of his teaching about critical morality's exclusions and requirements in politics and law; in fact, his teaching found prompt favor and recognition from the mid-1960s Labour government that superintended the liberalization of laws on pornography, abortion, homosexual acts, and divorce (Lacey, *A Life*, 274).

European states in the early twenty-first century move ever more clearly out of the social and political conditions of the 1960s into a trajectory of demographic and cultural decay; circumscription of political, religious, and educational speech and associated freedoms; pervasive untruthfulness about equality and diversity; population transfer and replacement by a kind of reverse colonization; and resultant internal fissiparation foreshadowing, it seems, ethnic and religious intercommunal miseries of hatred, bloodshed, and political paralysis reminiscent of late twentieth-century Yugoslavia or the Levant. Therefore the time seems ripe for a wider reflection on late twentieth-century political philosophies so characteristic, so suasive, so victorious, as Hart's.

That Hart had a political philosophy at all was an act of conscious resistance to skepticism. This resistance extended beyond the setting aside of methodological skepticism such as Quinton representatively articulated. It was particularly evident in Hart's repudiation of twentieth-century behaviorist reductionism, whether that took the form of Scandinavian or American legal "realism," reducing the normative to the predictive or magical or diagnostic; or of Hobbesian or Austinian accounts of choice and action as mere predominant desire and muscular contraction; or of mid-twentieth-century criminological/penological theories denying responsibility by treating human behavior as merely a more or less predictable cause of preventable harm.[50]

Yet the resistance was itself shaped and limited by Hart's own skepticism about something more foundational: the truth-value, and truth, of moral judgments intended as critical because asserted as true, sound, really justified. Only very late in his career did Hart allow himself to affirm in print this deep-going doubt.[51] But a determining consideration throughout *The Concept of Law* was that neither author nor reader, in taking a stand on issues in political or legal philosophy, need make any judgment about whether there are any "true principles of right conduct rationally discoverable"[52] or whether instead moral judgments are but "expressions of changing human attitudes, choices, demands, or feelings."[53] In that book, the explicit attempt

---

[50] So "skepticism" or its cognates appear as denoting an antagonist in almost all the nine essays in *Punishment and Responsibility*.

[51] See note 3, and H. L. A. Hart, "Who Can Tell Right from Wrong?" *New York Review of Books*, July 17, 1986, pp. 50–2.

[52] Hart, *Concept of Law*, 186.

[53] Ibid., 168.

to "evade these philosophical difficulties"[54] drives the reduction of law's rationale to survival, the later repudiated assimilation of moral judgment to articulation of positive ("consensus of convention") morality, and the pervasive refusal to identify a central case of the internal point of view.

In the discourse about the proper limits of the criminal law, the skepticism about morality is surely one primary motivation for the falling away from the level of Plato, Aristotle, and Mill to the essentially unphilosophical and irrelevant dialectic with Devlin. The popular success of that dialectic is a measure of the widespread loss of philosophical culture in the 104 years between *On Liberty* and *Law, Liberty and Morality*. For the first chapter of Mill's book makes the truly foundational issues explicit. It does so by its combined contentions (1) that state coercion may well be justifiable in the interests of the improvement of immature individuals or societies or to protect a state where relaxation of "the mental discipline" of any citizens might result in the overthrow of the state by "foreign attack or internal commotion" and (2) that the "salutary... effects of freedom" in accomplishing the necessary minimum of improvement in or of modern societies are "permanent" effects, so that the qualifications on the "principle of liberty" that were articulated in the first of those contentions can now, with us, be simply set aside. Hart criticized *On Liberty* for relying on a presumption of "middle-aged" psychological caution and stability to justify rejecting paternalism in relation even to uncontroversial harms.[55] Yet he, and with him the whole extensive academic and popular discourse he inspired, left unexamined the much more deep-going and far-reaching issues raised by each of those Millian contentions.[56]

---

[54] Ibid.

[55] Hart, *Law, Liberty and Morality*, 33. Hart accordingly accepted a limited measure of paternalism in relation to more or less physical or psychosomatic harms.

[56] See further John Finnis, "Hart as a Political Philosopher," in *Philosophy of Law*, 276–9.

12

John Rawls and the task of political philosophy

PAUL WEITHMAN

John Rawls was born on February 21, 1921. This makes him considerably younger than most of the thinkers treated in this volume, who were born around the turn of the twentieth century or well before that. Rawls was born almost forty years after Carl Schmitt (b. 1888) and more than sixty years after John Dewey (b. 1859). The year Rawls was born, Isaiah Berlin turned twelve and fled Russia with his family to settle in England. Of the eighteen thinkers commemorated here, only five others – Michel Foucault (b. 1926), Alasdair MacIntyre (b. 1929), Jürgen Habermas (b. 1929), Charles Taylor (b. 1931), and Richard Rorty (b. 1931) – were of roughly Rawls's generation.

Generational divides are not all that puts Rawls in the minority in this volume. But for Dewey and Rorty, he is the only American by birth. With the qualified exceptions of Dewey[1] and Rorty,[2] he is the only one whose thought emerged from a formation in liberal Protestantism. Although Dewey wrote his dissertation on Kant and there are obviously Kantian themes in Habermas's work, Rawls is the most Kantian of the thinkers treated here. Like Taylor and MacIntyre, and unlike most of the others, Rawls's intellectual roots run through the Oxford of the mid-twentieth century (where Rawls spent a critical year with Berlin and Hart). More

I am grateful to Catherine Zuckert and Robert Adams for helpful comments on an earlier draft.

[1] The qualification is that although Dewey was raised in a liberal Protestant household, he does not seem to have made the study of Protestant theology that Rawls did, and his work does not show the result of engagement with its theological doctrines. On Dewey's religious upbringing, see Robert Westbrook, *John Dewey and American Democracy* (Ithaca, NY: Cornell University Press, 1991), 6, 22. For Rawls's study of Protestant theology, see Robert Adams, "The Theological Ethics of the Young Rawls and Its Background," in *A Brief Inquiry into the Meaning of Sin and Faith*, by John Rawls, ed. Joshua Cohen and Thomas Nagel (Cambridge, MA: Harvard University Press, 2009), 24–101.

[2] Rorty was the grandson of the Protestant ethicist Walter Rauschenbusch. I group Rorty with the qualified exceptions because he was not raised in the theological traditions of his grandfather.

than anyone else discussed in this volume, Rawls found the techniques, the rigor, and the inherited problematics of analytic philosophy congenial. He was considerably more sympathetic to utopian political thinking than most others, asking what an ideally just liberal democracy would be like. He developed a systematic philosophical theory to answer that question.

In this chapter I say nothing about Rawls's formation in liberal Protestantism, although I do believe there are interesting connections between this formation and the views on which Rawls later relied in *Theory of Justice*. Some of the other distinguishing features I just cited are obviously connected. Rawls's affinity for analytic philosophy is no doubt part of what led him to Berlin, Hart, and Oxford in the 1950s – where, Berlin later claimed, Oxford-style analytic philosophy began in his rooms.[3] Less obviously, Rawls's Kantianism is connected – in ways I explain later – to his modest utopianism, or his ideal theorizing.

The least important of the differences between Rawls and the majority of the figures commemorated here may be the generational and geographic ones. Strauss, Voegelin, Hayek, Simon, and Arendt were all refugees – as was Berlin, albeit at an earlier time and from a different foe. Habermas came of age in early postwar Germany. Yet Rawls, too, was profoundly affected by the rise of Nazism and World War II. Understanding how these events affected him is important to understanding how he saw his task as a philosopher.

This may be a surprising claim. Rawls spent his professional life developing a conception of justice that was suitable for regulating the basic institutions of a liberal democracy under modern conditions. Some of his remarks suggest that he wrote out of profound dissatisfaction with utilitarianism[4] and a concern to overcome a deep tension within the democratic tradition.[5] My opinion is that this picture of Rawls's motivations ignores his long-running concern with intuitionism. Although Rawls is often thought to have brought up intuitionism early in *Theory of Justice* only to put it aside, I read him as engaged in a two-front war – against utilitarianism and intuitionism – throughout the book. Yet this qualification does not fundamentally alter the view of Rawls's motivations that his remarks suggest. That view might still be summarized by saying that Rawls tried to frame a conception of justice suitable for a modern liberal democracy, while addressing

---

[3] Isaiah Berlin, *The First and the Last* (New York: New York Review of Books, 1999), 28.
[4] John Rawls, *A Theory of Justice*, rev. ed. (Cambridge, MA: Harvard University Press, 1999), xvii–viii.
[5] John Rawls, *Collected Papers*, ed. Samuel Freeman (Cambridge, MA: Harvard University Press, 1999), 305.

problems internal to democratic thought and avoiding the shortcomings of competing theories in analytic moral philosophy.

I do not say that this summary is wrong, but I do believe it leaves out something important, the addition of which *would* fundamentally alter the picture. What it leaves out is hinted at in the closing lines of "Idea of an Overlapping Consensus," in which Rawls writes that "political philosophy assumes the role Kant gave to philosophy generally: the defense of reasonable faith. In our case this becomes the defense of reasonable faith in the real possibility of a just constitutional regime."[6] That essay does not explain why the possibility of a just constitutional regime was ever in doubt, why it is important to show that such a regime is possible, or why – having shown that it is – Rawls thinks our attitude toward the possibility of such a regime should be described as "reasonable faith" rather than as, say, "justified belief." The closing pages of the preface to the paperback edition of *Political Liberalism* suggest some answers. In this chapter I want to follow up these hints and suggestions to sketch a fuller and more accurate picture of Rawls's motivations, drawing on *Theory of Justice* and on his *Lectures on the History of Moral Philosophy* for occasional support.

Is a stable, just society possible?

In *Theory of Justice*, Rawls remarks, "Historically one of the main defects of constitutional government has been the failure to insure the fair value of political liberty. The necessary corrective steps have not been taken, indeed, they never seem to have been seriously entertained. . . . Essentially the fault lies in the fact that the democratic political process is at best regulated rivalry."[7] Thus Rawls thinks that the ordinary conduct of politics, even in societies that purport to be liberal and democratic, raises the question whether political outcomes really depend on exercises of power, regulated by constraints that fall short of what justice requires. Whether remedies are possible and whether just constitutional government is sustainable depend on *why* corrective steps "never seem to have been seriously entertained" and *why* actual "democratic process is at best regulated rivalry."

In *Political Liberalism*, Rawls intimates that the events of the twentieth century suggest troubling answers to these questions. He writes, "The wars of this century with their extreme violence and increasing destructiveness,

---

[6] Ibid., 448; see also John Rawls, *Political Liberalism* (New York: Columbia University Press, 1996), 172.
[7] Rawls, *Theory of Justice*, 198–9.

culminating in the manic evil of the Holocaust, raise in an acute way the question whether political relations *must* be governed by power and coercion *alone*."[8] I think what Rawls has in mind is this. In light of the "extreme violence and increasing destructiveness" of the twentieth century, and the "manic evil of the Holocaust," we have to take seriously the possibility that human beings are not the kind of creatures who *can* create and sustain a just constitutional regime. We have to take seriously the possibility that "political relations must be governed by power and coercion alone" and that "democratic process [can be] at best regulated rivalry" because – given the inner dynamics that move us – members of the human species can do no better. In this way, by raising doubts about our nature, the events of the twentieth century raise doubts about the very possibility of a just liberal democracy that the Rawls of "Overlapping Consensus" says political philosophy has to address.

Why should political philosophy address them? Why should political philosophy try to show that a just constitutional regime is a "real possibility"? The story of Hitler's ascendancy in Weimar shows what can happen, Rawls thinks, when a society "no longer believe[s] that a decent liberal parliamentary regime [is] possible."[9] That in itself shows why faith in the real possibility of such a regime is important. Furthermore, if we cease to believe such a regime is possible because we come to believe others are incapable of a sustained commitment to justice, then we will become self-serving and cynical ourselves, prone to act unjustly to preempt the unjust actions we anticipate from others.[10] I believe Rawls thinks it is a basic fact of our motivational structure that considerations of justice are less likely to move us if we think our efforts will be in vain or if we think others will return evil for good. Therefore if we do not believe that a just regime is possible – and possible because our nature is such that we could sustain it – then we are unlikely to make individual and collective commitments to justice.

I believe Rawls found a similar line of thought in Kant. Speaking of Kant in his *Lectures on the History of Moral Philosophy*, Rawls says, "[H]e believes that we cannot sustain our devotion to the moral law, or commit ourselves to the advancement of its a priori object, the realm of ends or the highest good as the case may be, unless we firmly believe that its object is possible."

---

[8] Rawls, *Political Liberalism*, lxii; emphases added.
[9] Ibid., lxi.
[10] Here I rely on *Political Liberalism*, lxii. I also rely on Rawls's revealing but neglected remark in *Theory of Justice* that citizens' mutual knowledge that they possess a sense of justice is the preferred way to avert the hazards of a generalized prisoner's dilemma; see *Theory of Justice*, 238 n. 8.

This firm belief requires "practical faith" that it is possible to realize these objects in the world.

What, Rawls asks, is the content of practical faith that has the realm of ends as its object? He replies that "we can believe that a realm of ends is possible in the world only if the order of nature and social necessities are not unfriendly to that ideal."[11] That the "order of nature" includes *human* nature is clear from Rawls's remark that practical faith "require[s] certain beliefs about *our* nature and the social world."[12] So according to Rawls, Kant thinks that we can sustain our commitment to the moral law only if we believe that human nature is not unfriendly to the realization of a realm of ends in the world. Similarly, I believe, Rawls thinks that we – and I take the "we" to refer both to members of the well-ordered society and to Rawls's readers – can sustain our commitment to the principles of justice and to bringing about a just society only if we think human nature is not unfriendly to the realization of that society in the world.[13]

To show that a just society is possible, Rawls needed to say what a just society would be like. Working out a conception of a just society required a theory of justice, with principles of justice as its centerpiece. But while saying what principles of justice would regulate a just society and what its institutions would be like is necessary for showing that a just society is possible, it is not sufficient.

It may be thought that, at this point, Rawls needs to show that we can make the transition to a just society from the unjust societies in which we live. This is not, however, a matter Rawls ever takes up in any detail.[14] One reason he does not, I think, is that this transition will differ from society to society. Saying very much about how those transitions would or could be made would require knowing and saying a good deal about political conditions in the societies to which his work is addressed. Detailing those conditions is not, Rawls may think, a task philosophers are equipped to handle.

The reading of Rawls that I have sketched here suggests two further reasons why Rawls does not discuss questions of transition. First, on my reading, Rawls does not merely want to show that a just society is possible. He wants to show that what makes it possible is that human beings have a

---

[11] John Rawls, *Lectures on the History of Moral Philosophy*, ed. Barbara Herman (Cambridge, MA: Harvard University Press, 2000), 319.
[12] Ibid.; emphasis added.
[13] See Robert M. Adams, "Moral Faith," *Journal of Philosophy* 92, no. 2 (1995): 80.
[14] See the schematic remarks at *Political Liberalism*, 164–8.

"moral nature." By that he means "not . . . a perfect such nature, yet one that can understand, act on and be sufficiently moved by a reasonable political conception of right and justice."[15] By that, I think he means a capacity *reliably* to "understand, act on and be sufficiently moved by a reasonable political conception of right and justice." Rawls may think that some forms of moral motivation – associated with heroism, with episodically mustering the political will to make our world more just, or with the readiness to do good to those who hate us – are or entail the capacity to be moved by moral considerations under nonideal circumstances. Yet the capacity for a settled disposition to act justly is a capacity for reciprocity. Showing that we have this capacity requires showing that we would regularly be moved by considerations of justice when we believe that others are similarly moved. And so it does not require showing that we are "moved by a reasonable political conception of right and justice" under the imperfect conditions of an unjust society in transition: It requires showing that we would be so moved in the conditions of a well-ordered society. Furthermore, if it cannot be shown that we would develop a settled disposition to be just even under just institutions with perfect compliance, then it is surely questionable whether we do have a moral nature. Yet if we would develop that disposition in a well-ordered society, then questions about transition can be confronted later. Thus the well-ordered society serves as a minimal – and hence a first – test that humanity must pass.

If the conjectures of the previous paragraph are right, then the Kantian problem I have said Rawls set for himself accounts for two features that distinguish Rawls from others discussed in this volume: his development of a philosophical theory and his amenability to utopian thinking.

What Rawls does need to show is that members of a just society could sustain it, or as Rawls puts it, he needs to show that a just society would be stable. The argument for stability proceeds in two stages in *Theory of Justice*. In the first, executed in chapter 8, Rawls shows that members of a just society would acquire a sense of justice as a normal part of their moral and psychological development. The sense of justice is, in effect, a disposition to cooperate. To show that society would be stable, and stable for what Rawls later calls "the right reasons,"[16] he needed to show that each member would *voluntarily* maintain and act from – and would know that others would voluntarily maintain and act from – their disposition to cooperate.

---

[15] Ibid., lxii.
[16] See, for example, Rawls, *Collected Papers*, 589.

The alternatives are social breakdown or a heavy reliance on penal devices. Rawls completes the second stage of the argument, executed in chapter 9, by demonstrating that members of a just society would affirm that their disposition to cooperate is good for them. It follows that a stable, just society is possible and that political philosophy has vindicated "reasonable faith in the real possibility of a just constitutional regime."

Why does the stability argument show that a just society is a *"real* possibility" rather than a merely logical one, coherent but remote and unlikely? The argument does not appeal to highly improbable claims about human motivation nor is stability said to depend on heroic or supererogatory action. Rather, both stages of the stability argument draw on what Rawls thought are plausible and reasonable psychological claims, together with claims about the educative effects of just institutions. It is therefore reasonable to suppose that creatures with our nature who grow up in a just society could sustain it. Because the argument draws on relatively weak psychological assumptions, it shows that such society is a "real possibility" for us and that we have a "moral nature" rather than a nature that is "unfriendly" to justice. The argument therefore vindicates reasonable faith in the goodness of humanity or vindicates it sufficiently to answer our need for "practical faith."

Rawls, stability and the analytic tradition of moral philosophy

I have tried to bring to light a task that Rawls assigns to political philosophy, to show how that task reflects both the impact of twentieth-century history and the influence of Kant, and to tie the execution of that task to Rawls's theoretical ambitions and his amenability to realistic utopianism. Another of the features of Rawls's work that I cited at the outset as distinguishing him from other thinkers recognized in this volume is his work in the analytic tradition of moral philosophy.

What counts as analytic philosophy has by now become so unclear that it is easy to forget what analytic moral philosophy was during the time Rawls worked on *Theory of Justice*. It is therefore easy to miss the dispatch with which Rawls departed from it. Early in *Theory of Justice*, Rawls says rather peremptorily that "definitions and analyses of meaning do not have a special place" in the theory.[17] This methodological remark, his distinction between the concept and the conception of justice,[18] his later equation of

---

[17] Rawls, *Theory of Justice*, 44.
[18] Ibid., 5.

concept with meaning,[19] and his insistence that substantive conceptions are what is really of interest quickly placed Rawls's work at some distance from the defining techniques of classical analytic philosophy.

Of course, in the broader sense of the phrase "analytic philosophy" and its cognates, Rawls may seem so obviously to be an analytic philosopher that the fact does not call for comment. What does call for comment, in light of the contents of this volume, is why Rawls should have thought that analytic philosophy could contribute to the understanding of politics.

I cannot give the complete answer to this question here. To see part of the answer, and a part that contemporary analytic philosophers may overlook, we need to return to the task I have said Rawls sets himself. To show that a just society is possible, Rawls needed to show that a just society would be stable for the right reasons. To show that, he needed to show that members of a just society would develop a sense of justice. And to show *that*, Rawls needed to say something about what a sense of justice *is*.

One of the central questions of analytic moral philosophy at midcentury was the nature of moral motivation. Is moral action motivated by a desire, and if so, what is that desire a desire for? How is the desire connected with moral knowledge? How is it connected with feelings of approval or disapproval for morally good or right acts? Is what makes an act good or right the fact that it is approved of? If so, whose approval matters? Can that approval attach to anything whatever, or does the nature of morality somehow impose limits on moral approval and disapproval? Does it thereby impose limits on what we can desire to do – and what we can in fact do – under color of morality?

Rawls's task demanded that he consider the answers to these questions that were offered by the best of contemporaneous moral theory. He argues that the answers offered by both utilitarians and intuitionists were badly flawed. Rawls's criticisms of utilitarianism are too widely known to be belabored here. His critique of intuitionism has received far less attention. The most forceful part of that critique is found in his trenchant discussion of the intuitionist doctrine of the "purely conscientious act." According to that doctrine, "the highest moral motive is the desire to do what is right and just simply because it is right and just, no other description being appropriate."[20] Rawls does think that members of the well-ordered society normally have a desire to do what is just for its own sake. Yet he also argues

---

[19] Rawls, *Political Liberalism*, 14 n. 15.
[20] Rawls, *Theory of Justice*, 418.

that if the doctrine of the purely conscientious act were right, then the desire to do what is right would be what we might call – in deference to a phrase he uses elsewhere – a "pure preference," a preference Rawls likens to "a preference for tea rather than coffee."

Rawls does not say that pure preferences are irrational. Yet someone who has a pure preference cannot cite reasons for trying to satisfy it that suffice to justify her action to others. If the doctrine of the purely conscientious act is right, this is just the predicament of someone who has a preference for acting justly. She cannot cite sufficient reasons for her preference because "no other description" of what she desires is appropriate; the object of her desire is "a distinct (and unanalyzable) object." If asked why she desires to do what is right, she has nothing to say beyond that it is right. Her desire may not lack any reasons at all, but it "lacks any *apparent* reason" (emphasis added).[21] And if her sense of justice "lacks *apparent* reason" – if she lacks reasons for being just that are apparent to others – then others cannot have any assurance that she will voluntarily maintain and act from it. Mutual assurance of voluntary compliance is necessary if a just society is to be stable for the right reasons. If Rawls was to show that members of the well-ordered society have that assurance, then he had to find some alternative to the intuitionist account of moral motivation.

He found that account in social contract theory. Intuitionists like Ross and Prichard held that "the highest moral motive is the desire to do what is right and just simply because it is right and just, *no other description being appropriate*" (emphasis added).[22] They thought no other description was appropriate because they thought that the object of the desire to do what is right is "distinct and unanalyzable." Rawls argued that it is not simple and unanalyzable and so can be described in a variety of ways, saying that "the [social contract] theory of justice supplies [a variety of] descriptions of what the sense of justice is a desire for."[23] In *Theory of Justice*, the sense of justice is not just a desire to do what is right for its own sake. It is also a desire to act from the commonly acknowledged moral beliefs of a just society, a desire to act from principles that are supremely regulative of a social union of social unions, and a desire to act from principles that would be chosen in the original position. Rawls argues that members of a just society would all have – and all know that all others have – desires they can satisfy only by

[21] Ibid.
[22] Ibid.
[23] Ibid., 499.

attaining these objects. So all have – and know that all others have – desires that they can satisfy only by being just. Rawls thus exploits this variety of descriptions to argue that his version of social contract theory can solve the assurance problem on which intuitionism founders.[24]

It is sometimes said that twentieth-century political philosophy began in 1971, with the publication of *Theory of Justice*. Of course, that claim is unfair to other great political thinkers of the last century, including those whose work is discussed in this volume. Because Rawls produced a work of power and scope within the analytic tradition, and because he identified and addressed so many of the central problems of political philosophy, his work is recognized as being of continuing philosophical interest by those who work in analytic philosophy as it is now practiced. Yet it is easy for contemporary moral and political philosophers to forget the extent to which Rawls altered the landscape of their fields, so that other problems that once bulked large are now submerged. We will miss something important about Rawls's contribution and about what Rawls was trying to do if those problems slip out of collective memory: Recovering his critique of a view that was prominent when he began his work goes some way toward confirming the reading of Rawls's project that I have sketched here.

Self-respect, stability, and political context

I have argued that Rawls took up the problem of showing that a just society is possible in part because of the impact of twentieth-century history on him. I have not yet maintained that he looked to the historical events of the twentieth century for solutions or that he thought the failures of the twentieth century provided clues to what a just society must be like if it is to be possible. Let me now offer a tentative and highly speculative suggestion.

A just, liberal society will be stable only if the forces that would undermine it are absent or peripheral. Having noted that the elites of Weimar Germany "no longer believed a decent liberal parliamentary regime was possible,"[25] Rawls may have identified some of those forces, at least, by asking *why* they no longer thought such a regime was possible. He may have thought they blamed the forces of democracy for the political and economic humiliation that Germany suffered at Versailles and in the

---

[24] The arguments to which I refer here are found in section 86 of *Theory of Justice*. I lay out these arguments in my *Why Political Liberalism?* (New York: Oxford University Press, 2010).

[25] Rawls, *Political Liberalism*, lxi.

1920s.[26] Rawls may have concluded, for this reason among others, that a just constitutional regime is a "real possibility" if – but only if – it provides the political and economic bases for individual and collective self-respect.

Rawls describes the social bases of self-respect as the most important of the primary goods.[27] Its importance is clear from an especially interesting – and, I would say, an especially contentious – set of claims on which he relies heavily. He states one element of that set most clearly in an essay called "Fairness to Goodness." Rawls says there that "strong or inordinate desires for primary goods on the part of individuals and groups, particularly a desire for greater income and wealth and prerogatives of position, spring from insecurity and anxiety."[28] The anxiety Rawls has in mind is status anxiety. Clearly such anxiety, if widespread, could destabilize a just society by moving people to seek more than their fair share under principles of justice. It might not move them to cheat on their taxes or otherwise break the law, but it might move them try to change the law so that greater economic inequalities were allowed and political power was, in effect, available for purchase.

Yet Rawls argues in *Theory of Justice* that the need for status is answered by public recognition as a free and equal citizen. This public recognition is manifest in a just constitution, in the justification of laws and policies bearing on constitutional essentials, and in the respect citizens show one another in the public forum. This recognition removes the source of status anxiety. Secure in their status as free and equal, citizens do not destabilize their society's just distribution of wealth or power: "No one," Rawls says rather optimistically, "is inclined to look beyond the constitutional affirmation of equality for further political ways of securing his status."[29] In *Law of Peoples*, he draws on Aron to argue that a liberal people composed of citizens who are satisfied – in part because they are satisfied with their status as free and equal – will have no reason to undertake aggressive war.[30] The traditional causes of aggressive war, such as national ambition, the lust for national glory, the desire to secure access to resources or to enlarge their territory or their markets, will not get a sufficiently strong grip on them.

---

[26] On the need for terms of peace that do not humiliate, see Rawls, *Collected Papers*, 569; see also principle 5 on p. 567.

[27] Rawls, *Theory of Justice*, 486.

[28] Rawls, *Collected Papers*, 277.

[29] Rawls, *Theory of Justice*, 477.

[30] John Rawls, *The Law of Peoples* (Cambridge, MA: Harvard University Press, 2001), 47. Rawls discusses the conditions of defensive war at 89–91.

Thus the bases of self-respect do a great deal of work in arguments for domestic and international stability, and therefore they do a great deal of work in the argument that a just society is possible. I have doubts about the crucial step in the argument, the premise I said is expressed in "Fairness to Goodness," because I am inclined to think that there are many causes of the "strong or inordinate desire for primary goods." Developing this doubt into an objection requires showing that these other causes would engender desires for income and wealth that would destabilize the justice of a well-ordered society. Because Rawls may have the resources to argue that they would not, and that a just society would also keep those causes in check, I do no more here than register a doubt. What matters for present purposes is this. If reflection on the collapse of Weimar was part of what led Rawls to appreciate the importance of this primary good, then the history of the twentieth century – which had such profound effects on other thinkers in this volume – had an even deeper effect on Rawls than I initially suggested: It not only set the questions to which his theory of justice responded but it also had some effect on the content of the theory.

Rawls's political turn

The influence of Rawls's theory on contemporary moral and political philosophy would be almost impossible to exaggerate. Yet despite the overwhelming success of *Theory of Justice*, in the middle 1980s Rawls famously began to re-present his view as what he called a "political liberalism." In describing his view as a "political liberalism," Rawls meant to distinguish it from other liberal political philosophies, such as those of Kant and Mill. He thought that these two philosophers, like many before them, tried to derive political principles from claims about human nature or the good human life. While never denying that his theory was in some sense "Kantian," he insisted that his own view was founded not on ambitious philosophical claims that purport to be true of human beings anywhere and everywhere, but on ideas about the nature of citizenship that are common coin in the liberal democracies to which his work was addressed. Political philosophy must start modestly, Rawls maintained, if its conclusions are to be acceptable in diverse, liberal societies.

Rawls recast his view because there were clearly identifiable arguments in the original presentation of justice as fairness with which he later became dissatisfied. It is possible to explain the changes Rawls made in his theory only by locating those arguments, laying them out with care, supplying missing premises when necessary, and asking where Rawls might have thought those arguments went wrong. By doing this, it is possible, I believe, to pinpoint key premises he came to reject as implausible and others that he modified to facilitate his political turn.

I cannot undertake the work of explaining Rawls's transition to political liberalism here.[31] For now, suffice it to say that the arguments in *Theory of Justice* with which Rawls became dissatisfied are found in his treatment of stability. I believe that his characterization of a sense of justice and his account of how a sense of justice is acquired underwent important but subtle changes between *Theory of Justice* and *Political Liberalism*. Rawls also came to believe that he had relied on unrealistic assumptions when he argued that members of a just society would judge their sense of justice to be part of their good. According to the treatment of stability in *Political Liberalism*, citizens' mutual knowledge that all would cooperate in sustaining just institutions depends on "the existence and public knowledge of a reasonable overlapping consensus."[32] If Rawls's later work vindicates our practical faith in humanity, it does so by showing that, under the influence of just institutions, we can live as free and equal citizens. Because the arguments for stability were so central to Rawls's project, the changes demanded a new family of concepts not used in his original presentation. The alterations triggered reverberations throughout his theory. It is a mark of Rawls's very great intellectual honesty that he acknowledged shortcomings in his earlier work and took the steps he believed necessary to fix them.

After Rawls's death in 2002 I, like many other of Rawls's students, paid tribute to his life and character, trying to say why the man and not just the work so deeply influenced us. I shall not repeat the tribute here.[33] In conclusion, I shall say only that this volume may well commemorate other great political thinkers who were also great human beings. Yet as I find it hard to believe that any of them was a greater philosopher, so I find it hard to believe that any of them was a better person than John Rawls.

---

[31] For an extended treatment, see my *Why Political Liberalism?*
[32] Rawls, *Political Liberalism*, 392.
[33] My tribute was published as "John Rawls: A Remembrance," *Review of Politics* 65, no. 1 (2003): 5–10.

13

Richard Rorty: liberalism, irony, and social hope

MICHAEL BACON

Richard Rorty (1931–2007) was born in New York City to a family of progressive intellectuals. Shortly after his birth his parents broke with the American Communist Party after realizing how much it was controlled by Moscow. Yet they remained firmly on the left, arguing for economic redistribution and social reform. In an autobiographical essay published in 1992, Rorty writes, "I grew up knowing that all decent people were, if not Trotskyites, at least socialists."[1]

Rorty writes that his political views were formed as a child when, working as an office boy, he read press releases detailing the injustices regularly meted out to labor unions. Yet he also speaks of his having "private, weird, snobbish, incommunicable interests."[2] These focused initially on collecting wild orchids during childhood summers spent in rural New Jersey, but gradually turned to imaginative literature, in particular to Proust's *Remembrance of Things Past*. A theme that runs through his political writings is the relationship between one's private hopes and one's public responsibilities. Attending the University of Chicago from the age of fifteen, he writes: "Insofar as I had any project in mind, it was to reconcile Trotsky and the orchids. I wanted to find some intellectual or aesthetic framework which would let me – in a thrilling phrase which I came across in Yeats – 'hold reality and justice in a single vision.'"[3]

At Chicago he initially sought such a vision in the work of Plato. However, during the course of his undergraduate studies he came to think that the Platonic quest to get "beyond hypotheses" was doomed to failure, because there is no neutral standpoint from which different hypotheses

---

[1] Richard Rorty, "Trotsky and the Wild Orchids," in *Philosophy and Social Hope* (Harmondsworth: Penguin Books, 1999), 6.
[2] Ibid.
[3] Ibid., 7.

might be evaluated. By the time he moved to Yale to study for a doctorate, Plato had come to be eclipsed in his mind by Hegel. Hegel held that philosophy is "its time held in thought." For Rorty, this understanding of philosophy suggests that we might draw on the circumstances of our time to "weave the conceptual fabric of a freer, better, more just society."[4]

Rorty received his PhD in 1956. His first academic post was at Wellesley College, where he taught for three years before moving to Princeton University. In early work in the philosophy of mind he was a proponent of "eliminative materialism," the view that cognitive science might eventually provide an account of the mind that would enable humans to set aside reference to mentalistic terms such as "belief" and "desire." In the 1970s, his focus became issues in metaphilosophy. In *Philosophy and the Mirror of Nature* (1979) Rorty criticizes the idea that knowledge is a matter of mental or linguistic representation of the external world. Essays published in the 1970s and collected together in *Consequences of Pragmatism* (1982) developed this view by bringing out its connections with the pragmatism of Peirce, James, and Dewey. He came to identify more and more with pragmatism, in particular viewing his position as "fully continuous with Dewey's."[5]

Philosophy and the Mirror of Nature was extremely successful, attracting a readership not only in philosophy but also across the arts and humanities. Looking back at the book, however, Rorty lamented that it did not touch the question that had first led him to philosophy, of how to hold reality and justice in a single vision. In 1982 he took a post as professor of humanities at the University of Virginia, a position that provided him the opportunity to look beyond analytic philosophy. During his time there he published widely on both analytic and Continental philosophy, attempting to highlight parallels and connections he found between them. In 1989 he published *Contingency, Irony, and Solidarity*. That book presupposes the account of language and knowledge presented in *Philosophy and the Mirror of Nature* but is of far wider compass, drawing freely not only on figures in philosophy but also on novelists such as Proust, Nabokov, and Orwell. It also marks a significant change in Rorty's view of the relationship between the private and the public, because in it he argues that there is no need to weave together one's private passions and one's social responsibilities. As he remarks, "This book tries to show how things look if we drop the demand

---

[4] Ibid., 11.
[5] Richard Rorty, *Objectivity, Relativism, and Truth: Philosophical Papers, Volume 1* (Cambridge: Cambridge University Press, 1991), 16.

for a theory which unifies the public and private, and are content to treat the demands of self-creation and of human solidarity as equally valid, yet forever incommensurable."[6]

Contingency, Irony, and Solidarity sketches what Rorty calls "the ideally liberal society." In such a society, liberal institutions are seen as the product of historical contingencies that do not have, nor stand in need of, philosophical justification. The book was widely criticized for what many took to be the air of light-mindedness it adopts toward political questions. Rorty addresses this concern in subsequent essays and in his book *Achieving Our Country: Leftist Thought in Twentieth-Century America*. Published in 1998 shortly after he moved to Stanford University as professor of comparative literature, *Achieving Our Country* is an account of what Rorty takes to be the successes and failures of the American left, as well as suggestions for political action and social reform.

Liberalism as a philosophical and a political project

Rorty is often identified with postmodernism. Although he once embraced the label, it is a description with which he grew unhappy, and in his later writings he distanced himself from it. One reason for this distance is that the term came to be used in so many different ways that it was simply unhelpful. Yet a more significant reason is that postmodernism, in the eyes of many, is associated with a rejection of the aspirations and legacy of the European Enlightenment. For Rorty the Enlightenment constitutes the single most significant contribution that philosophers have made to Western culture. Its importance lies in challenging the belief that respect and obedience are owed to traditional forms of authority, such as that of revealed religion. For the philosophers of the Enlightenment, authority itself needs to be vindicated through the exercise of reason.

Although committed to the Enlightenment, Rorty thinks it important to distinguish between what he regards as its two legacies: the philosophical and the political. These gave rise to two different sets of questions. Philosophical questions concern the foundations of liberalism, specifically whether liberal institutions are justified by a source such as natural right or human nature. Political questions in contrast concern the desirability of liberal institutions and their advantages when compared to alternatives. Rorty's thesis is that

---

[6] Richard Rorty, *Contingency, Irony, and Solidarity* (Cambridge: Cambridge University Press, 1989), xv.

liberals can give up Enlightenment philosophy without endangering liberal institutions. He writes, "[A]bandoning Western rationalism has no discouraging political implications. It leaves the Enlightenment political project looking as good as ever."[7]

By distinguishing between the philosophical and political elements of the Enlightenment, Rorty departs from classical liberalism. The liberals of the seventeenth and eighteenth centuries attempted to ground liberty in an account of natural right. Natural right was itself derived from different sources. Locke argued that natural right is guaranteed by God; Kant, that it involves a priori principles of reason. Yet in each case, liberal institutions were seen as resting on philosophical foundations, with government being justified insofar as it protects prepolitical rights (in particular, those of private property).

Rorty presents his own thoughts on liberalism not by examining the classical figures but by discussing more recent critics of liberalism. In their *Dialectic of Enlightenment*, critical theorists Max Horkheimer and Theodor Adorno claim that the challenge the Enlightenment presented to traditional forms of authority came to undermine the convictions of the Enlightenment itself. As a result of its striving for emancipation through the exercise of critical reason, the Enlightenment came to show up the absence of its own foundations by undercutting notions of rationality and human nature. Horkheimer and Adorno conclude that liberalism thus deprived itself both of its philosophical foundations and its source of social cohesion, leaving it intellectually and morally bankrupt.

Rorty shares this understanding of Enlightenment philosophy. However, he thinks it a mistake to conclude that Enlightenment liberal institutions are thereby threatened. "Horkheimer and Adorno assumed that the terms in which those who begin a historical development described their enterprise remain the terms which describe it correctly, and then inferred that the dissolution of that terminology deprives the results of that development of the right to, or the possibility of, continued existence. This is almost never the case."[8] Rorty acknowledges the advances heralded by Enlightenment metaphysics, but thinks that metaphysics only a halfway measure. The rhetoric of figures such as Locke and Kant retained the religious need for

---

[7] Richard Rorty, *Truth, Politics and "Post-Modernism": The Spinoza Lectures* (Amsterdam: Van Gorcum, 1997), 36.
[8] Rorty, *Contingency, Irony, and Solidarity*, 56.

human projects to be underwritten by a nonhuman authority. In his view, it is possible, and important, to go beyond them: "[T]he democracies are now in a position to throw away some of the ladders used in their own construction."[9]

The connection that writers such as Horkheimer and Adorno see between the philosophical and the political projects of the Enlightenment may, Rorty claims, "reflect nothing more than a historical coincidence."[10] He also argues that the perceived need to identify philosophical foundations for liberal institutions is undesirable, because the search for foundations can potentially stand in the way of securing justice and freedom. Like Dewey, he argues that although the classical liberals provided an important justification for freedom and toleration, their approach later came to stand in the way of necessary social reform. Dewey argued that the change in social conditions brought about by economic rights benefited some but created new relations of dependence for others. Rorty similarly argues that the emphasis placed on rights can be seen as conservative, enshrining the problems and beliefs of a particular time and place. For example, he notes that no less a liberal than Thomas Jefferson affirmed the absolute truth that all men are endowed by their creator with inalienable rights, but that he could do so while simultaneously owning slaves.[11]

In support of the suggestion that liberal institutions might be defended even while Enlightenment philosophy is set aside, Rorty discusses writers whom he takes successfully to have mounted just such a defense. He views Dewey, together with Michael Oakeshott, Isaiah Berlin, and John Rawls, as theorists who, in dispensing with Enlightenment rationalism, are able to offer a defense of liberal institutions stronger than that put forward by earlier figures. These theorists can be said to be pragmatists who sought to justify liberal institutions by drawing on the beliefs and practices of modern pluralist societies. Rorty proposes "that we see such writers as these as the self-canceling and self-fulfilling triumph of the Enlightenment. Their pragmatism is antithetical to Enlightenment rationalism, although it was itself made possible (in good dialectical fashion) only by that rationalism. It can serve as the vocabulary of a mature (de-scientized, de-philosophized) Enlightenment liberalism."[12]

---

[9] Ibid., 194.
[10] Rorty, *Truth, Politics and "Post-Modernism,"* 36.
[11] Richard Rorty, *Truth and Progress: Philosophical Papers, Volume 3* (Cambridge: Cambridge University Press, 1998), 167.
[12] Rorty, *Contingency, Irony, and Solidarity,* 57.

Postmodernist bourgeois liberalism

Rorty is a liberal, but what exactly does he mean by liberalism? We can best answer this question by locating his writings in the context of discussions in which he participated. In the late 1970s and 1980s, the central issue in Anglophone political theory was that which has become known as the liberal–communitarian debate. Prompted in part by the publication of Rawls's *A Theory of Justice* in 1971, writers such as Michael Sandel, Michael Walzer, and Alasdair MacIntyre criticized liberalism for ignoring the particular contexts within which people live their lives. In different ways, they attacked what they took to be the undue emphasis that liberals place on individual rights and their related failure to attend to the particular circumstances of justice.

In his earliest writings in political theory, Rorty was sympathetic to communitarianism. In particular he wrote appreciatively of Sandel's critique of Rawls's Kantian idea of a self standing outside of culture and history. Rorty's own Hegelian attempt to defend liberal institutions and practices without reference to Kantian notions of ahistoric rationality and morality was first outlined in a paper with the title "Postmodernist Bourgeois Liberalism" (1983).[13] By "bourgeois" he means the rights and freedoms that are (ideally) guaranteed in liberal democracies. By "postmodernist" he means a willingness to set aside the perceived need to provide a justification for those rights and freedoms of the kind sought by Kantian liberals such as Ronald Dworkin and (as he then thought) Rawls. Postmodernist bourgeois liberalism is historically contingent through and through, accepting that liberal institutions and practices are the products of particular circumstances and that our loyalties to them stem from nothing more than those contingencies.

Although Rorty came to regret associating himself with postmodernism, he never departed from his understanding of liberalism as being historically contingent. However, he did come to refine his understanding of both the communitarians on the one hand and Rawls on the other. In a paper written in 1984 titled "The Priority of Democracy to Philosophy," he presents communitarians like Sandel as maintaining "that liberal institutions and culture either should not or cannot survive the collapse of the philosophical justification that the Enlightenment provided for them."[14] As in his response to Horkheimer and Adorno, he contests the claim that

---

[13] Rorty, "Postmodernist Bourgeois Liberalism," in *Objectivity, Relativism, and Truth*, 197–202.
[14] Rorty, "The Priority of Democracy to Philosophy," in *Objectivity, Relativism, and Truth*, 177.

liberalism stands or falls with the philosophical justifications that have been provided for it, arguing that there is no sense "in which liberal democracy 'needs' philosophical justification at all." Although liberalism may "need philosophical articulation, it does not need philosophical backup."[15]

The claim that liberal democracy does not require philosophical backup has alarmed those who think that, if we follow Rorty, nothing can be said to critics of liberalism.[16] Yet this is to confuse two different claims. There is no justification of liberalism that will necessarily persuade every rational person, but this is not to claim that there is nothing to be said at all. Rorty writes, "I do not know how to 'justify' or 'defend' social democracy . . . in a large philosophical way (as opposed to going over the nitty-gritty advantages and disadvantages of the alternatives [critics of liberalism] propose)."[17] Although a philosophical justification is unavailable, one can seek to justify liberalism by arguing for its concrete advantages. He suggests that the best way to do so is through invidious comparison: "[T]he justification of liberal society [is] simply . . . a matter of historical comparisons with other attempts at social organization – those of the past and those envisaged by utopians."[18]

As he became more critical of communitarians such as Sandel, Rorty became more sympathetic to Rawls. He came to argue that Rawls presents the best contemporary philosophical articulation of liberalism. In *A Theory of Justice*, Rawls sets himself the task of outlining a theory of justice for modern societies. In later works, notably *Political Liberalism*, he addresses more explicitly the need for such a theory in order to secure political stability in the context of moral and religious diversity. According to Rawls, the pluralism of what he terms "reasonable comprehensive doctrines" (specifically, moral, religious, and philosophical doctrines) means that public policy and institutions cannot legitimately be structured around any particular one. The "fact of pluralism," the fact that there is a reasonable diversity of such doctrines, means that it would be unreasonable for any of them to be privileged in matters of public concern. Instead, he proposes what he calls a political conception of justice, in which the institutions and laws of modern societies are structured around a broadly liberal understanding developed out of the beliefs and values of reasonable citizens. Rawls explicitly distances

---

[15] Ibid., 178.
[16] See, for example, Stephen Mulhall and Adam Swift, *Liberals and Communitarians* (Oxford: Blackwell, 1992), chap. 8.
[17] Richard Rorty, "Thugs and Theorists: A Reply to Bernstein," *Political Theory* 15, no. 4 (1987): 577–8 n. 20.
[18] Rorty, *Contingency, Irony, and Solidarity*, 53.

this position from classical liberalism: "Political liberalism is not a form of Enlightenment liberalism, that is, a comprehensive liberal and often secular doctrine founded on reason."[19] Rather than drawing on controversial moral, theological, or philosophical premises, the political conception of justice is justified by reference to ideas that are embedded in the culture of contemporary liberal democracies.

In "The Priority of Democracy to Philosophy" Rorty endorses this political understanding of liberalism. That essay provides what he calls a historicist interpretation in which the Kantian side of Rawls is treated as a rhetorical flourish and in which the Hegelian, historicist, side is central. Rawls is taken to be addressing specific circumstances, specifically the legacy of the wars of religion following the Protestant Reformation. In a society that has come to accept, as Rawls puts it, that justice is its first virtue, no philosophical justification of the kind sought by the classical liberals will be needed. Rorty writes, "Such a society will become accustomed to the thought that social policy needs no more authority than successful accommodation among individuals, individuals who find themselves heir to the same historical traditions and faced with the same problems."[20]

If we grant Rorty's interpretation, we can see him as answering a question that Rawls himself left hanging. In the paperback edition of *Political Liberalism*, Rawls remarks, "It is a great puzzle to me why political liberalism was not worked out much earlier: it seems such a natural way to present the idea of liberalism, given the fact of reasonable pluralism in political life. Does it have deep faults that preceding writers may have found in it that I have not seen and these led them to dismiss it?"[21] We can imagine Rorty replying on his behalf that earlier liberals were working with a vocabulary that assumed liberalism needed justification by reference to Enlightenment reason, an assumption that we are now only learning to live without.

The strength of Rawls's writings, according to Rorty, is that they address the particular circumstances of modern pluralist societies while avoiding the unattractive extremes of either relativism or of an Archimedean point outside of culture and history. He thinks of Rawls as offering a midway between these two alternatives in his suggestion that the principles of justice might be the subject of what he calls an "overlapping consensus." Some commentators have thought that an overlapping consensus is merely

---

[19] John Rawls, *Political Liberalism* (New York: Columbia University Press, 1996), xl.
[20] Rorty, *Objectivity, Relativism, and Truth*, 184.
[21] Rawls, *Political Liberalism*, 374 n. 1.

a matter of comprehensive doctrines happening to agree on certain principles. Rorty disagrees, maintaining that in an overlapping consensus citizens do not endorse the principles of justice because their comprehensive doctrines already share them, but rather that it is the result of their actively seeking to work with holders of different such doctrines: "[A]n overlapping consensus is not the result of discovering that various comprehensive views already share common doctrines, but rather something that might never have emerged had the proponents of these views not started trying to cooperate."[22] There is no guarantee that an overlapping consensus will be secured, and it may be that what Rawls calls a "mere *modus vivendi*" is the most that can be achieved. However, ideally it will be possible to go beyond that to secure an overlapping consensus on a fair constitutional settlement.

Self-creation and irony

Rorty's most sustained presentation of his thoughts on political theory is made in his book *Contingency, Irony, and Solidarity*. There he concludes that his youthful desire to bring justice and beauty together into a single vision was mistaken and that both should be accommodated separately. This accommodation is realized in the "ideally liberal society," one that gives up on the very idea of a single kind of human life. Such a society provides a set of rights under which individuals are treated equally in certain respects, leaving them free to pursue their ends within the framework provided by those rights, consistent with the enjoyment of those freedoms by other members of society who have different views of the good. As Rorty puts it, "J. S. Mill's suggestion that governments devote themselves to optimizing the balance between leaving people's private lives alone and preventing suffering seems to me pretty much the last word."[23]

Rorty takes freedom to be a form of what Berlin called negative liberty, a matter of the absence of obstacles that interfere with one's actions. In conceiving of freedom in this way, he departs from Dewey. Dewey was a proponent of greater citizen participation in democracy, arguing that an active community life is a prerequisite for individual freedom. In contrast Rorty expresses no attraction to a life of civic participation and distances

---

[22] Richard Rorty, *Philosophy as Cultural Politics: Philosophical Papers, Volume 4* (Cambridge: Cambridge University Press, 2007), 52 n. 17.

[23] Rorty, *Contingency, Irony, and Solidarity*, 63.

himself from Dewey's defense of participatory democracy.[24] Although he describes himself as a Deweyan, he nowhere attends to the details of Dewey's political writings and looks to other philosophers to exemplify the kind of freedom he has in mind. In *Contingency, Irony, and Solidarity*, the most significant such philosopher is Nietzsche. Nietzsche is a philosopher of self-creation who identified the importance of appropriating and redescribing experiences rather than accepting inherited descriptions. As Rorty writes, "To create one's mind is to create one's own language, rather than to let the length of one's mind be set by the language other human beings have left behind."[25]

According to Rorty, the ideally liberal society is one in which citizens are free to create autonomous lives for themselves. He is careful, however, to distinguish the kind of autonomy he favors from that proposed by Kant. For Kant, autonomy is a matter of self-legislation in which one's choices are made by reason and not influenced by experience. In contrast, the sense of autonomy Rorty favors is a matter of embracing contingency – in particular, of seeing one's self and those things that are central to one's identity as the result of such contingencies, and re-creating them through continual redescription.

Rorty examines these different understandings of autonomy by turning to Freud. Freud distinguished the ascetic life from the aesthetic life. The ascetic life concerns purity and is characterized by the attempt to purge from oneself all that is accidental and contingent in order to achieve a keener awareness of one's true self. In contrast, the aesthetic life is marked not by purity but by self-enlargement, by "the development of richer, fuller ways of formulating one's desires and hopes, and thus making those desires and hopes themselves – and thereby oneself – richer and fuller."[26] In place of the ascetic pursuit of true self, the aesthete embraces the creation of narratives within which she tells the story of her life. Rorty identifies self-creation with the aesthetic life, emphasizing that such a life depends on what it has inherited. Rather than seeing the autonomous person as inventing a wholly new world for herself, she should be seen as drawing

---

[24] Richard Rorty, *Achieving Our Country: Leftist Thought in Twentieth-Century America* (London: Harvard University Press, 1998), 104. He also rejects the suggestion, made by Robert Westbrook and Cheryl Misak, that Dewey's epistemology can be worked up into an account of deliberative democracy (Richard Rorty, "Dewey and Posner on Pragmatism and Moral Progress," *University of Chicago Law Review* 74, no. 3 [2007]: 918).

[25] Rorty, *Contingency, Irony, and Solidarity*, 27.

[26] Richard Rorty, *Essays on Heidegger and Others: Philosophical Papers, Volume 2* (Cambridge: Cambridge University Press, 1991), 154.

on and redescribing what has gone before. On this point, Rorty departs from Nietzsche. There "can be no fully Nietzschean lives, lives which are pure action rather than reaction – no lives which are not largely parasitical on an un-redescribed past and depending on the charity of as yet unborn generations."[27]

The importance accorded by Rorty to self-creation through redescription is central to his claim that the citizens of the ideally liberal society will be "ironists." Ironists place self-creation at the heart of their identity by standing in a specific relation with their "final vocabulary." Such a vocabulary is final because the words of which it consists – "good," "right," "kindness," etc. – cannot be backed up by noncircular argument. If the use of those words is questioned, the only response is to appeal to other beliefs whose justification depends at least partly on the belief being questioned.

I shall define an "ironist" as someone who fulfills three conditions: (1) She has radical and continuing doubts about the final vocabulary she currently uses, because she has been impressed by other vocabularies, vocabularies taken as final by people or books she has encountered; (2) she realizes that argument phrased in her present vocabulary can neither underwrite nor dissolve these doubts; (3) insofar as she philosophizes about her situation, she does not think that her final vocabulary is closer to reality than others, that it is in touch with a power not herself.[28]

Rather than seeking to purify herself from doubt, the ironist grasps the inescapability of contingency. She undertakes self-creation through redescription, but recognizes that there is no way to move beyond all description to what Rorty calls "Reality as It Is in Itself."[29]

The figure of the ironist has attracted considerable criticism, the two most significant charges being that irony is highly elitist[30] and that it is incompatible with conviction, leading to the denigration of shared values and ways of life.[31]

The concern with elitism can in part be mitigated if we see that Rorty seeks to extend the life of self-creation to every citizen. Once again he illustrates how this might be accomplished by reference to Freud, who is said to democratize Nietzsche by showing how the detail of everyday life

---

[27] Rorty, *Contingency, Irony, and Solidarity*, 42.
[28] Ibid., 73.
[29] Rorty, *Truth and Progress*, 72.
[30] See, for example, Roy Bhaskar, *Philosophy and the Idea of Freedom* (Oxford: Blackwell, 1991).
[31] See, for example, Susan Haack, "Vulgar Pragmatism: An Unedifying Prospect," in *Rorty and Pragmatism: The Philosopher Responds to His Critics*, ed. Herman J. Saatkemp Jr. (London: Vanderbilt University Press, 1995).

provides the material from which one might forge a life for oneself: "For Freud's account of unconscious fantasy shows us how to see every human life as a poem – or, more exactly, every human life not so racked by pain as to be unable to learn a language nor so immersed in toil as to have no leisure in which to generate a self-description."[32]

Irony is also said to preclude any committed engagement with social questions, because it encourages a detached, even sneering, attitude toward such questions. In Rorty's view, however, the recognition of contingency need have no deleterious consequences for conviction. For if there is no such thing as a belief or conviction that swings free of contingency, recognizing its absence cannot alter the strength of our convictions. In *Contingency, Irony, and Solidarity* he writes that "the fundamental premise of this book is that a belief can still regulate action, can still be worth dying for, among people who are quite aware that this belief is caused by nothing deeper than contingent historical circumstances."[33] Elsewhere, he makes the point more strongly, suggesting that irony not only is consistent with moral and political conviction but might also positively enhance a certain kind of liberal toleration. Awareness that their beliefs are contingent can, he claims, make citizens less dogmatic and more willing to consider alternative descriptions: "It helps make the world's inhabitants more pragmatic, more tolerant, more liberal, more receptive to the appeal of instrumental rationality."[34]

Private irony and public hope

Self-creation is one of the aims of ideal liberal society. The second aim concerns one's responsibilities to one's fellow citizens. Rorty captures this relation of responsibility with reference to a suggestion made by Judith Shklar, who defines liberals as people for whom "cruelty is the worst thing we do."[35] She contrasts cruelty with sin: Whereas sin is transgression against God, cruelty is a matter of inflicting pain on another human being. There is no inherent conflict between sin and cruelty, but someone who regards cruelty as the worst thing we do necessarily relegates sin to at most a secondary concern.[36] Rorty takes up Shklar's distinction between sin and

---

[32] Rorty, *Contingency, Irony, and Solidarity*, 35–6.
[33] Ibid., 189.
[34] Rorty, *Objectivity, Relativism, and Truth*, 193.
[35] Rorty, *Contingency, Irony, and Solidarity*, xv.
[36] Judith N. Shklar, "Putting Cruelty First," in *Ordinary Vices* (London: Belknap Press of Harvard University Press, 1984), chap. 1.

cruelty by presenting liberals as people who take their duties to be owed exclusively to their fellow human beings.

In itself, the injunction to avoid cruelty tells us nothing about what cruelty might be or how it is to be avoided. Some commentators have thus pressed Rorty to provide a definition of cruelty.[37] However, this request is not to the point. To specify cruelty's necessary and sufficient conditions implies that we are in a position to give a definitive account of what is and is not cruel, but Rorty's claim is that we are never in this position. Once again, his argument here recalls that of Dewey, who worried that liberal rights might enshrine new forms of injustice. Like Dewey, Rorty argues that liberal societies need to be constantly reminded of the ways in which the current arrangements of rights and freedoms have a negative impact on certain people.

The need for such a reminder is evidenced in Rorty's view of Mill. Although Rorty thinks that the attempt to balance private interests and passions with social responsibilities constitutes the last word in political theory, he also thinks that the nature of that balance will vary according to circumstance. Thus, for example, he takes Rawls to have added to Mill the claim that the exercise of freedom requires economic redistribution.

Philosophers such as Mill and Rawls have a role to play in alerting us to cruelty, but Rorty thinks that more useful are those who sensitize us to the details of particular forms of suffering. These he calls "the specialists in particularity – historians, novelists, ethnographers, and muckraking journalists."[38] Such people bring into focus the details of particular lives. Novelists are especially helpful in this regard. Writers such as Nabokov and Dickens provide details of forms of cruelty (committed either by individuals or by institutions) that we had not previously considered, of cruelty inflicted on people with whom we may not have concerned ourselves.

Rorty has been widely challenged for his insistence on a firm distinction between the public and the private, which has been taken to ignore the feminist claim that "the personal is the political."[39] We should note, however, that he is not insisting on a categorical division between the private

---

[37] See, for example, John Horton, "Ironism and Commitment: An Irreconcilable Dualism of Modernity," in *Richard Rorty: Critical Dialogues*, ed. Matthew Festenstein and Simon Thompson (Cambridge: Polity, 2001).

[38] Rorty, *Objectivity, Relativism, and Truth*, 207.

[39] See, for example, Nancy Fraser, "Solidarity or Singularity? Richard Rorty between Romanticism and Technocracy," in *Reading Rorty: Critical Responses to Philosophy and the Mirror of Nature (and Beyond)*, ed. Alan R. Malachowski (Oxford: Basil Blackwell, 1991).

and the public, only that the one is often irrelevant for the other. Yet he recognizes that this is not always so. There is a role for ironic redescription in public life:

As I am a liberal, the part of my final vocabulary which is relevant to [public] actions requires me to become aware of all the various ways in which other human beings whom I might act upon can be humiliated. So the liberal ironist needs as much imaginative acquaintance with alternative final vocabularies as possible, not just for her own edification, but in order to understand the actual and possible humiliation of the people who use these alternative final vocabularies.[40]

By way of illustration, Rorty points out that, having secured women the vote, the American left forgot the ways in which women continued to suffer prejudice. To overcome this prejudice, society needed to be redescribed so that "the male-female distinction is no longer of much interest."[41] He applauds feminists for having exposed hitherto unrecognized instances of cruelty and thus expanding the frontiers of our imaginations and moral world.

Rorty's political writings are not limited to political theory and its relationship to imaginative literature. In pieces written for journals such as *The Nation* and *The New Republic* he makes concrete suggestions for social and institutional reform. In his 1998 book *Achieving Our Country* he proposes what he called a "People's Charter." At the top of his list of suggestions is reform of campaign financing.[42] He also proposes universal health insurance, public financing of primary and secondary education, and dramatically increased rates of income tax to pay for these programs.[43]

In his contributions to public debate, Rorty's immediate focus is contemporary America. However, his hopes are not limited to the United States but extend beyond both America and the European democracies. As he remarks, the historicist account of liberalism he offers in no way entails giving up on the "attempt to build a cosmopolitan world-society – one which embodies the same sort of utopia with which the Christian, Enlightenment, and Marxist metanarratives of emancipation ended."[44] Rorty himself epitomizes the notion of the liberal ironist, ready to reread and revise the thinkers he encounters in order to offer redescriptions of issues in political theory and political life.

---

[40] Rorty, *Contingency, Irony, and Solidarity*, 91–2.
[41] Rorty, *Truth and Progress*, 227.
[42] Rorty, *Achieving Our Country*, 99.
[43] Richard Rorty, "First Projects, Then Principles," *The Nation*, December 22, 1997.
[44] Rorty, *Objectivity, Relativism, and Truth*, 213.

Suggestions for further reading

Rorty, Richard. *Achieving Our Country: Leftist Thought in Twentieth-Century America.* London: Harvard University Press, 1998.

———. *Contingency, Irony, and Solidarity.* Cambridge: Cambridge University Press, 1989.

———. "Postmodernist Bourgeois Liberalism." In *Objectivity, Relativism, and Truth: Philosophical Papers, Volume 1,* 197–202. Cambridge: Cambridge University Press, 1991.

———. "The Priority of Democracy to Philosophy." In *Objectivity, Relativism, and Truth: Philosophical Papers, Volume 1,* 175–96. Cambridge: Cambridge University Press, 1991.

———. *Truth, Politics and "Post-Modernism": The Spinoza Lectures.* Amsterdam: Van Gorcum, 1997.

Part IV
Critiques of liberalism

14
Jean-Paul Sartre: "in the soup"

WILLIAM LEON MCBRIDE

Like all the other writers considered in this volume, Jean-Paul Sartre (1905–1980) was a figure of the twentieth century, which is no longer our century. What this means goes far beyond a mere mathematical statement, based on an arbitrary division of time. Although not surprising given this arbitrariness of the decimal and centile divisions, there are numerous continuities between his world and ours today – for example, there are still many living human beings who interacted with him, as with most of the other figures discussed here – it is also importantly true that the milieu in which he flourished is a distant memory. As he himself said in an interview with John Gerassi, conducted thirty-five years earlier but only published in 2009, there are still many "who remember what France was like twenty years ago. It was [even as late as 1968] in the center of the world.... Paris was the most stimulating city in the world.... Today, that's all gone. No one has the illusion that we are the center of the world."[1] With some sadness, I must agree, as did Gerassi, with Sartre's assessment, projected from 1974 to the present time. For some reason, Sartre, in these interviews, repeatedly employed a banal and not very common metaphor, "in the soup," which for him meant "in the thick of things," deeply involved. That was indeed his own situation at midcentury, the century of which Gerassi himself, in the title of a short biographical work, called Sartre "the hated conscience,"[2] and which Bernard-Henri Lévy, although a Sartre critic of sorts, has simply identified as Sartre's century.[3] Although these identifications may be somewhat hyperbolic, they do point to the confluence of major political events and ideas of which Sartre was at the center.

---

[1] John Gerassi, ed., *Talking with Sartre: Conversations and Debates* (New Haven: Yale University Press, 2009), 267.

[2] John Gerassi, *Jean-Paul Sartre: Hated Conscience of His Century* (Chicago: University of Chicago Press, 1989).

[3] Bernard-Henri Lévy, *Le Siècle de Sartre* (Paris: Bernard Grasset, 2000).

As he readily admitted, Sartre at the beginning of his intellectual career was not a political theorist. True, he published one short article in an international journal of legal philosophy at the age of twenty-two, but his writings of the next decade and a half were divided between studies of philosophical psychology (the emotions, the imagination) inspired in large measure by the movement of Husserlian phenomenology, on the one hand, and philosophically oriented works of literature, on the other. His short novel, *Nausea*, which he had reworked over a period of several years, together with his collection of short stories, *The Wall (Le Mur)*, gave him a certain notoriety at or just before the very time (late 1939) he was called up for military service, as a meteorologist, at the outset of the so-called phony war between France and Germany. While Hitler was consolidating his hold on Czechoslovakia and marching east through Poland, the "phony war" consisted of some skirmishes, but no major battles, and it ended in the surrender of the Vichy government and the beginning of the Nazi occupation of France. Like many other French soldiers, Sartre was confined to a *Stalag*, where the experience of communal living in very close quarters with fellow captives influenced him profoundly, as he often emphasized in later years. It was a short period of captivity, approximately nine months, after which Sartre escaped as many others did – French prisoners were not a top priority of the German authorities – and returned to Paris. He helped organize a clandestine, essentially nonviolent, resistance group that, apparently at his suggestion, took the name "Socialism and Freedom" (Socialisme et Liberté); its members prepared and circulated some pamphlets, but it soon dissolved. Meanwhile, he completed his long philosophical magnum opus, *Being and Nothingness*, which he had begun writing before the war; it was published during the middle of the Occupation period, in June 1943. In that same month, his play *The Flies*, with a classical Greek theme and a veiled antioccupation message, had its successful premiere.

Thus Sartre, who had spent a fellowship year at the French Institute in Berlin during the period (1933–4) when Hitler was gradually assuming dictatorial powers and the systematic persecution of German Jews began – and who had bidden farewell in 1936 to one of his good friends, Fernando Gerassi (John's father), when the latter left Paris to fight in Spain within two days of hearing the news that Francisco Franco had launched the civil war there that would bring the Falangists to power – nevertheless remained relatively untouched by political events during his early years. The word "relatively" is appropriate. The short story that gave the volume

Le Mur its title concerns an imagined event during the Spanish Civil War when a soldier is captured and threatened with execution if he fails to reveal the whereabouts of one of his comrades, and the final story of the book, *Childhood of a Leader (L'Enfance d'un chef)*, describes the growth and development of an adolescent from a well-to-do French family as he becomes an adherent of the right-wing, virulently anti-Semitic party Action Française. Even in *Being and Nothingness* one can find some flashes of political insight; a good, although by no means unique, example is Sartre's brief analysis of the re-creation of the past, particularly the ties with the Marquis de Lafayette, that took place in the United States when it entered World War I – and of how the alternative choice of siding with Germany at that time would have led to a different re-creation of other past ties.[4] Yet it was the wartime occupation, with its combination, somewhat peculiar to France among the countries of Europe, of *some* "business as usual" (scholarly publications, theater) and constant fear and despair for the future, which Sartre well describes in his essay "Paris sous l'occupation,"[5] that changed everything.

Paris was liberated by the Allied armies in late August 1944. Very soon thereafter, in fact within less than a year, the vogue called "existentialism" broke out, and Sartre was at its center. At first he did not flaunt this word, the several origins of which date from prewar times, as a label for his own thought and that of his friend and colleague Simone de Beauvoir, but the popular usage soon overtook them, so to speak, and they accepted it. Like any such label that captures the popular imagination, including the mass media, its applications soon spread far beyond the philosophy of *Being and Nothingness*, even in its more popularized versions. "Existentialism" came to stand for a certain type of literature and, ultimately, a vaguely defined but in any case unconventional way of life as well. As such, it became all the rage not only in France but also in much of the rest of Western Europe and in the Americas. This was the case at the level of popular culture even while, contrary to the dismissive claims of some, the serious and rather complex systematic philosophy of *Being and Nothingness*, with its emphasis above all on the reality of human freedom, was being taken very seriously (and on

---

[4] Jean-Paul Sartre, *Being and Nothingness*, trans. Hazel Barnes (New York: Philosophical Library, 1956), 500.

[5] Jean-Paul Sartre, "Paris sous l'occupation," in *Situations*, vol. 3 (Paris: Gallimard, 1949), 15–42. This essay is preceded by the very brief essay "La République du silence," which begins with Sartre's famously ironic assertion that "we" (the French) had never felt so free as under the German occupation.

the whole more positively than negatively) by professional reviewers as early as 1944.[6]

Yet Sartre and many of his close colleagues, while not repudiating the publicity and adulation that had begun to come their way, were becoming increasingly preoccupied with "the political," in the broad sense of that term. In the narrower sense, the newly liberated life of politics in France took on considerable complexity, which it would be impossible and some-what irrelevant to summarize here. However, certainly among its foremost features was the popularity of the French Communist Party (CP). Active even before the war, suffering a serious setback when Stalin signed his infamous although short-lived pact with Hitler (which resulted in the resig-nation from the party of one of Sartre's close personal friends, Paul Nizan, who was then killed during the "phony war"), but rebounding in popu-larity as a result of the subsequent, unquestionably strong commitment to the Resistance of its most militant members, the CP was preferred by up to 25 percent of French voters in some postwar elections – a percentage that has considerable weight in a multiparty system. Thus "it was not by accident," as orthodox Marxists, with their strongly deterministic beliefs, liked to say and write, that some leading French intellectuals decided to create a journal that would deal at both an experiential and a theoretical level with the new realities of the postwar situation; this meant above all, although not exclusively, domestic and international political realities at the experiential level and, at the theoretical, the increasing importance of the thought system that the communists claimed to be upholding, Marxism. This journal was given the name *Les Temps Modernes*, after Charlie Chaplin's film *Modern Times*. Sartre became its first editor, a position that he contin-ued to hold for many years thereafter, and its initial editorial board included luminaries of diverse viewpoints, such as the liberal democrat Raymond Aron. As enunciated in its original "Presentation" and in editorials (most of them actually written but not signed by Sartre's long-time collaborator, Maurice Merleau-Ponty) over some years following, the journal's purpose was to promote the thought of a strong non- (but not anti-) communist left. Aron and some others soon dropped out, but the journal, although its circulation was never spectacularly large, exerted a considerable influence both in France and to some extent even abroad for a very long time.

---

[6] For documentation of this, see my article "Les premiers comptes rendus de *L'Être et le néant*," in *La Naissance du "Phénomène Sartre": Raisons d'un succès 1938–1945*, ed. Ingrid Galster (Paris: Éditions du Seuil, 2001), 185–99. For example, the well-known British philosopher A. J. Ayer published a rather disapproving but respectful review of Sartre's work in the July 1945 issue of the journal *Horizon*.

One of Sartre's first serious essays in political theory, "Materialism and Revolution," first appeared in an early issue of *Les Temps Modernes*. This appearance reflected a publication pattern with respect to political writings that was to continue almost uninterruptedly until the appearance of Sartre's major, more lengthy, sociopolitical works, above all his *Critique of Dialectical Reason*. There are no doubt "purists" who would like to distinguish sharply Sartre's shorter political essays, often if not usually occasioned by ongoing historical events, from his more systematic sociopolitical work, of which the *Critique* is the leading instance; even Sartre himself, particularly in interviews, sometimes showed a tendency to think this way. To draw such a strong distinction, however, seems to me to be misleading and counterproductive, and "Materialism and Revolution" – which, ninety pages in length in its book version,[7] can hardly be called a short essay – is a good illustration of my point. It deals head-on with the central ontological claim of the self-styled orthodox Marxists of the Communist Party – namely, that there is only matter and determinism prevails in human history – and it dismisses this claim as a mere myth, an unproven faith. This is hardly an "occasional" sort of claim. In that essay, Sartre goes on to note that the communists have enjoyed considerable success with the dogma of materialism (among other reasons, because it reinforces workers' psychological feelings of equality, rather than inferiority, vis-à-vis the ruling classes), but contends that the justifiable goal of ending oppression should rather be advanced through a philosophy that affirms the reality of human freedom instead of the fallacy that is philosophical materialism.

Among the other important political writings of this period of Sartre's career, basically the fifteen years from 1945 to 1960, special note should be taken of at least four: *Anti-Semite and Jew* (in French, *Réflexions sur la question juive*, a more revealing title); *What Is Literature?*; "The Communists and Peace"; and "Stalin's Ghost." (*Search for a Method* was originally composed and published, first in Polish translation, during exactly the same period as "Stalin's Ghost," namely fall/winter 1956–7, but I shall deal with it later as the preface to the *Critique of Dialectical Reason* that it eventually became.) Sartre's study of anti-Semitism, which he wrote very soon after the liberation of Paris but published somewhat later and in segments, is especially valuable for showing in detail how the anti-Semite creates his or her image of the Jew, who is then demonized, as we might express it today (Sartre speaks of Manichaeism). What helps establish this study as something of a

---

[7] Jean-Paul Sartre, "Matérialisme et révolution," in *Situations* 3:135–225.

breakthrough essay is the fact that the psychological mechanisms analyzed by Sartre in it closely resemble those manifested by racists of other stripes as well.[8] Among the essay's many other valuable points is Sartre's extended criticism of the type of individual whom he denominates "the democrat," by which he means the sort of well-intentioned liberal who affirms the abstract humanity of everyone and hence refuses to acknowledge that there exists a "Jewish question" at all. Although the defects of such a position may seem obvious to most theorists today, Sartre's identification of them was rather original for its time. On the other hand, *Anti-Semite and Jew* is very deficient in its understanding of the significance of tradition in Judaism, a deficiency that Sartre in his last years was to work to overcome by assiduous study of that tradition with his Jewish secretary, Benny Lévy (not to be confused with Bernard-Henri Lévy), and his Jewish adopted daughter, Arlette Elkaïm Sartre.

What Is Literature? (1947) is Sartre's spirited, historically informed defense of a notion that had already been proclaimed in the pages of *Les Temps Modernes* and had been attacked especially by those who opposed its political agenda, namely, that of *littérature engagée*, committed or "engaged" literature. In it, he discusses the varying roles of writers in past historical periods, with special, highly critical emphasis on the late nineteenth-century cult of "art for art's sake," which had had the indirect political effect of reinforcing the status quo; he was to return to this theme in his mammoth, late-life study of one of the greatest exemplars of this cult, Gustave Flaubert, titled *The Family Idiot*. In *What Is Literature?* Sartre again attacked the decadent, wooden Marxism of official Communist Party ideologists and confronted such difficult issues as the problem of challenging the supremacy of the bourgeoisie when the majority of one's readers are inevitably going to be members of that class and the question of the relationship between politics and morality. Clearly, as he saw it, committed literature had to be written from a moral perspective, and yet at the same time it had to avoid the type of doctrinaire, unthinking moralism that was so well exemplified by the orthodox communist writers.

The ensuing, midcentury years were the period of the height of the Cold War; at the same time, they were marked by the unfolding, often painful, process of decolonization, the hot wars in Korea and Indochina, the Cuban revolution of Fidel Castro, and what we can perceive in retrospect as the

---

[8] See, for example, Lewis Gordon, *Bad Faith and Antiblack Racism* (Atlantic Highlands, NJ: Humanities Press, 1995), which makes extensive use of Sartrean philosophy.

beginning of the unraveling of the Warsaw Pact and the Soviet Union. Sartre's name – already very well known, as I have pointed out, through the existentialist vogue of the immediate postwar years – came into great prominence with respect to all of these events, and that is why there is considerable justification in B.-H. Lévy's having referred to the twentieth century, or at least the middle part of it, as Sartre's century, the time when he was deeply "in the soup." Sartre wrote several significant essays dealing with and criticizing colonialism and neocolonialism, the most enduringly famous being no doubt his provocative preface to Frantz Fanon's *The Wretched of the Earth*, published in 1961 when the French government was still asserting its sovereignty over Fanon's adopted land of Algeria. He wrote *L'Affaire Henri Martin* (1953) in defense of a French sailor, a member of the Communist Party, who had advocated resistance to the government's war in Indochina and had been imprisoned; some years later, Sartre joined in solidarity with Bertrand Russell in their unofficial "trial" of alleged American war crimes in Vietnam. He traveled extensively, most notably to the Soviet Union, about which he at one point expressed a degree of enthusiasm that he later came to regret, and to Cuba to become acquainted with its new ruler, Castro, about whom he underwent a similar sequence of changing attitudes. Perhaps the simplest way of grasping the disenchantment that Sartre experienced vis-à-vis the political pretensions of the ruling circles of the communist world (he had never felt any sense of enchantment with the Western powers) is to contrast the messages of the two previously mentioned essays, "The Communists and Peace" (1952 and 1954) and "Stalin's Ghost" (1956/7).

Sartre was incited to write "The Communists and Peace" by events that occurred in Paris while he was on vacation in Italy. The French Communist Party had organized demonstrations against the appointment of U.S. General Ridgway as the new commander of NATO. The French government reacted very strongly to these demonstrations, in the process arresting the leader of the French Communist Party, Jacques Duclos. Overcome with anger by this turn of events, Sartre immediately wrote the first part of his long essay with a view to showing that, historically speaking, the Soviet communists and their affiliated parties elsewhere supported efforts to maintain peace worldwide. In the second portion of the essay, he examined the relationship between the communists and the working class in a situation in which, despite claims to the contrary by Trotskyite groups and others, the Communist Party was, according to him, the only effective political voice actively supporting workers' demands; this part was written after subsequent demonstrations called by the communists had failed to attract the expected numbers of supporters. Finally, in a more historically based third part of the essay written a year and a half later, he discussed the sociopolitical aspects of the evolution of the French working class since the defeat of the Paris Commune some eighty years earlier. The period during which he was writing this essay (and many other works as well) also marked his break, first with Albert Camus over a review of the latter's *The Rebel* in *Les Temps Modernes* – a review that was sharply critical of the book's attempt to discredit aspirations to political revolution and that aroused Camus' extreme ire – and then, more gradually, with Maurice Merleau-Ponty over many matters, beginning with their differing interpretations of the causes of the outbreak of war in Korea.

In early 1956 the new secretary general of the Soviet Communist Party, Nikita Khrushchev, gave his famous address, intended just for party faithful but soon circulated worldwide, in which he indicated something of the scope of Stalin's crimes and initiated the period known as the Thaw. In some of the countries of the so-called Eastern Bloc, most notably Hungary and Poland, a certain degree of intellectual and even political freedom began to be exercised. As we now know, a Soviet invasion of Poland was narrowly averted. Not so in the case of Hungary, where Soviet troops rushed in to crush a popular uprising and a new government that had been formed in response to it. The title of the essay that Sartre wrote as a reaction, "Stalin's Ghost," already makes the essential point of this lengthy analysis of the events. Although this terminology implies merely a "haunting" – unsettling, discouraging, reprehensible, but not yet the demise of the Soviet system itself – the essay as a whole evinces the increasing disenchantment that for Sartre was to become total and utterly irreversible after the somewhat similar events that took place twelve years later in Czechoslovakia.

So much for the more strictly political aspects of Sartre's career at the height of his fame and influence, aspects that, as I have been assuming throughout and have tried to show through my references to a few of his essays, cannot be detached from his more purely theoretical positions. We may now turn to the latter as they are expressed in Sartre's great 750-page tome, the *Critique of Dialectical Reason*, volume 1, which is preceded in its French version by the essay *Search for a Method* and was to have been followed by a second volume; the latter was never completed, but it was eventually published posthumously in a book of more than 450 pages.

Search for a Method – in French, *Questions de méthode*, and *Marksizm i Egzystencjalizm* in the Polish version in which it first appeared – was originally a byproduct of the Khrushchevian Thaw, which had permitted the editor of a Polish journal to prepare an issue on contemporary French philosophy and to solicit contributions from noncommunists as well as communists. Sartre accepted his invitation and wrote a forthright *tour d'horizon*, taking as its initial focus what Continental European philosophers sometimes call "philosophical anthropology": the question, treated by Sartre as a methodological one, of how to understand human behavior in a social context. (He was later to introduce his very lengthy Flaubert study by saying that it was an instantiation of the sought-after method as applied to a single individual. That it required so many pages and still remained incomplete, lacking the planned fourth volume on Flaubert's masterpiece, *Madame Bovary*, might be considered somewhat discouraging to any would-be proponents of this method.) Two possible candidates for the desired method that Sartre discusses and rejects as partial and inadequate are Freudianism and American behavioral sociology. What he proposes instead is what he calls a three-stage "regressive-progressive method," originally proposed by the sociologist-philosopher (and erstwhile Communist Party intellectual, who had once written a scathing attack on Sartre's existentialism) Henri Lefebvre. This method involves first a phenomenological description of the society under investigation, followed by an analytic ("regressive") movement tracing underlying historical and other factors, completed by a reconstruction of the existing state of affairs but with a new, deeper understanding of it based on the findings of the "regressive" inquiry. Both Lefebvre and now Sartre took this methodological procedure to be in keeping with Marxist theory.

As the original Polish title implies, *Search for a Method* is above all an attempt to connect such a methodologically sophisticated, nondogmatic Marxism with existentialism. Sartre asserts at the outset that Marxism is the dominant philosophy of the present era, on which even its most severe critics must focus, and proposes existentialism as a subordinate but necessary complement to it. The existentialist component is necessary because, as Sartre emphasizes again and again, orthodox Marxism has become sclerosed, has stopped, and has failed to take seriously the question of the free and complex human individual. For example, he says that contemporary dogmatic Marxists write as if individuals had no childhoods and were born only on earning their first salaries.[9] He expresses agreement, in principle, with the central Marxist idea that human beings are shaped by material conditions – shaped, not totally determined – but ridicules the sort of thinking

---

[9] Jean-Paul Sartre, *Search for a Method*, trans. H. Barnes (New York: Alfred A. Knopf, 1963), 62.

exemplified by the early Russian Marxist, Plekhanov, who maintained that if Napoleon had not existed some other individual like Napoleon would have acted in such a way as to bring about the same historical outcome. He stresses, by contrast, his important idea, from *Being and Nothingness*, of individual human beings as characterized by their *projects* toward the future, and he begins to make some connection, which will become much clearer in the *Critique*, between this notion and that of historical "totalization," one of his principal proposals for understanding societies from within and in terms of their development across time. (For him, the contrast term to this is "totality," a reifying external perspective on societies and history.) He introduces the notion of scarcity as an important explanatory concept for understanding all of human history up to the present. He concludes the first part of *Search for a Method*, as he might well have concluded the entire work, with the assertion that, with the eventual overcoming of scarcity, the philosophy of Marxism will no longer be needed and a robust philosophy of freedom will take its place.

It is reflection on the historical context of *Search for a Method* that, perhaps more than any of the specific events that I have mentioned in connection with some of his earlier essays, led to my opening remark to the effect that this milieu is now a distant memory. In truth, his now seemingly shocking claim that Marxism is the dominant philosophy of the era can realistically be seen as a simple statement of fact for the time at which the essay was written: Marxism simply *was* the dominant philosophy in France and in much of the rest of Europe and some other parts of the world, although not so in the Anglo-Saxon countries. This is no longer the case, even if one should wish to argue that it still *should* be the case in light, for example, of the continued enormous importance of economic factors, vast inequalities of income and resources worldwide, and so on. One of the principal historical reasons for this changed intellectual landscape is surely the sclerosis of the official Marxism, in both its theory and its practice, that Sartre emphasizes so strongly in this very essay. He does so again, from time to time, in his *Critique of Dialectical Reason*, in the unfinished second volume of which he focuses for hundreds of pages on the Stalinist "*déviation*" (detour, or deviation) of the 1930s, which he says has led everyone worldwide to reconsider fundamental sociopolitical and historical issues in the context of the "One World" (he uses, somewhat surprisingly, the English expression) in which we now live. Yet we may well find other, more purely theoretical and ahistorical or transhistorical reasons for the decline of Marxism's dominance in the underlying structure of Sartre's *Critique* itself.

What I mean by this is that the *Critique* – which (in volume 1) purports to move from a very abstract level, through an analysis of various social formations, up to the point of actual, concrete history – is framed in such a way as to consign to the dustbin of history, so to speak, a fundamental assumption common to the thought of Sartre's most obvious dialectical predecessors, Hegel and Marx, namely, the assumption of inevitable progress. Sartre, who insists throughout the *Critique* that his principal goal is explanation, not justification or condemnation, plainly asserts that the dialectic as he conceives it is reversible. In fact this assertion is borne out by his painstaking analyses of its progressive stages, which are roughly as follows. It begins with human beings, conceived above all under the rubric of "praxis" (a term taken most directly from Marx and intended to emphasize human action as opposed to its more purely theoretical terminological counterpart in *Being and Nothingness*, "being-for-itself"), acting on "inert matter" (corresponding to "being-in-itself" from the earlier work) in a milieu of scarcity. The basic social structure of this initial stage is what Sartre calls "seriality" or "the series": Human beings in this initial state, although they are free in some basic existential sense, are forced to eke out their existence, in the context of what Sartre calls the "practico-inert," in such a way as to take on many of the characteristics of inert matter without, at first, any hope of being able to take control. Seriality is characteristic not only of early human societies, however, but is to be found in many contemporary situations as well: Sartre gives us, for example, some unforgettable descriptions of commuters queuing for a bus; of citizens listening impotently, in millions of homes, to a government-controlled radio station; of the functioning of the stock market; and the like.

In dramatic contrast to seriality is the situation in which, usually in light of some severe perceived menace, human beings coalesce to try to overcome their passive social existence through what Sartre calls the "group." His foremost illustration of this concept is the action taken by the residents of the Quartier Saint-Antoine in Paris: Fearing an attack on their neighborhood by royal troops who regarded them as suspect, they more or less spontaneously gathered to take action – in this case, to capture the prison, the Bastille, which loomed at the entrance to the quarter. The initial condition of this type of *"groupe à chaud,"* or group in fusion, is one of common praxis, with no recognized leader – although even with respect to this most unified, homogeneous form of social structure Sartre rejects the idea of its being an organism and maintains that each participant retains a certain modicum of individual freedom. Yet soon the need is felt to organize, to distribute tasks, and ultimately, through various stages from oath taking (swearing allegiance to the group) to the creation of a function of "sovereignty" to further institutionalization and eventually bureaucracy, the erstwhile group falls back into a state of passivity not entirely unlike the seriality of the initial stages of the *Critique*. With of course many complex variants, this is the general condition of modern society.

This very brief sketch of an enormously rich, still underrated work, full of interesting analyses and descriptions – in part somewhat (but not exactly) reminiscent of Hobbes and of other contract theorists, in part reminiscent of Hegel and Marx, but withal highly creative and original – should at least make clear just how far it is from Hegelian or Marxian triumphalism. True, there is a footnote in which Sartre speaks of the possibility of "group praxis forever,"[10] which would be the goal of socialism, but no reader who follows the analyses seriously is likely to come away with strong expectations of a future along these lines. Nor is the posthumously published volume 2 – featuring Sartre's lengthy analysis of Stalinist practices in the 1930s as part of a projected, but never completed, much longer study of "the intelligibility of history" (as its subtitle would have it) as a process (or rather many, increasingly interconnected processes) of "totalization" – likely to reverse this ultimately negative impression.

In his last years, Sartre concluded that Marxism was at base too hopelessly deterministic for him any longer to consider himself a Marxist at all; his own expectations for the world's future, as expressed in interviews with Benny Lévy, his secretary, that were published (in a newspaper) just before his death under the title *Hope Now*,[11] are far from sanguine. Although Sartre divided those final years, as blindness began to overtake him, between political activism and continuing his work as a writer, particularly of the Flaubert volumes, and although a number of posthumous publications (particularly the unfinished *Notebooks for an Ethics* from the late 1940s and the lectures that he was to have given at Cornell University before deciding to cancel them as a protest against the U.S. government's escalation in Vietnam in the 1960s) shed much additional light on both his sociopolitical and ethical thinking, the *Critique of Dialectical Reason* must be seen in retrospect as occupying pride of place in his post–World War II career. It is both the culmination, as I have attempted to situate it, of so much that went before and a distinctive

[10] Jean-Paul Sartre, *Critique of Dialectical Reason*, trans. A. Sheridan-Smith (London: NLB, 1976), 309.
[11] Jean-Paul Sartre and B. Lévy, *Hope Now: The 1980 Interviews*, trans. A. van den Hoven (Chicago: University of Chicago Press, 1996).

monument to the age in which it was written and published, an age of which the form of life was in fact growing old. Perhaps it may be said to illustrate Hegel's dictum that the owl of Minerva spreads its wings with the falling of dusk.

Suggestions for further reading

Sartre, Jean-Paul. *Being and Nothingness*. Translated by Hazel Barnes. New York: Philosophical Library, 1956.
_____. *Critique of Dialectical Reason*. Translated by A. Sheridan-Smith. London: NLB, 1976.
_____. *Search for a Method*. Translated by H. Barnes. New York: Alfred A. Knopf, 1963.

15

Michel Foucault: an ethical politics of care of self and others

ALAN MILCHMAN AND ALAN ROSENBERG

The name Michel Foucault seems to be inseparable from a discussion of power, that preeminent political concept. Politics, the political, permeates almost everything that Foucault wrote, just as it was a focal point of his life. One seminal feature of the Foucauldian way, we believe, was his juxtaposition of *ethics* and *politics*. Indeed, as he sought to weave the several strands of his thinking together in the last years of his life, Foucault came to see politics as an ethics – not understood as normative rules or a moral code, but as the self's relation to itself, the way one constitutes oneself as a subject. For us, Foucault's ethical turn of the early 1980s did not lead him away from the domain of the political, but rather in the direction of a reconceptualization of politics as an ethical politics. Finally, we contend that it was an adumbration of an ethical politics of care of self and others that Foucault was engaged in at the time of his death in 1984.

Foucault is known for his rejection of the originary, foundational, ahistorical *subject*, which has shaped the Western metaphysical tradition from Plato and Aristotle to Kant and Hegel. Foucault's "subjects" – discussion about them and their genealogies fill the pages of his books, lectures, and interviews – are historically constituted on the bases of determinate apparatuses (*dispositifs*) and discourses (*discours*), which are themselves the outcome of contingent and changing *practices* to which they are integrally linked. An apparatus is the network of power relations, strategies, and technologies on the bases of which a mode of subjectivity is constituted. A discourse constitutes the specific network of rules and procedures on the bases of which "truth" is established in a given historical time and place, the criteria for establishing what Foucault terms the forms of "veridiction." What these apparatuses and discourses, as well as the different modes of subjectivity that they produce, share is their *historicity*.

One strand of modern philosophy, beginning with Kant's question – "What is Enlightenment?" – with which Foucault explicitly identified himself, revolves around the problem: Who are we at present? In the opening lecture of his course at the Collège de France in 1983, Foucault elaborated on his own vision of philosophy: "It seems to me that philosophy as the surface of emergence of a present reality, as a questioning of the philosophical meaning of the present reality of which it is a part, and philosophy as the philosopher's questioning of this 'we' to which he belongs and in relation to which he has to situate himself, is a distinctive feature of philosophy as a discourse of modernity and on modernity."[1]

In a 1981 interview, Foucault was asked, "What has been your itinerary? What was the driving force of your reflection?" Given Foucault's emphasis on *genealogy* in his writings and his understanding of history, one might have expected an elucidation of the genealogy of his own thinking and texts, beginning with his first published book, *The History of Madness* (1961); then the volume that brought him fame, *The Order of Things* (1966); and finally his path-breaking studies of power relations, *Discipline and Punish* (1975), and of the ways in which relations of power shaped modern sexuality, *The History of Sexuality* (1976). Instead, Foucault answered, "You are asking me a difficult question. First because the driving line cannot be determined until one is at the end of the road."[2] Perhaps we can follow Foucault's lead here by starting with the issues that preoccupied him in the final cycle of lectures and courses, focusing on what has been termed his "ethical turn," and concentrating on just where his own "road," his own philosophical journey, was taking him when he died so prematurely in 1984.[3]

One fruitful way to describe Foucault's "histories," then, is that they are genealogies of the subject. However, as Foucault put it in his lectures at Berkeley and at Dartmouth in 1980, his histories have a definite "political dimension":

I mean an analysis that relates to what we are willing to accept in our world, to accept, to refuse, to change, both in ourselves and in our circumstances. In sum, it is a question of searching for another kind of critical philosophy. Not a critical philosophy that seeks to determine the conditions and the limits of our possible

---

[1] Michel Foucault, *The Government of Self and Others* (New York: Palgrave Macmillan, 2010), 13.
[2] Michel Foucault, "What Our Present Is," in *The Politics of Truth* (New York: Semiotext(e), 1997), 147.
[3] These are also the issues that have received the least critical and interpretive attention, and so, despite their importance within the Foucauldian way, they are also still relatively unexplored.

knowledge of the object, but a critical philosophy that seeks the conditions and the indefinite possibilities of transforming the subject, of transforming ourselves.[4]

Foucault signaled those possibilities as early as the (in)famous conclusion to *The Order of Things*, where he hinted at the prospect that the "arrangements" that created the modern subject might crumble, in which case one could "certainly wager that man would be erased like a face drawn in the sand at the edge of the sea."[5] Although many interpreters at the time read Foucault as having proclaimed the "death of the subject," consonant with his purported structuralism, it seems to us that Foucault was pointing to the historico-political conditions within our actuality for the creation of new modes of subjectivity. What was being erased was the foundational subject and its hypostasis within much of the Western philosophical tradition; the death was that of the humanist subject, the specific mode of subjectivity that, as Judith Revel has pointed out, was seen as "a solipsistic and a-historical consciousness, self-constituted and absolutely free."[6]

Foucault's philosophical journey – the elaboration of that critical philosophy – then led him to begin to articulate what we would term a *politics of care of self*, beginning around 1980; this project was ongoing at the time of his death. Foucault clearly articulated that project in November 1980 at the end of his second Dartmouth lecture:

Maybe our problem now is to discover that the self is nothing else than the historical correlation of the technology built in our history. Maybe the problem is to change those technologies [or maybe to get rid of those technologies, and then, to get rid of the sacrifice which is linked to those technologies.] And in this case, one of the main political problems nowadays would be, in the strict sense of the word, the politics of ourselves.[7]

Such a politics of care of self entails a genealogical analysis of both the historical contingencies and their attendant power relations, which produced our modern subjectivity, and the possibilities now contained within our present reality for creating new modes of subjectivity. Foucault's political theory, then, is a critical ontology of ourselves, a critique of who we are, the subjects that we have historically become, and the possibilities of fashioning ourselves differently.

---

[4] Michel Foucault, "Subjectivity and Truth," in *The Politics of Truth*, 179.
[5] Michel Foucault, *The Order of Things: An Archaeology of the Human Sciences* (New York: Vintage Books, 1994), 387.
[6] Judith Revel, *Dictionnaire Foucault* (Paris: Ellipses, 2008), 129.
[7] Michel Foucault, "Christianity and Confession," in *The Politics of Truth*, 230–1. The words in brackets have been added by the editor and are from the Berkeley lectures.

Foucault's analysis of power relations in modern societies, the various modes of domination, discipline, and control – what he termed *assujettisse-ment* and which we translate as "subjectification" – cannot be reduced to subjection or subjugation, with its implication of a passive subject. It also contains the possibility of *resistance* on the part of those who are subjec-tified. The importance of acknowledging the active role of the subject in *assujettissement* or subjectification became especially important in the late 1970s, when Foucault expanded the purview of his investigation of power relations beyond sovereignty and disciplinary power, with its "docile bod-ies," to include what he termed "governmentality." For Foucault, modern governmentality extended power relations beyond coercion and subjection to encapsulate the global administration of the lives of an entire population. At the end of the eighteenth and beginning of the nineteenth centuries in Western Europe, with the birth of liberalism, the whole of the life of the individual and that of the population as a whole – sexual, psychologi-cal, medical, educational, economic, and moral – came to be progressively invested by what Foucault designated as "bio-powers" and by the distinc-tion, imposed by a "social medicine," between the normal and the abnor-mal. However, governmentality, in investing the whole of life, implicates the person directly in the operation of its micro-powers and constitutes a veritable crossroads of technologies of domination and techniques of the self. Even as governmentality permits the spread of technologies of power into virtually every pore of individual and political life, within its ambit, as Johanna Oksala has put it, the subject "is now capable of turning back upon itself: of critically studying the processes of its own constitution, but also of subverting them and effecting changes in them."[8] Moreover, as Judith Revel has opined, it is possible that bio-powers could also be "the site of emer-gence of a counter-power, the site of the production of subjectivity which would constitute a moment of de-subjectification [*désassujettissement*]."[9]

Beyond subjectification, then, Foucault's ethical turn led him to explore a range of possibilities for fashioning one's own self – what he would designate as *subjectivation* in his 1982 lecture course at the Collège de France. Subjectivation is a project of "rejoining oneself as the end and object of a technique of life, an art of living,"[10] entailing a self-relation arising from the subject's own practices of freedom, from his or her own *choice*. It constitutes

---

[8] Johanna Oksala, *Foucault on Freedom* (Cambridge: Cambridge University Press, 2005), 165.
[9] Revel, *Dictionnaire Foucault*, 26.
[10] Michel Foucault, *The Hermeneutics of the Subject* (New York: Palgrave Macmillan, 2005), 333.

a fresh way of grappling with the question of the subject, although one that Foucault himself did not live to elaborate, but which seems to us to be integral to his ethical turn after the publication of the first volume of *The History of Sexuality*. It points to Foucault's growing interest in the prospects that the contemporary sociocultural world provides for the project of arts of living and the transfiguration of self.

This important distinction between *assujettissement* and *subjectivation* also corresponds to two distinct modes of *power*, a distinction that is obscured in English translations of Foucault because of the conventions of the English language itself. When Foucault speaks of *assujettissement* he links it to *pouvoir*, whereas when he speaks of *subjectivation* he links it to *puissance*. English makes do with the same word, "power," for each term, but *pouvoir* is power *over*, whereas *puissance* is power *to*; the former is linked to relations of domination and subjection, the latter to capacities for self-creation and de-subjectification.

Foucault explored the prospects for self-creation within the ambit of his treatment of *ethics*, which for him was integral to politics, and its link to the question of freedom. For Foucault, ethics concerns a self's relationship to itself, how we relate to our own self. It concerns how we "govern" our own conduct, which constituted what he termed an "ethical fourfold," two sides of which are especially relevant here: the ethical work one does on oneself in the effort "to attempt to transform oneself into the ethical subject of one's behavior" and the telos, the goal of fashioning a self, which is one's aim.[11] In Foucault's view, ethics is inseparable from *freedom*. Indeed, as he put it in one of his last interviews, "what is ethics, if not the practice of freedom, the conscious [*réfléchie*] practice of freedom? . . . Freedom is the ontological condition of ethics. But ethics is the considered form that freedom takes when it is informed by reflection."[12]

Yet exactly what kind of freedom is Foucault speaking of here? Is it an existential freedom, rooted in a purported ahistorical human nature? Is Foucault at the end of his life returning to the kinds of philosophical anthropology that he once so harshly criticized as groundless? In our view, such a conclusion is baseless. Is it some legal or constitutional freedom provided to its citizens by a polity or state? In our view, that too is not

---

[11] Michel Foucault, *The History of Sexuality*, vol. 2, *The Use of Pleasure* (New York: Vintage Books, 1990), 27.

[12] Michel Foucault, "The Ethics of the Concern of the Self as a Practice of Freedom," in *The Essential Works of Foucault, 1954–1984*, vol. 1, *Ethics: Subjectivity and Truth*, ed. Paul Rabinow (New York: New Press, 1997), 284.

the case here – although Foucault was not one to reject such "freedoms" where they existed. Foucauldian freedom seems to us to consist in our own groundlessness, in our possibility of unending change – changing ourselves, our subjectivity, changing the social, cultural, and political conditions and the apparatuses in which we contingently find ourselves. Such a conception of freedom, then, is integrally linked to the notion and practice of *refusal*, so powerfully expressed by Foucault: "Maybe the target nowadays is not to discover what we are but to refuse what we are. We have to imagine and to build up what we could be to get rid of this kind of political 'double bind,' which is the simultaneous individualization and totalization of modern power structures."[13]

Foucault's own exploration of those possibilities led him to the ancient Greco-Roman world, although, we believe, always with his eyes on our own actuality. In a series of discussions at Berkeley in 1983, Foucault distinguished between two projects focusing on care of self: One he termed a *techne* of the self and the other a *techne* of life. The latter project, characteristic of ancient Greece, "was to take care of the city, of his companions," not just one's self, although the decline of the polis would later shift the focus in the ancient world more exclusively to one's own self.[14] Although Foucault certainly explored the ways in which one's own life might become a work of art, as well as the space created in modernity for just such a project, he did not neglect the world of the political, the link between oneself as an artwork and the community in which one lives. Indeed, one implication of care of self, then, is care of *others*, of those with whom we share a communal life. Foucault's concern for self and its cultivation, then, is assuredly not solipsistic.

One dimension of treating one's life as an artwork, however, is care of self, the title of the second volume of what had originally been projected as *The History of Sexuality*. In one of his last interviews, Foucault was asked, "Could the problematic of the care of the self be at the heart of a new way of thinking about politics, of a form of politics different from what we know today?"[15] Foucault responded, "I admit that I have not got very far in this direction, and I would very much like to come back to more

---

[13] Michel Foucault, "The Subject and Power," in *The Essential Works of Foucault, 1954–1984*, vol. 3, *Power*, ed. James D. Faubion (New York: New Press, 2000), 336.

[14] Michel Foucault, "On the Genealogy of Ethics: An Overview of Work in Progress," in *Essential Works* 1:259–60.

[15] Michel Foucault, "The Ethics of the Concern of the Self as a Practice of Freedom," in *Essential Works* 1:294.

contemporary questions to try to see what can be made of all this in the context of the current political problematic."[16] Although death prevented Foucault from taking that path, it seems to us that what has been termed his "journey to Greece," his focus on the Greco-Roman world in his lecture courses after 1980, provides an indication of what such an ethical politics might look like.

In his lecture courses both in Paris (1981–4) and in Berkeley, Foucault explored the meaning and ramifications of the ancient concept of *parrhesia*, truth telling or "free-spokenness" (*franc-parler*), as both *techne* and ethos, a concept that he firmly linked to the political. An art of living, a culture of self, for Foucault, "required a relationship to the other. In other words: one cannot attend to oneself, take care of oneself, without a relationship to another person."[17] Such relationships are themselves *political* and require *parrhesia*. As Foucault explicates it, *parrhesia* involves "the affirmation that in fact one genuinely thinks, judges, and considers the truth one is saying to be genuinely true."[18] It "only exists when there is freedom in the enunciation of the truth, freedom of the act by which the subject says the truth,"[19] and there is a risk in one's free-spokenness "that the fact of telling the truth . . . will, may, or must entail costly consequences for those who have told it." Indeed, truth tellers, "parrhesiasts are those who, if necessary, accept death for having told the truth,"[20] for telling truth to power.

For Foucault, the concept of *parrhesia* was both a preeminent political concept and one directly linked to *democracy*. Although Foucault's last two lecture courses in Paris[21] both designate *parrhesia* as a fundamentally political concept, his discussion of that notion draws mostly on ancient texts and examples. Nonetheless, Foucault's concern with the history of the *present* leads him to forge explicit links with our own actuality in the person who engages in "critical discourse in the political domain," a certain type of philosopher, we would say, and in the figure of the revolutionary, "this person who arises within society and says: I am telling the truth, and I am telling the truth in the name of the revolution that I am going to make and that we will make together."[22]

---

[16] Ibid.
[17] Foucault, *The Government of Self and Others*, 43.
[18] Ibid., 64.
[19] Ibid., 66.
[20] Ibid., 56.
[21] *The Government of Self and Others* and the not yet translated *Le Courage de la vérité*.
[22] Foucault, *The Government of Self and Others*, 70.

Foucault's discussion of democracy in ancient Greece focuses on two conjoined elements, both of which would also seem to be integral to a modern conceptualization of democracy as a setting for a politics of care of self: first, *isegoria*, the equality of all citizens, the equal right to speak, to make decisions, and to actively participate in public life;[23] and second, *parrhesia*, which is added to the rights of a citizen and which entails a subject who has made a "parrhesiastic pact" that binds the subject both to speak the truth and to "take on the risk of all its consequences."[24] According to Foucault's concept of democracy, *isegoria*, equal rights, and *parrhesia* all exist within what he terms an "agonistic game," a rule-based communal framework, in which the speech, "the discourse of others, to which one leaves space alongside one's own, may prevail over your discourse. What constitutes the field peculiar to *parrhêsia* is this political risk of a discourse which leaves room free for other discourse and assumes the task, not of bending others to one's will, but of persuading them."[25] A modern democracy, then, would have to instantiate both equality and *parrhesia* in its own agonistic game, albeit with very different and broader conceptions of citizenship than prevailed even in the democratic polis of ancient Athens.

In his lectures on ancient democracy, Foucault was acutely sensitive to the danger of demagogy, to the fate of Periclean Athens, and to the need to distinguish between "good" and "bad" *parrhesia*. Good *parrhesia*, of which Pericles was an exemplar[26] and the ethical qualities of which are those of the parrhesiastic pact, is contrasted with the bad *parrhesia* linked to rhetoric and flattery of one's auditors. Bad *parrhesia* is where the aim of the "orator" is simply to win over the masses, typically by appeals to the basest of emotions and to fears; where it prevails, those who embody good *parrhesia* but cannot sway the masses with their own truth telling (*dire vrai*), who refuse to engage in demagogy, are "threatened with such measures, like expulsion – but these measures may go as far as exile, or ostracism, and also in some cases . . . death."[27] It is not difficult to see here a link with the practices of modern representative or plebiscitarian democracy and their charismatic leaders, as well as the ways in which the mass media and money function

---

[23] Ibid., 150–1.
[24] Ibid., 65. It also implicitly binds the citizens, who are no less responsible for the outcome of the decisions they have made than are those who first proposed them (ibid., 177).
[25] Ibid., 105.
[26] Ibid., 166–7. In his analysis of the *Orestes* of Euripides, Foucault points to the *autourgos*, the small peasant devoted to his land, as another exemplar of good *parrhesia*.
[27] Ibid., 181.

within them. Indeed, Foucault concluded his lecture on February 2, 1983, at the Collège on just such a note:

Well in a time like ours, when we are so fond of posing the problems of democracy in terms of the distribution of power, of the autonomy of each in the exercise of power, in terms of transparency and opacity, and of the relation between civil society and the state, I think it may be a good idea to recall this old question, which was contemporary with the functioning of Athenian democracy and its crises, namely the question of true discourse and the necessary, indispensable, and fragile caesura that true discourse cannot fail to introduce into a democracy which both makes this discourse possible and constantly threatens it.[28]

Meanwhile, good or ethical *parrhesia* "is anti-flattery in the sense that in *parrhêsia*, there is indeed someone who speaks and who speaks to the other, but, unlike what happens in flattery, he speaks to the other in such a way that this other will be able to form an autonomous, independent, full and satisfying relationship to himself. The final aim of *parrhêsia* is not to keep the person to whom one speaks dependent upon the person who speaks."[29]

Can the philosopher avoid the dangers, dare we say the risks, of political life by withdrawal into his or her study? Foucault was clear that that was not an option, and not just because the philosopher shares the life of the city, the community. Foucault also forges a direct link between *logos*, rational discourse, and *ergon*, action,[30] and although he is lecturing on Plato there, its implications for the modern philosopher and, of course, for Foucault himself seem clear: The philosopher must *act*, and act precisely insofar as he or she is both a philosopher and a "citizen." As Foucault forcefully argues, "Now the philosopher cannot be merely *logos* with regard to politics. To be more than just 'hollow words' he must take part in and put his hand directly to action (*ergon*)."[31]

In his final lecture course at the Collège de France, February–March 1984, just several months before his death, Foucault focused on the Cynics and Cynic *parrhesia*. Here, there appeared to be a sharp contrast with the Epicurean and Stoic schools with which Foucault had been concerned just a year earlier, when he first undertook to investigate the government of self and others: The Cynics enjoined a detachment from and a rejection of familial and civic ties, bonds of friendship, or loyalty to a city or polity. However, in their place, as Foucault showed, the Cynics enjoined a freedom

---

[28] Ibid., 184.
[29] Foucault, *The Hermeneutics of the Subject*, 379.
[30] Foucault, *The Government of Self and Others*, 218–19.
[31] Ibid., 219.

to instantiate and "accomplish the great task of ethical universality... the universality of all humans. An individual bond with individuals, but to all individuals, that is what characterized, in its freedom, but also in an obligatory way, the bond of the Cynic with all the other persons that constituted the human species."[32] In his or her care for the other, then, the Cynic embodied the qualities of "true political activity, true *politeuesthai*.... This *politeuesthai* [living and acting as a citizen] is no longer that of cities or of States, but of the entire world."[33]

What then is the relationship between democracy and a politics of care of self, to which Foucault was pointing at the end of his life? That was a project for which his final cycle of lecture courses was only a preparation, and one unfortunately cut short. The agonistic character of democracy on which Foucault insisted, linked to its parrhesiastic game, the framework within which truth telling functions, opens a path to a politics of care of self and care of others by its constant effort to expand the scope for new modes of subjectivity, by creating the space for the flourishing of a multiplicity of arts of living. A democratic politics would maximize those spaces and provide a critique of all those practices and discourses that seek to homogenize subjectivity, to make it uniform, and to narrow the scope of freedom.

Suggestions for further reading

In addition to Foucault's writings, to which this chapter points, readers seeking more information might consult the following.

Bernauer, James. *Michel Foucault's Force of Flight: Toward an Ethics for Thought.* Atlantic Highlands, NJ: Humanities Press International, 1990.
Binkley, Sam, and Jorge Capetillo-Ponce, eds. *A Foucault for the 21st Century: Governmentality, Biopolitics, and Discipline in the New Millennium.* Newcastle: Cambridge Scholars Publishing, 2009.
Dreyfus, Hubert L., and Paul Rabinow. *Michel Foucault: Beyond Structuralism and Hermeneutics.* 2nd ed. Chicago: University of Chicago Press, 1983.
Gutting, Gary, ed. *The Cambridge Companion to Foucault.* Cambridge: Cambridge University Press, 1994.
Revel, Judith. *Dictionnaire Foucault.* Paris: Ellipses, 2008.

---

[32] Michel Foucault, *Le courage de la vérité: Le gouvernement de soi et des autres II* (Paris: Gallimard/Seuil, 2009), 277; our translation.
[33] Ibid., 278.

16

Jürgen Habermas: postwar German political debates and the making of a critical theorist

WILLIAM E. SCHEUERMAN

Like few other intellectuals of his generation, Jürgen Habermas (1929–) has not only helped shape theoretical discourse in an astonishing array of scholarly fields (e.g., jurisprudence, the philosophy of social sciences, political theory or philosophy, and social theory) but has also consistently played a major role in cultural and political debates that have regularly garnered broad public audiences: In the Federal Republic of Germany, whose development Habermas has critically scrutinized pretty much since its founding, he has consistently and sometimes courageously checked revanchist political tendencies, repeatedly speaking out against antidemocratic and illiberal voices and trends.[1] To focus on Habermas's accomplishments as a "political philosopher" thus necessarily means ignoring many of his most significant contributions. Nonetheless, it remains appropriate to do so if only because his massive *oeuvre* speaks directly to one of political philosophy's main concerns since the 1960s.

With its dramatic portrayal of the decay of the classical liberal or "bourgeois" public sphere and its replacement by a late-capitalist "manufactured" public sphere, Habermas's landmark early work, *The Structural Transformation of the Public Sphere* (1962),[2] laid the foundations for most of his subsequent research. Since the outset of his career, Habermas has energetically undertaken to provide a theoretically sound account of freewheeling and unhindered public debate, which is able both to do justice to the realities

---

[1] See Martin Matustik, *Jürgen Habermas: A Philosophical-Political Profile* (Lanham, MD: Rowman & Littlefield, 2001).

[2] Jürgen Habermas, *The Structural Transformation of the Public Sphere: An Inquiry into a Category of Bourgeois Society*, trans. Thomas Burger (Cambridge, MA: MIT Press, 1989). For a useful collection of essays, see Craig Calhoun, ed., *Habermas and the Public Sphere* (Cambridge, MA: MIT Press, 1992), especially (given my purposes here) Seyla Benhabib, "Models of Public Space: Hannah Arendt, the Liberal Tradition, and Jürgen Habermas," 73–98.

of modern social complexity and ultimately to guide far-reaching political and social reform. As he has repeatedly argued, only a sufficiently demanding normative conception of the public sphere can redeem the original emancipatory promises of both the European Enlightenment and its most valuable political offspring, modern democracy. Even though his analysis has unavoidably shifted somewhat during his long career, he has frequently reiterated his original thesis that genuinely free and equal public debate – and with it, democratic politics – remains unsatisfactorily vulnerable under contemporary social conditions. Although he has abandoned much of the heavily Marxist framework that shaped *Structural Transformation*, he has remained critical of capitalism and firmly situated on the democratic left. Over the course of nearly five decades, his political and intellectual preoccupation with democratic deliberation's rich normative potential – as well as its more disappointing empirical fate – has encouraged Habermas to pursue many different problems in a mind-boggling variety of academic fields; his famous attempt to formulate an ambitious theory of what he calls "communicative action" stems directly from this preoccupation.[3]

Admittedly, his wide-ranging reflections have allowed even his most avid readers occasionally to lose the woods for the trees. Yet as one looks back at an intellectual career that now spans nearly six decades, the key question motivating Habermas's far-flung writings seems straightforward enough: How can we realize a robust democracy – and especially the requisite freewheeling public debate and exchange – in a seemingly hostile economic, social, and technological context? Moreover, how might we do so without sacrificing modernity's lasting political and social achievements?

Habermas's crucial early contributions to political theory should be grouped alongside a handful of other influential works from the same historical juncture, each of which was driven by a strikingly parallel interest in salvaging "the political" and, even more specifically, a vision of political action capable of countering the ominous authoritarian and totalitarian options widely embraced in the twentieth century. Like Hannah Arendt's *The Human Condition* (1958), C. Wright Mills's *The Power Elite* (1956) (both discussed in his early writings), and Sheldon Wolin's *Politics and Vision* (1960), the work of the young Habermas sought to rescue "the ideas of the public realm and a noninstrumental form of praxis from oblivion."[4] Like

---

[3] The key text here is Jürgen Habermas, *Theory of Communicative Action*, trans. Thomas McCarthy, 2 vols. (Cambridge, MA: MIT Press, 1984–87).

[4] See chapter 7 in this volume by Dana Villa, "Hannah Arendt: From Philosophy to Politics."

Arendt and Wolin, he worried deeply about the widespread tendency in modern political thinking to reduce the political to the social, economic, and technological. Like them as well, he was motivated by the quest to protect the special attributes of political action and especially public deliberation against inappropriately invasive inroads from other forms of activity.[5]

In contradistinction to Arendt and perhaps also Wolin, however, his instincts were always decidedly *modernist*; early on, Habermas bluntly rejected what he considered to be unduly nostalgic and theoretically misbegotten attempts to revitalize the political and philosophical legacy of classical antiquity.[6] These proclivities, in conjunction with his appreciative recourse to modern social theory and the social sciences, have made his work a more appealing starting point than Arendt's or Wolin's for those – typically situated on the political left – who share his more balanced assessment of modernity's latent political and social resources. In telling respects, the young Habermas was closer to the radical American sociologist C. Wright Mills, whose own fertile reflections from the same period also underscored the basically modern and liberal-democratic credentials of the public sphere, while similarly linking its decline to the ascent of modern capitalism and bureaucratization. Like Mills as well, Habermas early on evinced a clear grasp of classical Marxism's normative lacuna, even as he tried to employ an undogmatic version of it to make sense of the roots of recent democratic fragility.[7] Mills's anxieties about the fragility of public life must have hit home with this young German citizen of a fledgling post-totalitarian democracy not exactly well known in the 1950s for its lively political exchange and debate.[8]

From this angle, the intense fascination with Habermas's work derives partly from the same sources driving the huge interest in Arendt and others:

[5] See, for example, his critique of "technocracy" (as formulated especially in Jürgen Habermas, *Toward a Rational Society*, trans. Jeremy Shapiro [Boston: Beacon, 1971], 81–122), one of his main projects in the late 1960s.

[6] Habermas, *Structural Transformation*, 19. See also the many references to Arendt's work in the early essays collected in Jürgen Habermas, *Theory and Practice*, trans. John Viertel (Boston: Beacon, 1973). Interestingly, Habermas has cited Leo Strauss on various occasions, but has not systematically discussed his attempt to revitalize Greek political philosophy. However, *Structural Transformation* clearly provides an account of modernity fundamentally opposed to that offered by Strauss.

[7] Compare Mills's *The Marxists* (New York: Delta, 1962) to Habermas's early essays on Marxism, a number of which are found in *Theory and Practice*.

[8] See, for example, the great postwar satirist Wolfgang Koeppen's biting description of debate in the Bundestag from his classic *Das Treibhaus* (*The Hothouse*) (1953): "The fronts were rigid, and unfortunately it was inconceivable that someone could get up from the benches of the minority in opposition and convince the ruling majority that he was right and they were wrong. Not even a Demosthenes could succeed in changing the policy of the government in Bonn from the opposition benches; even if one spoke with angels' tongues, one would be preaching to deaf ears" (W. Koeppen, *The Hothouse*, trans. Michael Hofmann [New York: Norton, 2000], 183).

His writings tap into a ubiquitous unease among both ordinary citizens and politically minded intellectuals that something is "not quite right" in real existing liberal democracies, that political action and exchange too often seem shallow and somehow disconnected from fundamental matters, and that our major institutions appear unable to tackle the great issues of the day. Despite Habermas's attempt to address well-nigh *universal* political anxieties, the particular fashion in which he has done so has unavoidably been shaped by a *specific* political and historical context. As I hope to demonstrate in what follows, it would be a mistake to overlook the crucial fact – conveniently neglected by most Anglophone commentators[9] – that Habermas came of age intellectually in 1950s and early 1960s Germany and that his political theory can be fruitfully reconstructed not only as an effort at creatively "superseding" (in the Hegelian sense) the earlier theoretical accomplishments of the German Marxist left but also as an attempt to respond critically to the German right and its foremost midcentury representative, Carl Schmitt. In short, his political theory's seemingly abstract character should not mislead us into downplaying the particular political context, especially evident in a series of now pretty much forgotten political and legal debates from the early years of the Federal Republic, in which Habermas first sketched out his ideas.

Postwar German Marxism and the young Habermas

When reminiscing about his student days in Frankfurt during the 1950s, Habermas has occasionally mentioned Max Horkheimer's worries that he and other young leftist students would get hold of old copies of the *Zeitschrift für Sozialforschung*, which were safely locked away in the cellar of the newly rebuilt quarters of the Institute for Social Research, apparently to repress memory of its radical past. The young Habermas had already read Karl Marx, Georg Lukacs, Ernst Bloch, and Horkheimer and Adorno's *Dialectic of Enlightenment* (1944) before joining the Institute in Frankfurt, but he confesses to having initially had little knowledge of the interdisciplinary Hegelian-Marxist research program that the Institute had pioneered while in American exile.[10] Although his assistantship under Adorno quickly altered

---

[9] For an important exception, see Matthew G. Specter, *Habermas: An Intellectual Biography* (Cambridge: Cambridge University Press, 2010).

[10] Jürgen Habermas, *Autonomy and Solidarity: Interviews with Jürgen Habermas*, ed. Peter Dews (London: Verso, 1986), 94–5. See also Rolf Wiggershaus, *The Frankfurt School: Its History, Theories, and Political Significance*, trans. Michael Robertson (Cambridge, MA: MIT Press, 1995), 537–66.

this state of affairs, at least some credit for initiating Habermas into the rich tradition of interwar and especially German Jewish leftist thought should go to the jurist and political scientist Wolfgang Abendroth (1906–85), long the Federal Republic's only Marxist tenured professor, and whom Habermas in an appreciative 1966 *Die Zeit* essay described as a lonely "partisan fighter" in a "nation of fellow travelers."[11] The label was well chosen: The left-socialist Abendroth not only was active in the anti-Nazi underground and fought among anti-Fascist partisans but also spent his entire life involved in left-wing causes. He led the leftist charge against the disproportionately rightist academics – many of whom indeed had been active Nazis or at the very least fellow travelers – who dominated politics and law faculties in 1950s Germany.

Those familiar with Habermas's biography already know the unfortunate tale of Horkheimer's hostility to the young Habermas, whom the increasingly circumspect Institute director apparently considered too radical, and how Habermas was driven to disembark from Frankfurt and pursue his *habilitation* (or "second dissertation," traditionally required to pursue a German university career), *Structural Transformation of the Public Sphere*, under Abendroth's aegis at Marburg, a quaint but somewhat provincial college town just north of Frankfurt. What sometimes gets lost in the story, however, is Abendroth's relatively significant intellectual and political impact on the young Habermas. In crucial ways, Habermas's early work represented a creative engagement with an older tradition of creative leftist political and legal thought that Abendroth had almost singlehandedly managed to preserve in Adenauer's Germany.[12]

Abendroth represented a rare link not only to an indigenous Marxist tradition nearly extinguished by Nazism but also to the vibrant intellectual culture of left-wing Weimar jurisprudence and political theory.[13] A student of the prominent Weimar-era socialist jurists Hugo Sinzheimer and Hermann Heller, Abendroth made his main intellectual and political achievement in Adenauer's Germany by salvaging the original interpretation of the idea of a *sozialer Rechtsstaat* (social rule of law), which Heller (and, although usually forgotten, also the young Franz L. Neumann, later

---

[11] Jürgen Habermas, "Partisanenprofessor im Lande der Mitläufer," *Die Zeit*, April 29, 1966.
[12] Not surprisingly, *Structural Transformation* was dedicated to his Marburg teacher.
[13] For helpful surveys of Abendroth, see Friedrich-Martin Balzer, Hans Manfred Bock, and Uli Schöler, eds., *Wolfgang Abendroth: Wissenschaftlicher Politiker; Bio-bibliographische Beiträge* (Opladen: Westdeutscher Verlag, 2001); Barbara Dietrich and Joachim Perels, eds., *Wolfgang Abendroth: Ein Leben in der Arbeiterbewegung; Gespräche* (Frankfurt: Suhrkamp, 1976).

an affiliate of the exiled Institute for Social Research) had desperately advocated in Weimar's waning days. In Heller's view, as in the young Neumann's, the idea of the rule of law was no longer to be directly linked to economic liberalism. Potentially despotic forms of private economic power had to be tamed and regularized by regulatory devices if legal and economic security were to be achieved and political democracy survive. The rule of law could be successfully reconfigured in accordance with far-reaching social-democratic–style state interventionism.[14] In his much discussed "Zum Begriff des demokratischen und sozialen Rechtsstaates im Grundgesetz der Bundesrepublik Deutschland" (The conception of the democratic and social rule of law in the Basic Law of the German Federal Republic) (1954), Abendroth defended the original Weimar understanding of the notion of a social *Rechtsstaat* as an opening for radical reform and ultimately some type of democratic socialism.[15] In opposition to conservative Schmitt students like Ernst Forsthoff, Abendroth refused to interpret the Basic Law as a rigid codification of the economic and social status quo, and thus as little more than a constitutional basis for narrowly circumscribed correctives to an incorrigibly capitalist economy.[16] With the emergence of massive concentrations of economic power threatening "formal" democracy, in conjunction with the collapse of the classical liberal state/society divide, only a far-reaching democratization of both state and economy could realize the original humanistic ideals of the unfinished democratic revolutions. Although Abendroth admitted that the Basic Law entailed no express decision in favor of a socialist future, he insisted – to the outraged catcalls of right-wing law professors – that it not only *allowed* for a socialist Federal Republic, but in fact immediately required wide-ranging egalitarian social reforms that would propel West Germany in a leftist direction.

---

[14] Herman Heller, *Rechtsstaat oder Diktatur?* (Tübingen: Mohr, 1930). For a brief discussion, see William E. Scheuerman, *Between the Norm and the Exception: The Frankfurt School and the Rule of Law* (Cambridge, MA: MIT Press, 1994), 39–45. Weimar socialist legal discourse was of course one of Friedrich Hayek's main targets in his hugely influential postwar attempt to marry the rule of law to free-market economic policies.

[15] Wolfgang Abendroth, *Antagonistische Gesellschaft und politische Demokratie: Aufsätze zur politischen Soziologie* (Neuwied: Luchterhand, 1967).

[16] Article 20 of the Basic Law committed the Federal Republic to developing a "democratic and social rule of law." For an insightful discussion of the wide-ranging debate in which Abendroth, Habermas, and others were participating, see Peter C. Caldwell, "Is a 'Social *Rechtsstaat*' Possible? The Weimar Roots of a Bonn Controversy," in *From Liberal Democracy to Fascism: Legal and Political Thought in the Weimar Republic*, ed. Peter C. Caldwell and William E. Scheuerman (Boston: Humanities Press, 2000), 136–53.

As has been widely noted in the secondary literature, Habermas's *Structural Transformation* was deeply influenced by the Marxism of the early Frankfurt School and especially Adorno's devastating critique of capitalist "mass culture." However, the direct dependence of the work's concluding programmatic section on Abendroth's agenda is rarely mentioned. Like Abendroth, the young Habermas relied on a grand narrative about capitalist social transformation to help buttress a radical reading of the idea of a social *Rechtsstaat*, which he analogously interpreted as requiring democratization of the so-called neofeudal institutional configurations emerging in contemporary organized capitalism alongside the collapse of the classical liberal state/society divide.[17] Although perhaps somewhat more cautiously than Abendroth, Habermas pushed for a reform agenda possessing impeccable democratic socialist credentials. He offered a robust defense of social rights, arguing that social and economic transformations effaced traditional attempts to distinguish between "negative" and "positive" liberties: Even a basic measure of economic security, along the lines traditionally secured by classical liberal property rights, increasingly required of government that it intervene extensively in the economy. Any sensible attempt to resuscitate a critical public sphere attuned to contemporary conditions would need to employ novel modes of postliberal decision making and interest mediation. Echoing his Marxist teacher, Habermas even pointed to the possibility that advances in the "forces of production" and concomitant increases in social wealth might allow competing social interests to lose their "antagonistic edge."[18] Not surprisingly, in one of his own essays from the same period, Abendroth enthusiastically praised Habermas's study and its key ideas, understandably seeing in them a normative enrichment of his own proposals.[19]

More generally, Abendroth helped acquaint Habermas with – or at least provide him with professional and intellectual space to interrogate – broader leftist currents in 1920s and '30s political theory and jurisprudence.[20] To be sure, Habermas's writings always evinced greater appreciation than those of either Abendroth or his Weimar leftist forebears for normative political theory and especially the normative foundations of democracy. This greater appreciation always set him apart not only from Abendroth but also from the early Frankfurt School, which even at its best never developed a

---

[17] Habermas, *Structural Transformation*, 222–35.
[18] Ibid., 234.
[19] Abendroth, *Antagonistische Gesellschaft*, 272, 281–3.
[20] In email correspondence with the author, Habermas has confirmed the accuracy of this interpretation.

sufficiently well-grounded theory of law and democracy. Nonetheless, his far-reaching debts to leftist Weimar thought in *Structural Transformation* – and even more so in a crucial essay from the same period, "Zum Begriff der politischen Beteiligung" (On the concept of political participation), which served as a lengthy theoretical introduction to an empirical study he helped conduct in the late 1950s on the political attitudes of German students (*Student und Politik* [1961])[21] – remain indisputable. Especially in the latter essay, Habermas updated a core thesis that Neumann and Ernst Fraenkel (both also Sinzheimer students) had formulated in the 1930s: With the transition from competitive to monopoly or organized capitalism, the classical rule of law and especially the central place of the general legal norm necessarily found itself under attack.[22] Extensively citing the mostly Jewish émigrés – including another Institute affiliate from the 1930s, Otto Kirchheimer, whom Abendroth described as "the most talented and intelligent" of the Weimar socialist jurists[23] – now based in the United States, Habermas reiterated an argument that directly echoed their most radical writings: Organized capitalism was resulting in parliamentary decay, administrative as well as judicial discretion, and increasingly authoritarian forms of political domination. Directly taking up Heller's central claim from *Rechtsstaat oder Diktatur?* (Rule of law or dictatorship?) (1930), Habermas similarly prophesied that *either* decisive steps toward social democratization would have to be taken *or* new liberal democracies such as Germany faced nothing less than the terrifying prospect of a resurgence of political authoritarianism. Once again, he endorsed Abendroth's view – directly influenced by the Weimar debates – that social democratic interventionism could preserve the normative kernel of the rule of law by guaranteeing social rights as well as relatively predictable forms of state economic activity in accord with regularized legal and administrative procedures.

No wonder that an increasingly cautious and conservative Horkheimer was so hostile to this and other writings by the young Habermas: They must have brought back painful memories of 1930s Germany, for him an understandably traumatic period apparently best left buried deep in his psyche – and in the Institute basement.

---

[21] Jürgen Habermas, Ludwig von Friedeburg, and Christoph Oehler, *Student und Politik* (Neuwied: Luchterhand, 1961). Habermas's essay not only anticipated much of the subsequent interest in "participatory democracy" but also presciently identified some of its limitations. Oddly, the essay has never been translated, despite its potential interest to political scientists.

[22] William E. Scheuerman, "Social Democracy and the Rule of Law: The Legacy of Ernst Fraenkel," in *From Liberal Democracy to Fascism*, 74–105.

[23] Dietrich and Perels, eds., *Wolfgang Abendroth*, 146 (my translation).

Habermas has on many subsequent occasions praised Abendroth's political and intellectual integrity while gradually but unambiguously distancing himself from the reformist brand of Marxist democratic socialism always defended by his Marburg teacher. Apt appreciation for the fact that ours is necessarily a functionally differentiated society, Habermas has argued, proves inconsonant with holistic models of a planned democratic socialism in which the rightful autonomy of market mechanisms necessarily must be neglected.[24] In an essay published for a 1989 conference convened in honor of the belated English translation of *Structural Transformation*, Habermas again gratefully mentioned his debt to Abendroth, while conceding that in hindsight "one cannot but be struck by the weaknesses of a Hegelian-Marxist style of thought, all wrapped up in notions of totality, as is evidently the case with Abendroth's fascinating program."[25] Traditional socialists like Abendroth succumbed to a naive view of bureaucratic state intervention and failed to grapple sufficiently with the perils of *Verrechtlichung* (juridification), a negative form of legal regulation to which the mature Habermas has devoted significant analytic attention.[26] In his recent *Between Facts and Norms*,[27] which updates many of Habermas's long-standing political concerns in part by engaging extensively with Anglo-American jurisprudence and political philosophy, debates from Weimar and early postwar German political and legal theory seem peripheral, with Habermas openly criticizing interpretations of the rule of law having as their centerpiece the generality of the legal norm. Referring expressly to *Student und Politik*, Habermas now apparently sees some of its more radical theses as little more than an example of youthful exuberance: In his present view, its implicit reformulation of 1920s and 1930s Hegelian-Marxism was shaped inordinately by a tendentious view of the generality of the legal norm deriving from Carl Schmitt and especially his influential *Constitutional Theory* (1928), and then imported into left-wing German legal discourse by Neumann and others.[28]

Despite the theoretical distance from Abendroth, his impact remains palpable. Habermas continues to defend an interpretation of the social

---

[24] Jürgen Habermas, "What Does Socialism Mean Today? The Rectifying Revolution and the Need for New Thinking on the Left," *New Left Review*, no. 183 (September–October 1990), 3–21.

[25] Jürgen Habermas, "Further Reflections on the Public Sphere," in *Habermas and the Public Sphere*, 435–6.

[26] Habermas, *Theory of Communicative Action* 2:356–73.

[27] Jürgen Habermas, *Between Facts and Norms: Contributions to a Discourse Theory of Law and Democracy*, trans. William Rehg (Cambridge, MA: MIT Press, 1998).

[28] Ibid., 563 n. 75.

Rechtsstaat as calling for what he now dubs the "reflexive" reform of the social welfare state.[29] Although weak on concrete details, this model interprets the unfulfilled project of the social welfare state as necessitating substantially more ambitious measures than mere regulatory correctives to contemporary capitalism. In short, Habermas has never made his peace with the social and economic status quo or with a model of the welfare state as resting on paternalistic forms of administrative action chiefly aimed at preserving social order and warding off meaningful advancement by the disadvantaged. Even as its theoretical contours have obviously changed over the decades, the original demand for a far-reaching democratization of society has by no means vanished, although Habermas now tends to highlight the difficult challenges posed by social complexity and functional differentiation to conventional left-wing programmatic ideas. The systematic attempt in *Between Facts and Norms* to draw integral links between and among radical democratization, the rule of law, and a "reflexive" welfare state also contains significant remnants of Abendroth's original critical response to postwar German Schmittians who sharply *juxtaposed* the rule of law to an ambitious model of the welfare state, seeing the latter as necessarily incongruent with the former.

When contemporary leftist critics lament a lack of radicalism in Habermas's recent writings, what they in fact are addressing is the demise of a plausible model of democratic socialism along the lines once advocated by Abendroth. There can be no question that Habermas's skepticism remains understandable, however. His own caution about the possible contours of a fundamental alternative to the political and economic status quo, at the very least, provides expression to genuine dilemmas facing the democratic left today.

Habermas meets Schmitt

In another fashion as well, Habermas remains indebted to Abendroth and the jurists of the interwar left whose memory Abendroth helped preserve in postwar Germany: The target of much of his political and legal thinking remains Carl Schmitt (1888–1985), Germany's premier twentieth-century authoritarian right-wing legal thinker and, at least for a few years, the

---

[29] Ibid., 388–446.

eager "crown jurist of the Third Reich."[30] Although Schmitt was banned from university teaching after World War II, his students – for example, Forsthoff and Werner Weber – energetically updated many of his core ideas for the postwar era; in the legal academy and elsewhere, Schmitt's thinking remained enormously influential. Abendroth, as noted, waged a fierce battle with Schmitt's followers in debates about the social *Rechtsstaat*. A generation earlier, Neumann and Kirchheimer, the Weimar leftist lawyers who later served as the first-generation political and legal theorists of the Institute for Social Research, also focused their theoretical and political ire on Schmitt and his disciples. Habermas's writings similarly reveal an impressive familiarity with Schmitt's far-flung writings, along with deep political and moral revulsion.[31] On one reading of Neumann and Kirchheimer, they attempted to proffer a social democratic rejoinder to both Schmitt's normative dismissal of modern democracy and the rule of law and also his empirical diagnosis that "normativistic" legality inexorably must decay under contemporary political and social traditions. Interestingly, Habermas has pursued a parallel strategy of attack, repeatedly criticizing Schmitt and at times envisioning his own theorizing as best capable of providing the requisite antipode to the dangerous temptations of Schmitt's decisionism. In any event, opposition to Schmitt runs like a red thread throughout his political and legal theorizing: Schmitt is a key target not only in Habermas's early political writings but also in his latest discussions of globalization and the prospects of postnational democratization. As Habermas revealingly noted in a 1984 interview, "I was critical of decisionism from the very beginning – from the minute when I read Schmitt, for instance."[32]

Although Habermas was in fact deeply critical of Schmitt even at the outset of his career, his early political writings occasionally marshaled Schmitt and his disciples to document worrisome empirical trends – for example, the decay of deliberative parliamentarism – that Habermas, in contrast to Schmitt, hoped to counter.[33] In these first jousts with Schmitt, Habermas echoed Neumann and Kirchheimer by interpreting Schmitt's troublesome

---

[30] The literature on Schmitt is massive. Particularly relevant here is the detailed intellectual and institutional history of his impact on postwar German thought by Dirk van Laak, *Gespräche in der Sicherheit des Schweigens: Carl Schmitt in der Geistesgeschichte der frühen Bundesrepublik* (Berlin: Akademie Verlag, 2002).

[31] See, for example, Jürgen Habermas, "The Horrors of Autonomy," in *The New Conservatism: Cultural Criticism and the Historians' Debate* (Cambridge, MA: MIT Press, 1989), 128–39.

[32] Habermas, *Autonomy and Solidarity*, 194.

[33] This overlap leads some (most recently, Hartmut Becker, *Die Parlamentarismkritik bei Carl Schmitt und Jürgen Habermas* [Berlin: Duncker & Humblot, 1994]) to miss vital differences.

authoritarian political and programmatic preferences as reifying disturbing real-life empirical trends. When *Structural Transformation* described the ominous prospects of an executive-dominated plebiscitarian regime in which uncoerced debate, the rule of law, and parliamentary rule had been jettisoned for manufactured publics, legal arbitrariness, and plebiscitary acclamation, Habermas's description of its main components mirrored Schmitt's defense of mass-based authoritarianism.[34]

By way of countering a decisionist model of law and politics, Habermas revealingly turned to precisely that feature of classical liberalism that Schmitt had regularly scorned: Whereas Schmitt had denounced the liberal bourgeoisie as a mere "talking class" whose impulses were harmlessly apolitical at best and dangerously anarchistic and power dissolving at worst, Habermas proposed a deliberative conception of political legitimacy that hinted at the possibility of a fundamental transformation of the modern state and perhaps even the dissolution of "the political" as widely associated with coercion. *Pace* Schmitt, power and law *could* be reduced to *ratio*, if properly interpreted in a deliberative fashion. When combined with radical social democratic reforms, bourgeois society's most important gift to modernity might survive. New venues for effective critical publicity and deliberative will formation, in opposition both to Schmitt's normative wishes and his dreary empirical diagnosis, could perhaps be secured.

Habermas's lifelong quest to sketch out a defensible deliberative model of politics and law, grounded in a rigorous theory of communicative action, can be plausibly interpreted at least in part as an attempt to discredit Schmitt's political existentialism and antirationalism. When criticizing technocracy in *Toward a Rational Society* (1971), Habermas thus pointed to parallels between it and Hermann Lübbe's updated version of a politics of the "pure decision," whereas in *Legitimation Crisis* (1973), he interpreted Niklas Luhmann rather unsympathetically as a closeted follower of Schmitt and his decisionistic legal theory. The critical strategy in these texts was not so much that of "guilt by association" as an implicit acknowledgment of Schmitt's broad intellectual and political appeal, and thus the necessity of countering even relatively moderate reformulations of his ideas. In *Between Facts and Norms*, Habermas then moved beyond stock criticisms of decisionism to tackle Schmitt's specific contributions to political and legal scholarship. Here he defended judicial review in part by responding to Schmitt's Weimar-era polemics against Hans Kelsen's own earlier spirited defense in a famous

---

[34] For example, see the references to Schmitt and his disciples in *Structural Transformation*, chap. 21.

1931 debate.[35] He also tried to counter Schmitt's influential account of parliamentary decay in part by appealing to a theory of deliberative civil society: Even if modern legislatures are by no means freewheeling deliberative bodies, they operate in conjunction with a civil society in which public deliberation and debate, at least occasionally, remain vibrant. Revising the somewhat bleaker account found in his early writings, Habermas seemed more willing to admit that critical publics had survived, even if many factors continued to threaten them.[36]

In the last decade or so, Schmitt has made frequent appearances as a target of Habermas's emerging defense of global governance. The rather ambivalent record of "humanitarian military intervention" in the former Yugoslavia and in the Middle East has undoubtedly helped gain a second intellectual life for Schmitt's critique of so-called discriminatory wars, according to which liberal states typically mask their fundamental brutality and imperialistic intentions under the hypocritical mantle of humanitarian rhetoric and liberal international law. Even for leftist critics of NATO military intervention in Yugoslavia, for example, or the first UN-endorsed Gulf War, Schmitt now exercises a certain amount of drawing power, as readily apparent from the pages of the *New Left Review* and countless left-leaning academic journals around the world. With Schmitt's growing popularity in mind, Habermas in *The Divided West* and elsewhere has taken it on himself to remind Schmitt's latest fans of the troublesome fact that the critique of discriminatory war rests on an untenable vitalistic and existentialist "concept of the political."[37] Schmitt and those currently influenced by him conveniently obfuscate the crucial fact that interstate relations have undergone an ambitious process of legalization: Schmitt's anxieties about a reckless "moralization" of warfare, according to which liberal universalism necessarily reduces political rivals to subhuman foes, are both misleading and overstated, in part because they obscure constitutive features of contemporary legal development.

Even more ambitiously, Habermas has joined forces with Schmitt's most impressive nemesis in international political theory: Habermas is now busily reformulating Immanuel Kant's cosmopolitan vision of a global constitutionalization of law *without* a world state, seeking to defend a pacific yet

---

[35] Carl Schmitt, *Der Hüter der Verfassung* (Tübingen: Mohr, 1931); for Kelsen's reply, see *Wer soll der Hüter der Verfassung sein?* (Berlin: Rotschild, 1931).

[36] Habermas, *Between Facts and Norms*, 184–6, 241–4.

[37] Jürgen Habermas, *The Divided West*, trans. Ciaran Cronin (Cambridge: Polity, 2006); also, Jürgen Habermas, *The Postnational Constellation*, trans. Max Pensky (Cambridge: Polity, 2001).

nonstatist variety of cosmopolitan global governance – in other words, the anticosmopolitan Carl Schmitt's worst nightmare.

Recommended readings

Habermas, Jürgen. *Between Facts and Norms: Contributions to a Discourse Theory of Law and Democracy.* Translated by William Rehg. Cambridge, MA: MIT Press, 1998.

————. *The Divided West.* Translated by Ciaran Cronin. Cambridge: Polity, 2006.

————. *Legitimation Crisis.* Translated by Thomas McCarthy. Boston: Beacon, 1975.

————. *The Structural Transformation of the Public Sphere: An Inquiry into a Category of Bourgeois Society.* Translated by Thomas Burger. Cambridge, MA: MIT Press, 1989.

Recommended secondary sources

Dews, Peter, ed. *Habermas: A Critical Reader.* Oxford: Blackwell, 1999.

McCarthy, Thomas. *The Critical Theory of Jürgen Habermas.* Cambridge, MA: MIT Press, 1982.

Scheuerman, William E. *Frankfurt School Perspectives on Globalization, Democracy, and the Law.* London: Routledge, 2008.

Specter, Matthew G. *Habermas: An Intellectual Biography.* Cambridge: Cambridge University Press, 2010.

White, Stephen K., ed. *The Cambridge Companion to Habermas.* Cambridge: Cambridge University Press, 1995.

————. *The Recent Work of Jürgen Habermas: Reason, Justice and Modernity.* Cambridge: Cambridge University Press, 1988.

17
Alasdair MacIntyre on political thinking and the tasks of politics

ARTHUR MADIGAN, S.J.

To summarize Alasdair MacIntyre's contributions to political thought in a few words is something easier agreed to than done. For the most part his contributions to political thought are embedded in more general ethical discussions, found in a series of books and papers spanning six decades, and already the object of a considerable secondary literature. The aims of this chapter must then be modest: to trace briefly the evolution of MacIntyre's political thinking, to outline the position that he has held since the late 1980s, and to offer a brief evaluation of his contribution to political thinking in our time.

MacIntyre's first book was *Marxism: An Interpretation*. When he wrote this book MacIntyre thought of himself as both a Marxist and a Christian, or at least as someone trying to be both a Marxist and a Christian. In it he tried to argue for the compatibility of Marxism and Christianity, or at least for a more nuanced understanding of the relationships between them than was customary at the time. By 1968, when he published a revised version under the title *Marxism and Christianity*, he had ceased to be either a Marxist or a Christian.[1] Although the ins and outs of MacIntyre's long engagement with Marxism will not detain us here,[2] two texts are especially important for understanding his current position.

The first is "Notes from the Moral Wilderness."[3] The context of this essay is the late 1950s left's reaction to Stalinism. Its thesis is that, although Stalinism undoubtedly deserves to be rejected, contemporary liberalism

---

[1] Alasdair MacIntyre, *Marxism and Christianity* (New York: Schocken Books, 1968; Notre Dame, IN: University of Notre Dame Press, 1984).

[2] Paul Blackledge and Neil Davidson have brought together a long series of publications from MacIntyre's Marxist period in *Alasdair MacIntyre's Engagement with Marxism*, ed. Blackledge and Davidson (Leiden: Brill, 2008).

[3] Alasdair MacIntyre, "Notes from the Moral Wilderness," in *The MacIntyre Reader*, ed. Kelvin Knight (Notre Dame, IN: University of Notre Dame Press, 1998), 31–49.

provides no sufficient basis for the rejection. The essay documents the rejection of contemporary liberalism that has been and continues to be one of the constants in MacIntyre's thought.

Anyone who embraces Marx's criticism of capitalist society will be confronted with a raft of objections to the thought of Marx and Engels and to the practice of self-styled Marxist or communist regimes. The core of MacIntyre's response is found in the 1994 essay "The *Theses on Feuerbach*: A Road Not Taken."[4] Here he argues that Marx was unable to come to terms with certain basic insights in his own 1845 *Theses on Feuerbach* and that he then unfortunately turned away from philosophy into economics. The standard objections to Marx's economics and to later Marxism are thus largely irrelevant to the core of Marx's philosophy, and the collapse of communist rule in so many countries in the 1980s and 1990s does not amount to a refutation of Marx's philosophy.

Between "Notes from the Moral Wilderness" and "The *Theses on Feuerbach*" MacIntyre's thought developed in ways that took him far beyond Marx and Marxism. In *After Virtue* (1981) MacIntyre carried out a trenchant critique of the failure of what he termed the Enlightenment project of providing a rational justification for morality, which he saw as leading by stages to the amoralism of Nietzsche.[5] This project failed and was bound to fail because it attempted to justify an inherited morality without reference to the only context in which that morality made sense, namely, a teleological understanding of human nature that distinguished between human beings as they de facto are and human beings as they could be if they were to realize their nature or telos. Of course the classical exponent of a teleological understanding of human nature was Aristotle. And it was Aristotle whom MacIntyre came to see as the principal alternative to the failed Enlightenment project and to the ensuing amoralism of Nietzsche.[6] In *Whose Justice? Which Rationality?*, *Three Rival Versions of Moral Enquiry*, and *Dependent Rational Animals*, MacIntyre further developed his Aristotelianism in the light of Thomas Aquinas.[7]

---

[4] Alasdair MacIntyre, "The *Theses on Feuerbach*: A Road Not Taken," in *The MacIntyre Reader*, 223–34.

[5] Alasdair MacIntyre, *After Virtue*, 3rd ed. (Notre Dame, IN: University of Notre Dame Press, 2007).

[6] This is not to suggest that MacIntyre's judgment on the Enlightenment is entirely negative. In his "Some Enlightenment Projects Reconsidered," in *Ethics and Politics: Selected Essays, Volume 2* (Cambridge: Cambridge University Press, 2006), 172–85, he clearly sympathizes with the Enlightenment's aim of developing a public capable of rational debate on moral and political questions, but argues that the institutions the Enlightenment has given us have not provided a suitable forum for such debate.

[7] Alasdair MacIntyre, *Whose Justice? Which Rationality?* (Notre Dame, IN: University of Notre Dame Press, 1988); MacIntyre, *Three Rival Versions of Moral Enquiry* (Notre Dame, IN: University of Notre Dame Press, 1990); MacIntyre, *Dependent Rational Animals* (Chicago: Open Court, 1999).

The main business of this chapter is to summarize MacIntyre's Thomistic Aristotelian political thinking. However, because he came to clarity about the deficiencies of certain ways of thought and certain social forms before he came to clarity about his own constructive ethical and political position, it may be helpful to pave the way for the account of his constructive position by mentioning some of his principal targets (this list makes no claim to be exhaustive).

In "Three Perspectives on Marxism: 1953, 1968, 1995," MacIntyre criticizes political liberalism on three grounds.[8] First, liberalism means (among other things) the involvement of labor unions in capitalism and parliamentary politics, an involvement that weakens the power of labor and returns it to being nothing more than an instrument of capital formation. Second, liberalism is the politics of a set of elites and excludes the vast majority of people from participation in politics. Third, liberalism understands the political community and the state as means to the satisfaction of whatever desires individuals may happen to have; therefore it involves an individualism that is incompatible with any conception of the common good as more than the sum of individuals' preferences.[9] As MacIntyre points out in his 1984 lecture "Is Patriotism a Virtue?" the survival of any state depends on the willingness of some of its citizens (police, firefighters, military men and women) to risk life and limb in its defense, a willingness that makes no sense within the individualist ethics of liberalism.[10] Thus the survival of the liberal state depends on at least some of its citizens not accepting liberalism.

By liberalism MacIntyre does not mean simply that side of contemporary political debate that styles itself liberal or is so styled by others. In *Whose Justice? Which Rationality?* he writes,

Liberalism, as I have understood it in this book, does of course appear in contemporary debates in a number of guises and in so doing is often successful in preempting the debate by reformulating quarrels and conflicts with liberalism, so that they appear to have become debates within liberalism, putting in question this or that particular set of attitudes or policies, but not the fundamental tenets of liberalism with respect to individuals and the expression of their preferences. So so-called conservatism and so-called radicalism in these contemporary guises are in general mere stalking-horses for liberalism: the contemporary debates within modern political systems are almost exclusively between conservative liberals,

---

[8] Alasdair MacIntyre, "Three Perspectives on Marxism: 1953, 1968, 1995," in *Ethics and Politics*, 145–58.
[9] Ibid., 153–4.
[10] Alasdair MacIntyre, "Is Patriotism a Virtue?" in *Theorizing Citizenship*, ed. Ronald Beiner (Albany: SUNY Press, 1995), 209–28.

liberal liberals, and radical liberals. There is little place in such political systems for the criticism of the system itself, that is, for putting liberalism in question.[11]

The 2007 prologue to the third edition of *After Virtue* makes it clear that MacIntyre is no supporter of what is commonly thought of as political conservatism:

This critique of liberalism should not be interpreted as a sign of any sympathy on my part for contemporary conservatism. That conservatism is in too many ways a mirror image of the liberalism that it professedly opposes. Its commitment to a way of life structured by a free market economy is a commitment to an individualism as corrosive as that of liberalism. And, where liberalism by permissive legal enactments has tried to use the power of the modern state to transform social relationships, conservatism by prohibitive legal enactments now tries to use that same power for its own coercive purposes. Such conservatism is as alien to the projects of *After Virtue* as liberalism is.[12]

Thus for MacIntyre the differences between contemporary "liberalism" and contemporary "conservatism" are much less significant than is often supposed.

Critics of capitalism regularly object that an uncontrolled free market naturally leads and in fact has led to gross economic inequalities. MacIntyre's criticism is different. He is by no means opposed to free markets. His contention is rather that there are no free markets beyond the level of relatively small local communities: "Genuinely free markets are always local and small-scale markets in whose exchanges producers can choose to participate or not."[13] The capitalist economy is not a genuinely free market: "Market relationships in contemporary capitalism are for the most part relations imposed both on labor and on small producers, rather than in any sense freely chosen."[14] Yet this is by no means the worst injustice of capitalism. Although capitalism certainly brings about a rising standard of material prosperity, it also tends to educate people not to seek what they deserve but instead to seek whatever they happen to want. It teaches them to understand themselves primarily as consumers. It disposes them to *pleonexia*, the vice of wanting more and more, and so to injustice.

MacIntyre argues that capitalism involves a systematic exploitation of labor: "The more effective the employment of capital, the more labor

[11] MacIntyre, *Whose Justice? Which Rationality?* 392.
[12] MacIntyre, *After Virtue*, xv.
[13] Alasdair MacIntyre, "Politics, Philosophy and the Common Good," in *The MacIntyre Reader*, 249.
[14] MacIntyre, "Three Perspectives on Marxism," 149.

becomes no more than an instrument of capital's purposes, and an instrument whose treatment is a function of the needs for long-term profit maximization and capital formation."[15] This exploitation does not simply result in economic inequality; the economic inequality makes it impossible for the disadvantaged to take a meaningful part in a political process of deliberation about common goods. And even if the disadvantaged were to have a meaningful part in the political process, their education to *pleonexia* would render them unfit for rational deliberation.

MacIntyre regards the contemporary nation-state as the embodiment and protector of capitalism, liberalism, and individualism. Its politics is a sham politics, because the processes of voting and elections only appear to allow the electors a free choice of their representatives, a free choice among policies. In reality the electors have to choose between alternatives already narrowly defined for them by political elites. "Politically the societies of advanced Western modernity are oligarchies disguised as liberal democracies."[16] And the sham is barren inasmuch as there is practically no possibility of genuine political debate about first principles. Criticisms of the dominant liberalism are transformed into positions within the dominant liberalism. To win and hold power, dominant elites appeal to many different interest groups on the basis of many different and incompatible values.

Yet simply identifying and criticizing the incoherence of contemporary liberalism accomplishes little. Contemporary liberalism survives and flourishes precisely because of its incoherence:

The modern state . . . behaves part of the time towards those subjected to it as if it were no more than a giant, monopolistic utility company and part of the time as if it were the sacred guardian of all that is most to be valued. In the one capacity it requires us to fill in the appropriate forms in triplicate. In the other it periodically demands that we die for it. This deep incoherence in the modern state is not a secret, but the fact that it is plain for everyone to see of itself does nothing at all to undermine the modern state.[17]

The societies of advanced (liberal, individualist, capitalist) Western modernity are marked by a high degree of compartmentalization and an insistence on adaptability. Depending on the sphere in which they are operating – home, school, work, and so on – individuals are encouraged to

---

[15] Ibid., 147.
[16] MacIntyre, "Politics, Philosophy and the Common Good," 237.
[17] MacIntyre, "The *Theses on Feuerbach*," 227.

present themselves as different people with different attitudes. "A compart-mentalized society imposes a fragmented ethics."[18]

Against this background I now try to summarize what I take to be the main points of MacIntyre's political thinking. That thinking is embedded in an Aristotelian ethics in which good is prior to right. The most basic categories of this ethics are practices, the goods internal to practices, and the virtues necessary to sustain practices. MacIntyre defines a practice as

any coherent and complex form of socially established cooperative human activity through which goods internal to that form of activity are realized in the course of trying to achieve those standards of excellence which are appropriate to, and partially definitive of, that form of activity, with the result that human powers to achieve excellence, and human conceptions of the ends and goods involved, are systematically extended.[19]

By goods internal to a given practice he means those goods that can only be recognized and achieved by engaging in that practice, as opposed to external goods, such as money and prestige, that can be achieved in many different ways. To achieve the goods internal to a given practice, an agent needs to cultivate a range of virtues. MacIntyre defines a virtue as "an acquired human quality the possession and exercise of which tends to enable us to achieve those goods which are internal to practices and the lack of which effectively prevents us from achieving any such goods."[20]

MacIntyre understands a good human life as possessing a certain narrative unity, the unity of a quest for the good life. Yet this quest for a good life is not something that individuals can carry out on their own; the quest for a good human life is a cooperative venture. MacIntyre insists that there are such things as genuinely common goods – that is, goods that are genuinely shared across groups – as opposed to goods that are merely aggregates of the goods of individuals. Examples of genuinely common goods he regularly uses are the good of a good fishing voyage, shared across the crew, and the good of a well-playing string quartet, shared across the musicians.

Practices require the support of institutions, but the relation between institutions and practices is complex. Institutions can and often do under-mine, rather than support, practices and the goods of practices; hence the need for further virtues to manage institutions well and to offset their ten-dency not to support the practices that they were intended to support.

---

[18] MacIntyre, "Politics, Philosophy and the Common Good," 236.
[19] MacIntyre, *After Virtue*, 187.
[20] Ibid., 191.

Further, practices, communities, and the institutions founded to support practices are necessarily involved in the development of traditions. MacIntyre understands tradition not in the sense of a Burkean fixity but as a continuing argument about the goods internal to practices, how best to sustain and promote them, the ordering of these practices, and the institutions to support these practices. It is this dimension of inquiry that brings us to the political sphere. As communities of inquiry, political communities should be open to recognizing problems within their traditions and even open to the possibility that other traditions may have the resources to surmount these problems.

As MacIntyre understands it, political thinking is thinking about how to order practices, the goods internal to those practices, and the institutions that are intended to sustain practices. A political community "is constituted by a type of practice through which other types of practice are ordered, so that individuals may direct themselves towards what is best for them and for the community."[21] Political communities are thus necessarily communities of inquiry. Much of MacIntyre's political position is the spelling out of the implications of this point.

Good politics – there is no perfect politics – is an exercise of rational inquiry and debate in which everyone who has something to teach the group (and under this heading MacIntyre includes everyone) is allowed to teach it and no one who has something to teach the group is excluded. Political deliberation about the ordering of goods, practices, and institutions is the specific common good of a political community.

The achievement of common goods, and above all the achievement of the common good of political deliberation, requires a commitment of the group to treat one another, and especially not to treat one another, in certain specifiable ways. These obligations and prohibitions largely correspond to the precepts of the natural law as understood by Thomas Aquinas: "We come to know them practically as precepts whose binding authority is presupposed in any situation in which learning and enquiry between rational individuals about their individual and common goods can be advanced and by any relationship in which individuals can conduct themselves with rational integrity."[22] Therefore the precepts of the natural law are to be understood not as conclusions reached at the end of a process of rational inquiry but as preconditions for rational inquiry itself. "The exceptionless

---

[21] MacIntyre, "Politics, Philosophy and the Common Good," 241.
[22] Alasdair MacIntyre, "Natural Law as Subversive: The Case of Aquinas," in *Ethics and Politics*, 48.

precepts of the natural law are those which, insofar as we are rational, we recognize as indispensable in every society and in every situation for the achievement of our goods and of our final good, because they direct us towards and partially define our common good."[23]

Good politics must inevitably be fairly small scale, small enough that everyone can be heard, people can evaluate one another's character, and everyone's contribution can be assessed. This is precisely what is impossible in the contemporary nation-state, but it is possible at the level of the school, the parish, and similar communities. Thus for MacIntyre, politics, in the most important and positive sense of the term, takes place on a level "below" what is usually thought of as politics.

Given that political community is a community of rational inquiry and that the contemporary nation-state is hostile to such a form of community, MacIntyre advocates what he calls a politics of local community. In addition, given that local communities obviously find themselves in the context of a capitalist "free market" and liberal nation-states, they need to practice a politics of communal self-defense against the corrupting influence of the market and the state: "For the state and the market economy are so structured as to subvert and undermine the politics of local community. Between the one politics and the other there can only be continuing conflict."[24]

In a short statement "The Only Vote Worth Casting in November," written in the context of the U.S. presidential election in 2004, MacIntyre argues that there is no sufficient reason to vote for either of the two leading candidates and counsels abstention. By itself this statement might suggest that MacIntyre favors a complete disengagement from politics, but in fact his position is more nuanced. To defend and expand their freedom of action, local communities will need to engage with the "free market" and the liberal state; their task is to do so prudently and warily. MacIntyre certainly opposes the attempt to modify or take over the liberal state, whether in its older Marxist revolutionary form or its contemporary social democratic or communitarian form. Yet in "The Only Vote Worth Casting in November," he goes on to sketch the outline of a politics that might be and that ought to be:

What then are the right political questions? One of them is: What do we owe our children? And the answer is that we owe them the best chance that we can give them of protection and fostering from the moment of conception onwards.

[23] Ibid., 49.
[24] MacIntyre, "Politics, Philosophy and the Common Good," 252.

And we can only achieve that if we give them the best chance that we can both of a flourishing family life, in which the work of their parents is fairly and adequately rewarded, and of an education which will enable them to flourish. These two sentences, if fully spelled out, amount to a politics.[25]

MacIntyre thus combines a strongly critical view of contemporary politics with at least a faint hope for a better kind of politics.

MacIntyre's anti-individualism, antiliberalism, and insistence on the importance of common goods have led some observers to classify him as a communitarian, a label that he vigorously rejects. He sees communitarianism as one trend of thought within contemporary liberalism rather than as a genuine alternative to that liberalism:

Communitarians are apt to place great emphasis on their rejection of any merely individualist conception of the common good. But the communitarian conception of the common good is not at all that of a kind of community of political learning and enquiry participation in which is necessary for individuals to discover what their individual and common goods are. Indeed in every statement by the protagonists of communitarianism that I have read the precise nature of the communitarian view of the relationship between the community, the common good and individual goods remains elusive.[26]

MacIntyre's political thinking is thus Aristotelian in its focus on the achievement of goods specified by a shared human nature, especially on the achievement of genuinely common human goods. It is also Aristotelian in seeing deliberation about common goods as both a necessary condition for their achievement and as itself a major common good. MacIntyre corrects Aristotle's oversights with respect to women, natural slaves, and manual workers, here developing Aristotle along specifically Thomistic lines and beyond. More explicitly than Aristotle and Aquinas, he recognizes the importance of politics representing the interests of the young, the weak, and the incapacitated.[27] Where the Catholic political tradition has favored subsidiarity in the sense that higher social entities should assist lower social entities but not unnecessarily interfere with them, MacIntyre's politics of local community embodies what may be called a "subsidiarity from below," in the sense that local communities should take the initiative to increase their freedom from the influence of the "free market" and the liberal state.

---

[25] This statement is available at http://perennis.blogspot.com/2004/10/alasdair-macintyre-only-vote-worth.html.

[26] MacIntyre, "Politics, Philosophy and the Common Good," 246.

[27] This theme is particularly prominent in *Dependent Rational Animals*.

MacIntyre's political thinking retains a strong Marxist aspect in its critique of capitalism, of liberal modernity generally, and of the workings of the contemporary nation-state. Kelvin Knight has well characterized it as "revolutionary Aristotelianism." It is revolutionary not in the sense that it contemplates the violent overthrow of current regimes, but in the sense that it recognizes no allegiance to them: "If... claims to political allegiance can be justified only where there is the common good of communal political learning, then modern states cannot advance any justifiable claim to the allegiance of their members."[28]

Within the family of Aristotelian political theories, then, MacIntyre's view must be contrasted with those Aristotelian views that attempt or claim to have reached a synthesis with contemporary liberalism, in particular from the Americanizing Aristotelianism of Mortimer Adler and from the liberal or social democratic Aristotelianism of Martha Nussbaum. MacIntyre's position must also be contrasted with a contemporary liberal version of Roman Catholic social teaching that understands the common good as a set of background conditions enabling individuals to develop themselves and then makes the nation-state responsible for guaranteeing these background conditions. If I have understood MacIntyre correctly, he would find this too thin a conception of common good and common goods.

MacIntyre is hardly alone in criticizing the liberalism of our time, but his criticism is more basic and far-reaching than most. His reading of contemporary conservatism and radicalism as species of liberalism is particularly insightful, as is his insistence that a merely theoretical criticism of liberalism is insufficient; the criticism must also be practical, involving the construction and maintenance of small-scale political communities that can support the life of practices, common goods, rational inquiry, and the virtues.

MacIntyre presents his ethical and political thinking in a way that leaves it open to question and revision. In recognition of this openness, let me indicate two areas that seem to call for further study and development.

One such area is MacIntyre's derivation of the precepts of natural law from the requirements for communities of inquiry to function. If I have understood it correctly, the core of his argument is that, unless most members of a community of inquiry characteristically treat one another in certain ways and not in certain other ways, the community will not be able to function well, and it may not be able to function at all as a community of rational

---

[28] MacIntyre, "Politics, Philosophy and the Common Good," 243.

inquiry. Now this grounding of the precepts of natural law has significant advantages over the positing of natural rights as sheer facts in themselves – a view that to my knowledge MacIntyre still rejects as he did in *After Virtue*. Yet it would seem to invite questions: Does this mean that we only have duties toward people who are fellow members with us in some community of inquiry? Is the basis for respect not a common human nature or personhood as such, but rather membership in a community of inquiry? Thomistic natural law has generally been understood as stating duties that we have toward all other human beings, not only to those with whom we are engaged in common inquiries. One way to meet this difficulty might be to conceive of each and every human being as a potential fellow member of a community of inquiry. If we understand the human race in this way, then the duties deriving from the requirements of communities of inquiry might extend beyond the de facto boundaries of small-scale local communities of inquiry to include the whole human race.[29] Yet to make this move would be to introduce into MacIntyre's politics and ethics of small-scale local community a certain cosmopolitan element, and perhaps a better solution may be available.

A second area for development is the relationship between politics and technology. On the strength of his (not unqualifiedly) sympathetic portrayal of the Greeks and the medievals, and of his approving references to communities of hand-loom weavers, to fishing crews, and to vanishing family farms as schools of the virtues, MacIntyre has sometimes been charged with harboring a nostalgia for premodern societies and for what might be called premodern survivals within modernizing or modern societies. Although this charge is less than fair, it points to an area where MacIntyre's thought could stand to be further developed: the relationship between politics and technology. To what extent does the onward march (if that is what it is) of technology influence or even determine the form that the political life of a nation, or of a small-scale local community within a nation, has to take? How should small-scale local communities go about making up their minds about when to accept and when to reject new technologies? It would be a welcome development if Prof. MacIntyre were to turn his attention to these and similar questions.

---

[29] Although I have not found this idea in Prof. MacIntyre's writings, it was suggested to me by his remark that it is possible to understand a nation not only as the nation that it de facto is but also as a project yet to be achieved; see MacIntyre, "Is Patriotism a Virtue?" 223–4.

Suggestions for further reading

After Virtue remains fundamental for the understanding of MacIntyre's ethics and his overall philosophical position. For the specifically political dimension of MacIntyre's thought, the essays cited earlier from *The MacIntyre Reader*, edited by Kelvin Knight, and from MacIntyre's *Ethics and Politics: Selected Essays, Volume 2*, are most important.

Two brief introductions to MacIntyre's political thinking are Kelvin Knight, "Revolutionary Aristotelianism," in *Contemporary Political Studies*, ed. Iain Hampsher-Monk and Jeffrey Stanyer, Proceedings of the Political Studies Association 3 (Belfast: Political Studies Association of the United Kingdom, 1996), 885–96; and Mark C. Murphy, "MacIntyre's Political Philosophy," in *Alasdair MacIntyre*, ed. Mark C. Murphy (Cambridge: Cambridge University Press, 2003), 152–75.

A fuller study is Kelvin Knight, "A Revolutionary Aristotelianism," in *Aristotelian Philosophy: Ethics and Politics from Aristotle to MacIntyre* (Cambridge: Polity, 2007), chap. 4.

Kelvin Knight and Paul Blackledge, eds., *Revolutionary Aristotelianism: Ethics, Resistance and Utopia* (Stuttgart: Lucius & Lucius, 2008) is a useful collection of essays on MacIntyre's political thinking and its implications.

18

Another philosopher-citizen: the political philosophy of Charles Taylor

RUTH ABBEY

In paying tribute to Jürgen Habermas on his eightieth birthday, Charles Taylor described the octogenerian as

an exemplary public intellectual. He has never been content simply with writing, teaching, and discussing philosophy. Unremittingly and with great courage he has intervened in the important debates of our time.... One might almost say that theory and practice are organically linked in the thought of Habermas... [who] lives his philosophy, with a kind of passionate integrity.

Taylor goes on to portray Habermas as "articulating two profound changes in the consciousness of the later 20th Century," both of which center on the concept of dialogue. The first profound change, which was philosophical in nature, challenged the monological turn taken by modern Western philosophy with the work of René Descartes. The second occurred within Western political cultures through the growing demand that democracies become more fully representative of their populations' diversity. Seeking what Taylor calls a renegotiation of the political contract, groups previously excluded from the political mainstream agitated for fuller inclusion. As Taylor points out in his homage to Habermas, such renegotiation can only be conducted dialogically.[1]

Anyone familiar with Taylor's political philosophy will readily intuit how applicable his depiction of Habermas is to Taylor himself. Taylor too has been a philosopher-citizen, which, with its allusion to Plato, is the term he coins for Habermas. Taylor's own academic career has also been interwoven

---

[1] An abbreviated and translated version of Taylor's homage appears in "The Philosopher-Citizen," posted on the website *The Immanent Frame* (http://blogs.ssrc.org/tif/2009/10/19/philosopher-citizen/). Born in November 1931 (in Montreal, Quebec, Canada), Taylor is very close in age to Habermas.

with political participation.[2] Nicholas Smith demarcates three stages of Taylor's political involvement:[3] The first is his work with the New Left in Britain in the 1950s,[4] the second is with the Canadian New Democratic Party in the 1960s, and the third comes in his engagement in debates about Quebec's role in the Canadian federation in the 1980s and '90s.[5] Smith's list must be updated to include the fact that from 2007 to 2008 Taylor co-chaired a public inquiry into the treatment of cultural and religious differences in that province.[6] Thus within his native Canada, Taylor is a high-profile public intellectual who has intervened in several of his nation's political debates.

There is also an intimate connection between Taylor's political practice and his political philosophy. His reflections on nationalism and on democracy's need for greater inclusion to sustain its legitimacy and his influential account of the politics of recognition have all been directly affected by his experience of living and being politically active in Quebec. Residing in a country bordered by the world's largest and probably still most confident liberal democracy has also shaped Taylor's thinking about different styles and understandings of liberalism. Smith even contends that a proper appreciation of Taylor's political thought *requires* awareness of his political activity.[7] Two reasons seem to underlie this claim. The first is that Taylor's approach to political theory is problem driven. As Smith sees it, Taylor is not a systematic thinker but responds to issues as they emerge in the realm of

---

[2] Awarded a PhD in 1961 in philosophy from Oxford, Taylor returned to Canada for a post at McGill University in the Departments of Philosophy and Political Science. In 1976 he went back to Oxford to take up the Chichele Professorship of Social and Political Theory, but returned again to McGill in 1981. He retired from McGill in 1998, but remains an emeritus professor in the Department of Philosophy.

[3] Nicholas H. Smith, *Charles Taylor: Meaning, Morals and Modernity* (Cambridge: Polity, 2002), 12–17, 172–98.

[4] For Taylor's own reflections on this phase, see Charles Taylor, "On Identity, Alienation and the Consequences of September 11th: Interview with Hartmut Rosa and Arto Laitinen," in *Perspectives on the Philosophy of Charles Taylor*, ed. Arto Laitinen and Nicholas H. Smith (Helsinki: Societas Philosophica Fennica, 2002), 165–95.

[5] Many of the essays Taylor wrote during this period have been collected in *Rapprocher les solitudes: Écrits sur le fédéralisme et le nationalisme au Canada*, ed. Guy Laforest (Sainte-Foy, QC: Les Presses de l'Université Laval, 1992). The English edition is *Reconciling the Solitudes: Essays in Canadian Federalism and Nationalism*, ed. Guy Laforest (Montreal and Kingston: McGill-Queen's University Press, 1993). Introducing that collection, Laforest also emphasizes the life–work connection for understanding Taylor's political thought.

[6] For a synopsis of the commission's report and a discussion of its relationship to Taylor's political thought, see Ruth Abbey, "Plus ça Change: Charles Taylor on Accommodating Quebec's Minority Cultures," *Thesis Eleven* 99, no. 1 (2009): 71–92.

[7] Smith, *Charles Taylor*, 172.

political practice.[8] This is especially evident in his landmark essay "The Politics of Recognition," which examines the challenges of multiculturalism and identity politics for liberal democracies.

In connection with Smith's claim about the problem-driven nature of Taylor's thought, it is interesting to note that his contributions to political philosophy tend to appear in essays, rather than in his books. Although I am not suggesting that his large works *Hegel, Sources of the Self,* and *A Secular Age* make no contribution to political philosophy, they are not obviously or exclusively works within this genre. Taylor's more direct and focused investigations of issues that do fall squarely within the domain of political thought – such as freedom, democracy, nationalism, multiculturalism, rights, cross-cultural understanding, legitimacy, distributive justice, the liberal–communitarian debate, and the public sphere – take place in the essay format.[9]

The second reason Smith suggests for needing to appreciate the link between theory and practice is that Taylor's political thinking is motivated primarily by a desire to foster change. Smith imputes to Taylor the view that "the worth of political theory is inseparable from the quality of social criticism it informs and, beyond that, its capacity to transform social life for the better."[10] Taylor's concerns as a political philosopher thus emerge from the realm of practice, and he hopes that his responses will return to influence that practice. In this context it is important to note the nontechnical, relatively jargon-free style in which Taylor typically writes, making his ideas more accessible to a general audience than is the case with much professional philosophy. It would, after all, be self-defeating to strive to influence the practice of politics while writing in a highly technical, formal, forbidding, or exclusionary style. As Smith explains, "It matters to Taylor that his ideas are able to connect with the concrete concerns of ordinary thinking people. He has written extensively for a non-specialized, non-academic

---

[8] Ibid., 9. I agree that Taylor is no system builder, but we should not overlook the many areas of intersection among his views on and approaches to different topics. See, for example, Ruth Abbey, *Charles Taylor* (Princeton, NJ: Princeton University Press, 2000), 4–5. Indeed, Smith himself finds "a unified philosophical project" in Taylor's writings, revolving around the centrality of meaning in human life (Smith, *Charles Taylor,* 1).

[9] Taylor's short book, *Modern Social Imaginaries* (Durham, NC: Duke University Press, 2004) is an exception to this trend. Yet it is short and, as mentioned later, belongs to a larger project that is not essentially a work of political philosophy.

[10] Smith, *Charles Taylor,* 172. But see Ronald Beiner, "Hermeneutical Generosity and Social Criticism," in *Philosophy in a Time of Lost Spirit: Essays on Contemporary Theory* (Toronto: University of Toronto Press, 1997), 155–66 for a different assessment of the sort of social criticism to which Taylor's work gives rise.

readership."[11] On the basis of these reflections, it seems fair to infer that the organic link between theory and practice Taylor identifies in Habermas is also present in his own work.[12]

The third aspect of Habermas's contribution underscored by Taylor is also manifest in Taylor's own corpus. Dialogue is a central category in Taylor's political philosophy, as in his philosophy in general. For example, he advances a conception of the self as dialogical, and he thinks about political life, at least within democracies, along the model of a dialogue. Much has been written on these dimensions of Taylor's thought, but for now I want to suggest that this dialogical approach to politics leads Taylor to downplay the state's coercive power and potential. Consider that when he invokes Max Weber, as he often does, it is not so much his definition of the state as enjoying a monopoly on the means of coercion that Taylor refers to, but rather the important role Weber attributes to ideas in social life and change and his emphasis on meaning in social explanation.[13] In this regard Taylor contrasts markedly with John Rawls for whom, as Paul Weithman points out in this volume, the state's power to coerce was central in his thinking about justice.[14]

Having briefly reviewed the connection between Taylor's life and work, this chapter goes on to locate Taylor in the light of another of the threads uniting the chapters in this volume, which is how twentieth-century

---

[11] Smith, *Charles Taylor*, 11; see 9–10. Yet Taylor's magnum opus, *A Secular Age*, combines his inviting, conversational style with a number of neologisms, such as "neo- (paleo-, post-) Durkheimian," "the immanent frame," "the nova effect," "exclusive humanism," and "closed world structures."

[12] As his book's title indicates, Mark Redhead also underscores the intimate connection between theory and practice in Taylor's work: Mark Redhead, *Charles Taylor: Living and Thinking Deep Diversity* (Lanham, MD: Rowman & Littlefield, 2002). Although he mentions Taylor's earlier activism (5–7), Redhead's focus is Taylor's participation in Quebec politics (45) and, within that, on the third of Smith's stages – Taylor's role in debating the future of Quebec in the Canadian federation. Redhead contends that "simply to study Taylor's academic writings is to miss much of what is important about the unique perspective that Taylor brings to bear on the problem of political fragmentation" (17).

[13] See, for example, *The Malaise of Modernity* (Concord, ON: Anansi, 1991), 125 n. 16; *Sources of the Self* (Cambridge, MA: Harvard University Press, 1989), 203, 225–6. *Sources of the Self* and Taylor's more recent writings on religion in modern Western societies also draw heavily on Weber's notion of disenchantment, whereas *Varieties of Religion Today* (Cambridge, MA: Harvard University Press, 2002), 19, makes reference to charismatic leadership. At one point Taylor does, however, cite Weber on the state: see *Philosophical Arguments* (Cambridge, MA: Harvard University Press, 1995), 205.

[14] I am not proposing that Taylor is ignorant of or indifferent to the role of coercion in politics – see, for example, "Interpretation and the Sciences of Man" (1971), in *Philosophy and the Human Sciences: Philosophical Papers 2* (Cambridge: Cambridge University Press, 1985), 43. But it is not front and center in his thinking. It could be argued, however, that state coercion is the specter that haunts his recurrent concern with the social bases of cohesion in diverse democracies, for without some re-creation of these bases, democracies could descend into polities in which coercion plays a much more prominent role.

political philosophers responded to the rise of modern science and the influential belief that natural science could provide a paradigm for knowledge of the social and political world. It then traces the consequences of Taylor's position in this debate for another of the volume's key concerns, which is the diversity of views among prominent twentieth-century practitioners about what political theory is and how it should be done.[15]

Taylor is a central figure in the debate about the relationship between the human and the natural sciences. Indeed, Smith deems him to be "the most eloquent and influential advocate of the hermeneutic model of social science in the English-speaking world."[16] Ever since his first book, *The Explanation of Behaviour*, published in 1964, Taylor has refused the assimilation of the human to the natural sciences. His major reason for insisting on an unbridgeable difference between them is that "man is a self-interpreting animal . . . he is always partly constituted by self-interpretation."[17] This ontological claim injects an inescapably hermeneutic dimension into the human sciences, because if we wish to understand human behavior, we need some sense of the self-understandings informing it. Self-interpretations are crucial components of human identity and, therefore, of social and political reality.[18] For example, it would be impossible to give an account of an election by simply describing people's attendance at polling stations and marking of pieces of paper (or computer screens). A large part of what matters in understanding an election is knowing what the voters think they are doing in casting a vote.[19]

---

[15] In explicating Taylor's views on this last question, I draw from two essays from the early 1980s that have received little attention in the vast secondary literature about Taylor: "Political Theory and Practice," in *Social Theory and Political Practice*, ed. Christopher Lloyd (Oxford: Clarendon, 1983), 61–85, and "Use and Abuse of Theory," in *Ideology, Philosophy and Politics*, ed. Anthony Parel (Waterloo, ON: Wilfrid Laurier University Press, 1983), 37–59.

[16] Smith, *Charles Taylor*, 120. Space does not permit a comprehensive account of Taylor's views on the contrasts between the natural and the human sciences. For a fuller discussion, see Abbey, *Charles Taylor*, 152–65, and Smith, 120–8. For one of Taylor's more recent discussions of this issue, see Charles Taylor, "Gadamer and the Human Sciences," in *The Cambridge Companion to Gadamer*, ed. Robert J. Dostal (New York: Cambridge University Press, 2002), 126–42.

[17] Charles Taylor, "Self-Interpreting Animals," in *Human Agency and Language: Philosophical Papers 1* (Cambridge: Cambridge University Press, 1985), 72; see also 47. He had previously made this point in "Interpretation and the Sciences of Man," 54. In exploring this claim, Taylor situates himself as continuing the work of Dilthey, Heidegger, Gadamer, and Habermas ("Self-Interpreting Animals," 45; he also mentions Paul Ricoeur at "Interpretation," 15).

[18] For a fuller discussion of Taylor's views on these issues, see Abbey, *Charles Taylor*, 58–62, and Smith, *Charles Taylor*, 120–8. A more systematic approach to the study of self-interpretations inspired by some of Taylor's insights appears in Hartmut Rosa, "Four Levels of Self-interpretation," *Philosophy and Social Criticism* 30, no. 5/6 (2004): 691–720.

[19] Taylor, "Interpretation," 29.

As Taylor sees it, practices such as voting are necessarily laden with meaning: "A society is among other things a set of institutions and practices, and these cannot exist and be carried on without certain self-understandings."[20] To understand the meaning of a practice such as voting, or majority rule, or negotiation, it is essential to grasp its constitutive rules and norms. A norm is constitutive when "it is so related to the point of the practice, that no-one could be deemed to be engaged in that practice who wasn't sensitive to the norm."[21] In the interests of accuracy, we should refer here to the meanings – plural – of a practice, for not all members of a culture will always understand the practice in the same way. Yet the practices of politics should be the subject matter of political theory, according to Taylor, and these are inextricably bound up with meanings.

However, the meanings of such practices are not things that individuals cook up on their own; they become available to individuals via the wider political culture in which they live. So in attending to meanings, theories of politics must make reference to the wider political culture in which the actors operate.[22] Meanings exceed the ideas in the heads (and hearts) of individuals. Practices are intersubjectively formed and perpetuated: The meanings they contain are "the common property of the society . . . they are not [purely or exclusively] subjective meanings, the property of one or some individuals, but rather inter-subjective meanings, which are constitutive of the social matrix in which individuals find themselves and act."[23] So meanings therefore matter greatly in the study of politics, but the individual cannot be the basic unit of analysis for them. To understand the meanings any individual harbors, we must look beyond to the wider social milieu in which he or she is ensconced. Taylor is therefore adamant that apprehending the basic features of political life means rejecting the presumption of atomism that underlies mainstream political science: "What the ontology of mainstream social science lacks is the notion of meaning as not

---

[20] Taylor, "Political Theory and Practice," 62–3.

[21] Taylor, "Use and Abuse of Theory," 41. See also Taylor, "Interpretation," 34–5, which discusses John Searle's work on constitutive rules.

[22] Because political cultures vary from one another, very little can be said in universal terms (Taylor, "Interpretation," 32, 42, 47–8). This highlights another difference between the natural and the human sciences because the former aspire to universal explanations of their objects. In "The Nature and Scope of Distributive Justice," Taylor finds much to endorse in Michael Walzer's *Spheres of Justice*, such as the particularism and pluralism of his approach, along with its attention to social meanings. See Taylor, *Philosophy and the Human Sciences*, 289–317.

[23] Taylor, "Interpretation," 37; see also 39. The square brackets are my insertion, added in the interests of clarification.

simply for an individual subject; of a subject who can be a 'we' as well as an 'I.'"[24]

Underlining the centrality of intersubjective meanings in politics as Taylor does should not, however, be mistaken for identifying consensus. Dissent and critique are themselves parasitic on the existence of intersubjective meanings in a political culture. To change the world, critics must engage with and challenge the regnant interpretations held by their fellow actors.[25] The existence of intersubjective meanings embodied in institutions makes common meaning or convergence possible, for actors might agree on the value of democratic elections. Yet even when they do not, and no common meanings can be attained across the whole society, the debate about their value is still conducted intersubjectively.[26]

Practices thus lie at the heart of political life for Taylor. They are inherently meaningful, or rather bear a range of possible meanings for their participants, and those meanings are intersubjective. This does not require, however, that their meanings be fully explicit to all participants: The constitutive rules and norms of practices can be things that participants grasp intuitively, implicitly. These norms and rules are typically learned by doing, and the "test" of whether participants grasp them lies in their ability to carry on effectively with the practice. Conversely, Taylor suggests that being able to identify when the norm has been violated, to "call a foul" as he puts it, also indicates a practical grasp of that norm.[27] Participation in practices can therefore be pretheoretical or prearticulate: It is essential neither for practices' existence nor their transmission that they be fully and cogently articulated nor that this articulation be done in a theoretical manner. Yet Taylor's term "pretheoretical" could be something of a misnomer if it implies that a theoretical account of a practice will always and everywhere ensue. He allows, rather, that practices can exist and continue without any articulation of their meaning and logic in a theoretical fashion.[28]

---

[24] Taylor, "Interpretation," 40; see also 41. Some of these issues are explored in more detail in Charles Taylor, "Atomism" (1979), in *Philosophy and the Human Sciences*, 187–210, and Taylor, "Irreducibly Social Goods," in *Philosophical Arguments*, 127–45.

[25] Taylor, "Interpretation," 36–7.

[26] Ibid., 39.

[27] Taylor, "Use and Abuse of Theory," 42; "Political Theory and Practice," 62.

[28] Taylor, "Use and Abuse of Theory," 42, 46; "Political Theory and Practice," 63. Here Taylor's political thought intersects with his wider endorsement of the idea of embodied coping, in which he has been influenced by Merleau-Ponty, Heidegger, Wittgenstein, and Michael Polanyi. For a fuller discussion of this aspect of his epistemology, see Abbey, *Charles Taylor*, 178–90.

If meaning-laden, intersubjective practices are the stuff of political life, but they do not require theoretical articulation, a rather stark question arises about the purpose of political theory. At one point Taylor declares that "a theory is the making explicit of a society's life, i.e. a set of institutions and practices."[29] Yet this limited and conservative view soon turns out to be too bald a statement of political theory's purpose, for Taylor qualifies it by specifying that "*one of the things social theory does . . .* is make explicit the self-understandings which constitute our social life."[30] As I read him, Taylor nominates four possible functions for political theory vis-à-vis a society's practices.

All theory strives to supply a more formal and systematic articulation of a political practice or set of practices than that available to people through everyday awareness. Thus, according to Taylor, "social theory arises when we try to formulate explicitly what we are doing, to describe the activity which is central to a practice, and to articulate the norms which are essential to it."[31] In doing this, the theory need not capture all aspects of the practice, but can confine itself to identifying and connecting its most important ones. As I understand Taylor's position, this is a necessary component of political theory, and it is possible for a theory to stop there – to simply give an account of a political practice or practices. Theories "can have the function just of clarifying or codifying the significance which is already implicit in our self-descriptions."[32] Taylor suggests, however, that it is unusual for theory to stop at the explication of practices.[33] One possible explanation for this appears in his claim that people turn toward theory in times of trouble and confusion, when they perceive that commonsense understandings of their institutions and practices will not suffice. He thus identifies a "stronger motive for making and adopting theories" than the mere quest to codify the meanings of practices. This stronger motive is "the sense that our implicit understanding is in some way crucially inadequate or even wrong."[34] Theory's other possible roles thus include but go beyond this first function of articulation.

A second possible role for political theory is to buttress or reinforce and even improve a practice. By eliciting its central features, a theory can help the

---

[29] Taylor, "Use and Abuse of Theory," 46.
[30] Ibid., 49; emphasis added.
[31] Taylor, "Political Theory and Practice," 63.
[32] Ibid., 68.
[33] Ibid., 64 ("The framing of theory rarely consists simply of making some ongoing practice explicit").
[34] Ibid.; see also 62, 81, and "Use and Abuse of Theory," 51.

participants better understand what they are doing and why. Such enhanced self-understanding can, in turn, make them more effective practitioners. As Taylor says, "To have a good theory . . . is to understand better what we are doing; and this means that our action can be freer of the stumbling, self-defeating character that previously afflicted it; our action becomes less haphazard and contradictory; less prone to produce what we didn't want at all."[35]

A closely related, but I think separable, third possible role for theory is to strengthen the actors' commitment to a practice. By illuminating what the practice is about, the theory can distill what is good and laudable in it and thus renew the actors' attachment to the practice. As we have seen, norms and practices do not require theoretical articulation for their existence and transmission. Yet the norms informing a practice can become more powerful and more galvanizing when translated from the prearticulate realm to the articulate. As Taylor describes it, "An interpretation of our predicament can give added point to our practices, or show them to be even more significant than we had thought."[36] Theory can serve this process by making plain to the actors some of the tacit shared goods of their political life and thereby heightening their appreciation of those goods. This process is intensified when these norms become recognized in public life. Theory can thus move these meanings from the intersubjective to the common register, to use adjectives deployed earlier. Taylor further suggests that such public acknowledgment of shared goods can help mobilize the political will required for common action to preserve or develop them.[37]

Fourth, and finally, a political theory can undermine a practice. Marxist theory, for example, seeks to persuade people that a practice as central to Western societies as private property is inherently unjust and exploitative and should be overturned. Not all critical theories are as revolutionary in their implications as Marxism, of course; some might be less critical of society as a whole or might confine their attack to more localized practices. Yet however extensive the criticism, challenging social practices with a view to undermining them has been an important function of political theory in the modern Western tradition.[38]

[35] Taylor, "Use and Abuse of Theory," 53; see also 45, 52, and "Political Theory and Practice," 78.
[36] Taylor, "Political Theory and Practice," 70; see also 67, and "Use and Abuse of Theory," 46.
[37] Taylor, "Political Theory and Practice," 71.
[38] Taylor, "Use and Abuse of Theory," 45; "Political Theory and Practice," 64. It is useful to compare the functions of articulation that political theory fulfills with those of moral theory. See Abbey, *Charles Taylor*, 41–7.

In fulfilling its second, third, or fourth function enumerated here, theory has the potential to change practice. It can do this in different ways and to different degrees, but Taylor is adamant that a theory, once it has been accepted by a number of people, can affect the way a practice is carried out.[39] This introduces another reason why the natural sciences fail to provide a credible model for the human sciences, because theories in the former do not change their object. The object is independent of the theory, as Taylor sometimes puts it. The theory is separate from but applied to the object.[40] Of course, theories developed by the natural sciences can help manipulate and control their object: As Taylor concedes, in these sciences "part of what is involved in having a better theory is being able to more effectively cope with the world. We are able to intervene successfully to effect our purposes in a way that we were not able before."[41] Yet the subjects of these sciences are not self-interpreting, and theories about them can, by definition, shape neither their self-understanding nor actions based on those. This also means that political theories cannot be applied in the way that those aiming to emulate the natural sciences hope, because in the social sciences the object to which the theory is to be applied is not wholly separate from the theory. Instead, "[i]n politics . . . accepting a theory can itself transform what that theory bears on."[42]

Yet if Taylor is correct in the reasons he gives why the natural sciences are an ill-fitting model for the social sciences, the obvious question that arises is why so many have been, and remain, tempted to align the two. I can discern three related reasons that Taylor could forward to address this puzzle. The first is that the natural sciences have enjoyed huge prestige in the modern West, and social scientists want to enjoy some of the kudos. The second is that, as noted earlier, the natural sciences offer the promise of manipulating and controlling the world, and the desire to improve the human estate, as Bacon called it, and to promote commodious living, as Hobbes expressed it, is very strong in Western modernity. The hope is that political life could become more effective if we could develop a science of politics that allowed us to control and predict human behavior.[43] The third explanation why the natural science model so entices is that the social science to have

---

[39] Taylor, "Use and Abuse of Theory," 42, 45, 47, 53.

[40] Ibid., 47; "Political Theory and Practice," 70, 77.

[41] Taylor, "Political Theory and Practice," 61.

[42] Taylor, "Use and Abuse of Theory," 47; see also 40 ("Theory can't just be applied to human affairs because it also transforms").

[43] Taylor, "Political Theory and Practice," 61.

achieved greatest proximity to a natural science is economics. After all, the "economy" is supposed to be an independent object to which theories can be applied. The "economy" is supposed to be governed by its own laws, irrespective of actors' interpretations and self-understandings – or rather, those who fail to adjust their self-understanding to the lawlike demands of the economy are doomed to fail. The assumption seems to be that if the natural science model can be emulated in the economic domain, it can in others too – in politics, sociology, psychology. However, Taylor points out that centuries of effort have gone into establishing a seemingly independent domain of economics with its own apparent laws and patterns.[44] And he is adamant that however far economics might have traveled down the track of emulating a natural science, this path is not generalizable to the other social sciences.[45]

By way of conclusion it is illuminating to begin to consider to what extent Taylor's own practice as a political theorist conforms to his account of what political theory should be and do. (The constraints of space mean that this is regrettably a preliminary, sketchy, and therefore contestable treatment of this question.) As we have seen, Taylor suggests that people turn to political theory in times of trouble and confusion, when prevailing understandings of a particular practice seem inadequate. This suggestion can be connected to this chapter's claim that Taylor's own approach as a political theorist is problem driven: It responds to issues as they arise in the practical realm. Taylor also contends that political theory should focus on practices that are meaning laden and intersubjective and that vary to some degree from society to society. This recommendation is certainly borne out in his own work on modern social imaginaries where he outlines the shared understandings of modern Western institutions such as the economy, the public sphere, and popular sovereignty. However, it could also be argued that what Taylor is doing in this work falls into the first type of theorizing identified earlier, namely, supplying a formal and systematic articulation of a political practice or set of practices. The reason for this, I suspect, is that his work on modern social imaginaries developed as part of his wider ambition to track the rise of secularity in modern Western societies and to explain how it came to be that societies whose key institutions were once fully imbricated in a

---

[44] Taylor, "Use and Abuse of Theory," 47–8; "Political Theory and Practice," 75. Taylor, "The Economy as Objectified Reality," in *Modern Social Imaginaries*, chap. 5, discusses how the economy came to be seen as an independent and self-regulating domain.
[45] Taylor, "Political Theory and Practice," 77.

religious worldview became able to imagine those institutions independently of religion.

Some of Taylor's other work exemplifies the second role of political theory adduced earlier – namely, to buttress or reinforce and even improve a practice. By perspicuously eliciting its central features, a theory can help participants in the practice better understand what they are doing and why. This seems to capture Taylor's purpose in some of the essays mentioned earlier as illustrative of his tendency to interpret political life in dialogical terms. "The Politics of Recognition," for example, starts with the observation that some groups within Western society are making claims for the public recognition of their particularity. Taylor draws on resources from the history of political thought to provide some philosophical background to this development and lends this practice a psychological dimension by explaining how misrecognition can harm those subjected to it. Through elucidating the quest for recognition in this way, Taylor can give those who seek, as well as those who grant, recognition a fuller appreciation of the processes in which they are engaged, as well as a sense of the dangers involved in withholding recognition.

Likewise, in "The Dynamics of Democratic Exclusion," Taylor describes groups within Western democracies making bids to participate in politics on their own terms. He shows how democracy's inner logic of inclusion encourages this while its twin logic of exclusion pushes against it, for democracy requires a strong sense of collective identity. He concludes by gesturing toward more encompassing models of democracy that would embrace diversity. His analysis allows denizens of democratic societies to understand political processes in a more clairvoyant manner and to acquire a deeper appreciation of the ways in which diversity both stretches and strains democracy. Although it is not, as noted earlier, exclusively a work of political theory, *Sources of the Self* can be seen in this light, too. Seeking to enhance its readers' self-knowledge, it strives to illuminate "the modern identity as we live it today."[46] This work underlines what a multiple and complex entity the modern self is, and Taylor hopes that tracing the historical contours of this complexity will free people from the tendency to deny and stifle the plurality of goods that modern selves effectively, if not always knowingly, affirm.[47]

---

[46] Taylor, *Sources of the Self*, 319.
[47] Ibid., 106–7, 503, 511, 514, 520.

Yet because there is, as noted earlier, a relatively fine line between the second and third functions of political theory adumbrated in this chapter, it is possible to argue that these forays into political theory actually enact its third function – namely, to strengthen the actors' commitment to a practice, be it recognition or democratic inclusion.[48] This is especially so given Taylor's tendency to focus on the positive aspects of a practice. Indeed, my sense is that most of Taylor's work as a political theorist falls within the second or third role for political theory: There is little in his corpus that seeks to challenge, let alone to undermine, political practices. In many cases, the desired effect seems to be a more lucid awareness of what is going on in a practice and an accentuation of what is good in that. Yet this effect does not preclude criticism, because underlining what is valuable about a practice at the same time facilitates identification of its troubling aspects, thereby empowering its practitioners to "call a foul" and explain why they are doing so.[49]

As we have seen, Taylor insists that if we wish to understand human behavior, we must have some sense of the self-understandings that inform it. Self-interpretations are crucial components of human identity and, there-fore, of social and political reality. However, just as emphasizing intersub-jective meanings need not betoken consensus, so acknowledging the signif-icance of self-interpretations does not compel acceptance of them as final. Hermeneutic approaches to the social sciences are not limited to simply taking account of existing self-interpretations. Self-understandings are not incorrigible; some interpretations of actions and behavior are superior to others; and actors' self-understandings are amenable to revision when con-fronted with better interpretations. As Taylor puts it, "if the explanation is really clearer than the lived interpretation then it will be such that it would alter in some way the behavior if it came to be internalized by the agent as his self-interpretation."[50] Insofar as Taylor's work is about "transforming

---

[48] In "Plus ça Change" I suggest, albeit not in these exact terms, that this is what Taylor is trying to do in his report for the Quebec commission.

[49] As I have argued in reply to Beiner's critique of Taylor on the politics of recognition, Taylor provides some resources for a critique of the sort of pathological identity claims Beiner fears. Taylor shows how the dynamics of recognition have developed in the context of, and via some of the moral resources available in, the liberal democratic tradition. Its cardinal values include universality, equality, liberty, respect, reciprocity, toleration, and autonomy. Bids for identity expression that violate some or any of these norms can be subjected to criticism from within Taylor's framework. See Ruth Abbey, "Pluralism in Practice: The Political Thought of Charles Taylor," *Critical Review of International Social and Political Philosophy* 5, no. 3 (Autumn 2002): 98–123.

[50] Taylor, "Interpretation," 27.

social life" in the way Smith suggests, it is aimed primarily at changing self-interpretations.

That Taylor is attempting to alter or amend some of the ways in which his readers understand themselves is evident in his most recent work, *A Secular Age*. It is designed, in part, to affect how his religious and nonreligious readers alike interpret themselves by showing that a decline in religious belief is not a sine qua non of being modern. Shifting the terms of debate about the role of religion in Western modernity also involves destabilizing the (apparent) extremes in this debate as currently configured. Taylor wants to show that the supposed antagonists who seem to occupy, and seem to themselves to occupy, polarized positions have more in common than either realizes. Moving the exchange in a more productive direction thus involves rendering fragile the self-understandings of those who currently occupy its (apparently) opposite poles.[51]

Suggestions for further reading

Abbey, Ruth. *Charles Taylor*. Princeton, NJ: Princeton University Press, 2000.
Smith, Nicholas H. *Charles Taylor: Meaning, Morals and Modernity*. Cambridge: Polity, 2002.
Taylor, Charles. "The Dynamics of Democratic Exclusion." *Journal of Democracy* 9, no. 4 (October 1998): 143–56.
_____. "Nationalism and Modernity." In *The Morality of Nationalism*, edited by Robert McKim and Jeff McMahan, 31–55. New York: Oxford University Press, 1997.
_____. "The Politics of Recognition." In *Multiculturalism and "The Politics of Recognition,"* edited by Amy Gutmann, 27–73. Princeton: Princeton University Press, 1994.

---

[51] Taylor, *Secular Age*, 618, 624–5, 656, 674–6, 726–7. For a fuller discussion, see Ruth Abbey, "Theorizing Secularity 3: Authenticity, Ontology, Fragilization," in *Aspiring to Fullness in a Secular Age: Essays on Religion and Theology in the Work of Charles Taylor*, ed. Carlos D. Colorado and Justin D. Klassen (Notre Dame, IN: University of Notre Dame Press, forthcoming).

Index